Women and education

TAVISTOCK WOMEN'S STUDIES

Women and education

EILEEN M. BYRNE

TAVISTOCK PUBLICATIONS

First published in 1978 by
Tavistock Publications Limited
11 New Fetter Lane,
London EC4P 4EE
Printed in Great Britain by
Richard Clay (The Chaucer
Press) Ltd Bungay, Suffolk

© Eileen M. Byrne 1978

I S B N 0 422 75960 0 (hardbound)
I S B N 0 422 75970 8 (paperback)

This book is dedicated to three women: to my mother for her early battles against those who placed barriers in our paths; to the late headmistress of South Park High School for Girls, Lincoln, for her courageous determination that her girls should succeed against all adversity; and to P.M. for a lifetime of loyal patience and support without which I would never have lasted the course.

Contents

Contents

Acknowledgements

It is always difficult fully to acknowledge the generous help one receives while writing a research-based book. My foremost debt is to Lincolnshire County Council for the award of six months' special research leave to carry out the practical research, reading, and analyses which form the main basis of the book. It was timely in International Women's Year, and is much appreciated.

I owe a considerable debt to Dr Mark Abrams, to John Hall, and to Cathy Marsh of the SSRC Survey Unit in relation to the fifth-form survey. Dr Abrams kindly offered advice and resources for collation; John Hall most generously allowed me to plagiarize and adapt the questionnaire he devised for his own research into girls' attitudes; and Cathy Marsh shouldered the main burden of coding and programming the computer analysis of the 110 questionnaires, without which much of their value would have been lost.

To the headmistress and girls of the High School in the North, my warmest thanks both for their work and for their enthusiasm. I hope that they will recognize the life they have brought to the book by their comments and experience, although for obvious reasons, when quoting directly, I have changed the names of the girls for the purpose of the book.

Many librarians have contributed to the research, but especial mention is due to my colleagues in the NUT research department for early co-operation when the project was in its infancy; and to Jan Ayres at the library of the Royal Institute of Public Administration for her initiative and help.

Finally, that this has reached print is due both to Christine Moss and Sylvia Christie, as much for their faith as for their support and efficiency.

Most of the research and writing of this book took place before the author's appointment as Education Officer to the UK Equal Opportunities Commission. Work undertaken since then reflects the valued contribution of a network of colleagues and feminists in this country and elsewhere, and not my experience at the EOC. Nevertheless it should be made clear that all of the views and opinions expressed herein are my own, and in no way commit the EOC to a particular view or policy.

Preface

In 1965, the United Nations embarked upon a long-term programme to improve the status of women in all fields. A decade later 1975 was designated as International Women's Year and UNESCO declared its belief that 'in the long run, education will prove to be the most effective channel for achieving equality between men and women and ensuring the full participation of women in development'.

In the attention that was focused in 1975 on the status of women, and as the United Kingdom introduced its own legislation to promote equality between the sexes (the *Sex Discrimination Act, 1975*), the role of education has emerged as of increasing importance. As this book goes to press, indeed, we in the United Kingdom are reviewing two years of anti-discrimination legislation. In the public debate that this has provoked, the role of education and training has emerged as even more central than hitherto. This book is an attempt, at least partly, to fill the gap that exists in the general knowledge and consciousness of the actual, and of the desired, character of the education of girls and women and the situation of girls and women in education today.

It is not only an attempt to provoke new thought and to strengthen existing knowledge; it is an impassioned call to all educated women (and men) to accept their own responsibility and direct duty, to walk back down the ladder which they have climbed, and to build in all the missing rungs to help less fortunate girls and women (both here and abroad) to the freedom of status, career, and personal fulfilment to which only the fullest educational opportunity is the key.

My particular generation of women owe their secondary education to the *Education Act, 1944* of which we were the very first post-war beneficiaries in 1945. But less than 1 per cent of us reached higher education. We owe that, and indeed our careers, to the unshakeable determination of a few enlightened women and men who helped us to break the barriers of prejudice, repressive practices and regulations, and to lift us over the hurdles of stereotyped conditioning, under-expectation, and male competition, to high fulfilment.

Every reader of this book should accept in turn her or his own responsibility to fight to extend the reality of the equal opportunity, which we minority few have won (and maintained with such continuing difficulty), to all women everywhere, as an innate right and not as a kindly privilege. It is their just entitlement; it is this country's economic and social future.

Eileen M. Byrne
Marple Bridge
April 1978

ONE

Introduction – education for change

'We must think positively about how the position of
women in their own societies and in international affairs
could not only be improved, but their large potential
contribution be better utilized for the benefit of all.'

(KURT WALDHEIM,
Secretary General, United Nations, 1975)

The grandeur of an international canvas and the dignity of
policy clothed in the language of diplomacy do not make the
translation of Waldheim's challenge to all nations in International Women's Year the less real or the less relevant to every
classroom, lecture-hall, education office, or teacher–parents'
group in this country. Waldheim was talking to the government
of education quite as much as to the politicians who listen
through their earphones to the minuet dancing of international
affairs. He was talking to you, readers of this book – teachers,

13

education officers, planners, students, parents, men and women in the High Street. We ourselves, not Geneva, are the agents of change in our own country, town, or village.

Education has long been one of the most decisive of our life-chances, the key to equal opportunity and the ladder to advancement, since men first learned that literacy and communication in the hands of a few meant power, government, and the control of the many. Without education, and especially without *equal* educational experiences or skills and qualifications, men and women alike of certain classes and social groups have over the years been condemned to inferior lives in their personal development, in their choice of work, as citizens, and in their power to influence government, leadership, and the national decisions which affect their local lives.

But it is a double-edged tool. Before the coming of state education in the late nineteenth century, the careful rationing of education by an elite, with its comfortable sop to Cerberus by way of charity schools and Sunday schools for the children of the poor, was unquestionably the major cause of under-achievement in every civic and working sense, of the main body of the people, until they were given a more real educational choice and opportunity in this century. But the sophistication of a multidisciplinary state education has brought with it a new discrimination. The more simplistic differentiation by social class was a hallmark of the Taunton Commission in 1868 (secondary education until eighteen plus for the sons of gentlemen and the upper professions; a more commercially based and practical education until sixteen for the sons of the mercantile classes; and 'very good reading, writing and arithmetic' until thirteen plus for the artisans). No one will now admit to overt class differentiation in educational objectives (although hidden indirect distinctions can still be found). Yet we justify gross differentiation of curricula as between the sexes, and between rural and urban children, and between the intellectually gifted and the average, based on assumptions of hypothetical normative homogeneity as unthought and unresearched as the original class differentiation used to justify different educational objectives by social status and not by diagnosed needs.

It has been widely believed that the coming of state education brought equality of educational opportunity. In an otherwise admirably argued book, for example, a leading woman educationalist suggested as far back as 1961 that: 'It might be said that women have largely won the battle for equal educational opportunity with men ... this is largely true ...' (Ollerenshaw 1961 : 14). I believe Dame Kathleen might review that assumption now. I *question* it for the 65 per cent of less able girls in school; and for working-class women. Success has, as always, come to the middle-class girl in the grammar school (or academic stream in comprehensive schools) who has crept through the net to university or polytechnic. It has come in only parsimonious measure to the girl workers denied day release; to the middle-ability girl offered a less solid curricular 'option' than her brother; to the women denied further education and retraining because they are married and therefore 'kept' – as if education's only purpose were to provide bread and a roof over one's head.

I am more especially concerned with education for the twentieth and twenty-first centuries, and with the missing girl apprentices and women supervisors and technicians of a scientific and technological age, than with the intellectual minority of girls whose elite wings have helped them to fly up T. H. Huxley's ladder from the gutter to the university, despite the many missing rungs on the way. My deepest concern is with girls whose alternative to staying at home for forty years is not the professions – not even the skilled bench, the high wage packet bringing financial independence, the industrial training which gives her job security, responsibility, and mobility. It is low pay, canteen cleaning, helping with school meals, the typewriter, the unskilled labour market, short-term employment. The cause: a different, often inferior education planned perhaps with no conscious ill-intent by the men who represent 97 per cent of the government of education, but which nevertheless gives no foundation for a later career in either work or government.

Theories are of course still advanced that the opportunities are there, and if any under-achieving group – girls, the working classes, rural children – does not take advantage of them, it is because they do not wish to, are too lazy, or do not need the same chances of development; and by rationalization it is argued that a different, often inferior, education is therefore right. I am constantly (and wrongly) told that any girl of my generation could do what I have done, if only they had so chosen. This book is about why they could not, and often still cannot. It is about the planned differences of the educational menus we still offer to girls in a restricted cafeteria choice; about under-investment in girls and women; and about the contribution women could make socially and economically if we educated them as highly individual people in their own right, and not as future wives, mothers, nannies, secretaries, and other support services for husbands, sons, brothers, and (male) bosses. The educational future of women is a central theme also – a new future in the economic and political leadership, in the skilled and managerial rungs of employment; and their freedom to be Jean or Mary in their own homes and in their own right, and not merely Tom's wife or Jim's mother.

Span and limitations

To deal with so large and complex a subject as women and education is rather like attempting to catch the outside of a balloon, or to cut a sand dune. It eludes grasp, its shape changes with the tack adopted. Some conceptual barriers or limitations are necessary to break down this subject (which, by its influence, permeates all aspects of society and family and personal life) into manageable ideas. We need to define the differences in education and training that fit us either for high responsibility, or for the routine or unskilled labour market; for divergent analytical thinking, or for unquestioning acceptance of social stereotypes; for economic independence, or for existence as a dependent satellite or shadow of our spouses, our family, our friends, our field of employment, local community, social class.

Because therefore it is impossible in the span of one short book adequately to cover, leave aside debate, the entire field of education from pre-school through to education for retirement, some difficult choices have been made on priorities for detailed survey, and on direct or indirect omissions. These necessarily reflect my own ideology and experience, and I make little apology for them. The very concentration of themes and the selection of omissions should spur readers to re-examine their own identity of interest, and may suggest some legitimate areas for further study. Meanwhile readers may be helped by a conscious definition of some of the omissions.

There is for example only minimal reference to the private

sector of education in the UK. In fact, only between 5 per cent and 10 per cent of our pupils and students (depending on region) are educated privately (fewer in Scotland). Of these, most are either middle and upper class, or intellectually gifted, or financially secure, or all three. They command no priority at all in my over-riding desire to see reforms affecting the remaining 90 per cent of girls and women. And second, equality of educational opportunity came first to women from this sector – who have occupied themselves so far very little over the last century with the needs of the average girls and women educated under the vagaries of the state education and training system. A century of priority of investment in the upper classes, in the intellectually able, and in the 'future leadership of our country' has *not* in fact produced more top women than fifty years ago; nor fundamental reforms of discriminatory practices or inequalities affecting the average woman.

There is similarly a deliberate under-treatment of universities, and of women academics. The latter number about one per cent of the problems of under-achievement of women and are the best qualified to fight for their own equality – as well as for ours. The problems of women in higher education who teach from 8 per cent to 10 per cent only of school leavers are more than adequately covered by the work of Tessa Blackstone, Oliver Fulton, and others; by sharp contrast with an almost complete neglect of the position of women staff in the tertiary sector, who teach up to 30 per cent of the young men and women leaving our schools.

The history of the education of girls and women has been documented only relatively recently but there is, for interested readers, a growing bibliography now available, sufficient to make inclusion of any substantial similar coverage here, unnecessary. (The selected bibliography in this book gives brief introductory details for readers new to this field.) Far more central to the achievement of educational equality is knowledge of today's classrooms and of tomorrow's potential.

Finally, this work is unusual if not unique in making virtually no reference to American research, literature, or programmes. This is not to underestimate the pioneer influence of the USA, from the work of Susan B. Anthony, through Betty Friedan, to the American girl who challenged, legally, her right to a place at the prestigious (boys') Central High School in New York in

1975 (Novarra 1976). But the transfer value of American education, different in organization, culture, values, objectives, demography, and historical tradition, to that of the United Kingdom, is extremely limited. After twenty years of interdisciplinary work in the education service, moreover, I have found that education officers, planners, teachers, community and parent groups simply do not see or know enough of what takes place here – in our own country. To add a superficial and academic gloss of the American situation to an imperfect knowledge and understanding of our own practices, values, objectives, and achievements, is to pile Pelion on Ossa to the mountain of ideological confusion that now dominates the sex equality debate. Change in this country will come from an increased understanding of our own system – first and foremost. When we have clarity in our own field, we can usefully use comparative education as a tool for intellectual development or for social reform; but not until then will it be wholly productive. Finally, such comparisons as are politically or tactically useful are more appropriately set in a European, than a transatlantic, context.

It is of course impossible to discuss the education of women without looking at education for girls and boys as a whole, and at the differences that we have fashioned for them in our schools, or the different preconceived adult roles tailored for them by an unreflecting society, working on reflex and not on reason. It is, above all, the naive acceptance by our sophisticated Western society that the superficiality of plenty has meant the achievement of equality in education, that makes a review of the respective opportunities and achievements of women and men especially timely. Implicit in the argument underlying this book is an expectation that society must and will change but that it is unlikely to do so unless forced by a certain amount of ruthless logic and by social and political pressure to rethink the balance of economic adult roles of women and men. Change is a cyclical process. Teachers are reluctant to alter courses seen as 'relevant' to local outlets for less able leavers until employers change their expectations. Employers and local communities cannot change if their yearly injection of school leavers remains immutably the same in character and type.

In the continuing controversy about inequality in its wider sense, indeed, the education service has at least paid Jencks and Jensen the compliment earned by Tawney some fifty years earlier. It has acknowledged, for example, the seriousness of their arguments at the most minimal level of recognition, by conducting a public, thoughtful, and informed debate which draws on widely known, if conflicting, data and research for its reasoning. The analogous question of inequality of educational opportunity for girls and women, and of deliberate and discriminating differentiation of curricula for girls and for boys, has evoked, however, no such similar public reaction or debate. It is not yet 'respectable', in academe or government.

Even the first serious enquiries by HM Inspectorate in the United Kingdom into curricular patterns of education for the two sexes since 1923,[1] published in 1975, have sunk without trace in the deep pool of unresolved educational controversies, with barely a traceable ripple. The disturbing conclusions and unusually trenchant comments of their slender pages have been received with a now customary deafening silence. Some of the evidence and ideas that follow in later chapters here will seek to shatter that careful silence and replace it with a lively debate which can neither be lost in a Babylonian hubbub of traditional reaction, nor talked out like an unpopular Parliamentary Bill.

There are two or three fundamental principles whose definition (rightly or wrongly as readers may perceive them) underly the whole review of the educational rights of girls. One is the *defined* purpose of education. The second is the antithesis of inequality and of discrimination. The third is the principle that 'equal means the same' – not the specious 'equivalent'.

Equal means the same

The recognition of this aspect of the key role of education received its most recent formal accolade in 1967 when the United Nations passed one of its most far-reaching resolutions:

'All appropriate measures shall be taken to ensure to girls and women, married or unmarried, equal rights with men in education at all levels, and in particular

(a) equal conditions of access to and study in educational institutions of all types, including universities and vocational, technical and professional schools;

(b) the *same choice of curricula*, the *same examinations*, teaching staff *with qualifications of the same standard*, and school premises and equipment *of the same quality, whether the institutions are coeducational or not;*

(c) equal opportunities to benefit from scholarships and other study grants;

(d) equal opportunities for access to programmes of continuing education, including adult literacy programmes, and

(e) access to educational information to help in ensuring the health and well-being of families.'[2]

The rejection of this principle by educational planners, and their addiction to the highly questionable principle of equivalence, underlies the whole curricular debate about housecraft versus handicraft, physics or biology, separation for physical education, educating boys for work and girls for domestic life, motherhood and part-time work. It is central to the equality debate. It must now be faced by government and community alike, both of whom have evaded it so far by refusing to agree on any defined educational objectives at all. We are the only European country to reject responsibility for common, national educational objectives; and in doing so, we endorse and perpetuate inequalities of all kinds. The most serious of these is the *aggregation of inequality* from which girls and women suffer worse than their brothers. There is considerable research evidence that social class and intelligence are more decisive single factors of advantage or disadvantage than sex alone. Given however that there are a range of factors, the 'compound interest of inequality' becomes apparent. I suggest that there are five major indices of potential inequality which, where two or more are aggregated, create a cumulative cycle of underachievement which can only be overcome by positive, affirmative, interventionist programmes aimed at increasing resources, counteracting cultural and social barriers, and adding to the skills and experience. The five factors are:

(i) sex
(ii) lower social class
(iii) lower range of intelligence
(iv) residence in certain regions with a history of underachievement
(v) residence in rural areas.

This is emerging as a European pattern. France, Germany, and Italy all have problems of differential under-achievement as between regions. Rural, relative under-achievement is evident in Ireland and Italy, and is unquestionably a factor in the United Kingdom. Girls who are less able, Northern, of lower social class, and rural are quadruply disadvantaged.

For what are we educating girls?

It has always seemed to me that one major setback in achieving a balanced and full secondary education for girls, geared to a career for economic independence and a choice of external and internal roles in family and community, is the consistent and unaccountable refusal of the education service to define agreed *national* minimum objectives. The following quotation, for example, is disturbingly typical of current debates in the educational media. A Chief Education Officer of a large rural county was reported verbatim in the *Guardian* on January 7, 1975:

> 'There isn't the respect for educated people that there used to be. I was brought up that if you read Greats and had sensitivities and were fairly decent to people, you were educated. You could tell who were and who weren't. But today teachers don't know. Administrators don't know. It's less and less clear just what we are supposed to produce.'

He controlled a budget of over £24 million a year. We might well question how such an incoherent philosophy of education could possibly produce any clarity of educational purpose or practice in sharing out that budget. Statements abound moreover like that which opens L. C. Taylor's otherwise admirable book on *Resources for Learning* (1971): 'It is impossible to define exactly the purpose of secondary education.' I utterly refute this evasive approach. It is perfectly possible to define realistic 'Monday morning' practical aims and, indeed, it is difficult to see how the education service can spend £6 billion each year without knowing what purposes and objectives it expects to achieve, by what methods and priorities in allocating these resources. But the traditionally insoluble debate about the aims of education, which has filled publishers' bookshelves over the years, enables us comfortably to evade answering questions like, why do some groups of children (girls, rural children, immigrants, those in the North) appear so consistently to under-achieve?

Further, because monitoring is also impossible against unknown and undefined factors, well-worn placebos like 'examinations don't mean one is educated' or 'you can't measure education', become the traditional defensive reflex against demands for accountability for the different actual standards of achievement and expectation of different groups and classes of children in our care. In this case, it is the girls who still lack the physics, maths, and technical studies that would lead to recruitment to further education, industrial training, a break into the world of men's work and skilled wages, instead of the unskilled assembly line. Qualifications do matter. One major cause of failure to acquire equal pay is in my view the unequal training and therefore lesser skills of women, which prevent them from doing really comparable work. One is reminded of the recommendation of Lloyd George's Committee of the War Cabinet on Women in Industry sixty years ago that

'Good training is the factor which comes next to good health in increasing the value of women in industry. The removal of all educational disabilities of women and the provision of equal facilities for technical training and apprenticeships is urged.' (HM Government 1919:170)

The Committee said equally bluntly that

'The prejudice of male workers must share the responsibility with the prejudice of employers for the fact that the training of women is deficient ... Technical dexterity is certainly attained by women to a degree not inferior to men.'

(1919:170)

It does not follow that achievement of equal qualifications will necessarily and alone achieve equal promotion and advancement; but it does follow that failure to reach the same level of qualification as men will actively debar women from access to advanced training programmes, recruitment, and advancement. Graduates may choose to drop out of managerial roles and become clerks; but clerks cannot choose to become managers unless they are trained and qualified for leadership roles.

Whether or not the leadership of the education service is allowed to continue to evade clearer definitions of the purposes of educating both boys and girls, which underlie their organization of education (and their discriminatory allocation of resources to achieve their allegedly unknown objectives), I am suggesting a number of perfectly definable objectives which, in my view, the education service must accept if we are to survive economically and individually into the twenty-first century. They all have clear implications for the establishment of some form of national basic secondary curriculum up to the age of sixteen common to both sexes (which does not, however, necessarily imply control of *how* subjects are taught, of what curricular content should be included, nor of what precise educational media and books to use). I am outlining some of the objectives below because the whole argument of this book is set against the assumption that these are desirable, acceptable, necessary, and attainable. If these objectives are rejected, girls will continue to be educated for a home-based domestic role or for short term, lower-paid employment; and if they are accepted for both sexes, there can be no justification whatever for allowing the imposition of a different curriculum for each sex. I propose in fact to nail a flag to the mast, and indeed several pennants as well, on this question of objectives. The purpose of education is perfectly definable. Objectives are measurable. Educational achievements are measurable both at personal and at school and college levels. *Input* (that is resources of staff, money, buildings, equipment) is measurable against specific educational purposes – for example, the achievement of literacy; of the five GCE/CSE passes in basic subjects which are the key to entry to nine-tenths of all further education courses above craft level; of a sound scientific base for later retraining. *Output* (that is pupils' and students' educational achievements) is also measurable – the success rate or the take-up of examinations; pupils can or cannot read, spell and add; they do or do not go on to further and higher education, skilled employment, or unskilled work; they can or cannot reason from evidence observed. Finally our consistent deliberate refusal actually to monitor the direct relationship of discriminatory practices of resource-allocation, both to educational achievement and to success of defined objectives, is one major and direct cause of continuing and worsening inequality between the sexes, and between social classes.

Let me therefore first define what I consider to be the objectives of educating young people – girls and boys strictly alike. *Personal fulfilment* and individual excellence have always been accepted in theory as the first and principal aim of education, and the present government of education, mostly trained over twenty-five years ago, are quite likely to quote Sir Percy Nunn's still relevant seminal work of the 1920s on educational principles: 'The primary aim of all educational effort should be to help boys and girls to achieve the highest degree of individual development of which they are capable (Nunn 1945, preface).

But as long as girls' schools remain deficient in comparable facilities for teaching maths, science, and the background to technology, and boys' schools lack any teaching in the home-crafts and parenthood; as long as boys are denied activities like ballet education because they are 'unmasculine', or equivalent facilities for music, drama, and cultural subjects; as long, in fact, as the curriculum remains stereotyped into girls' subjects and boys' subjects for which different practical investment is made, then personal fulfilment will remain an unattainable goal for many of both sexes.

Yet even the influential government-sponsored Central Advisory Council has reinforced an ideology of a 'different but equal' education which can owe nothing to education for individuality. The Crowther report put the (regrettable) seal of its approval on the pressure to educate boys for a career and girls for a different 'relevance', which I personally reject as educationally unacceptable: 'It is true that there is a broad distinction between boys' and girls' interests which is *rightly* reflected in curriculum planning' (Crowther Committee 1959:para 170, my italics).

The Committee found it '*natural*' that the strength of the vocational test of relevance (i.e. to future work) should be more frequent in boys than in girls, 'for a good many of whom wage earning is likely to seem a more temporary preoccupation' (1959:para 172). The Committee, however, did recommend that the tendency to regard physics and maths as masculine empires, and biology and literature as feminine, should be corrected, not accepted or indeed accentuated by the tendency for certain subject areas to be taught by men or women only and thus become sex-linked.

Second only to this in my view is the need to educate both sexes for the best job or *career* of which we are capable – which 86 per cent of the boys *and 88 per cent of the girls* and 89 per cent of their parents rated as a major school objective in the Schools Council's survey of nearly 5,000 pupils in 1968. (The *teachers*, however, rated this very lowly – only 28 per cent of heads and 47 per cent of teachers thought this important.) Production of the country's skilled manpower (womanpower) is also essentially a task of education and training, however much the academic may shy away from it. There are many factors for change that make a healthy scepticism about many of the current attitudes towards the education of girls gain momentum. Our bland refusal to take on manpower planning below the prestigious level of nuclear physicists and tame economists at Westminster leaves us regularly bereft of enough gas fitters; of electricians to repair our deficient old domestic systems; of plumbers to deal with burst pipes and pouring over-flows; all of the service industries in fact. Where are the extra medical technicians to man all the kidney machines, service the thalidomide aids, provide electronic backup for brain and heart surgery, and keep Queen Mary's, Roehampton, and Stoke Mandeville Hospitals at peak working? How do we find the missing dental auxiliaries; or maintenance technicians for all those washing machines and freezers? What could be more suitable for girl school leavers as well as for the retrained lost generations of mature women who are too far along their current road to take on a completely new full career, than to retrain for part-time technical work in the service industries in their own locality with regular 'topping up' retraining courses at the local college of further education?

The employment field is constantly changing. Education for later retraining in this century of mobility, recession, technological development, and consumer demand is of growing importance – and implies clearly a common measurable minimum secondary base – back to common core. Education for full participation in government is a social and economic need which has so far been recognized for boys but sidestepped for girls – despite their generally higher exercise of social responsibility. Education for leisure comes back to personal fulfilment and can no longer legitimately be interpreted as merely flower arranging and cake icing for women and car maintenance or basketball for men. Education for parenthood, for community welfare, education in personal relationships, is in my view equally needed for both sexes. Neither boys nor girls should continue to accept that the pastoral role is a feminine pre-rogative, or that it is unmasculine to enter the caring professions or to show gentleness and thought in family relationships. Mopping up broken hearts or mending broken emotions is a two-fold responsibility of both sexes. So is mopping up the mess left by inadequate governmental actions over the years. Poverty, bad housing, deprivation, social breakdown, mental illness, handicap, rehabilitation after crime – women predominate in the remedial professions which stitch together parts of society that largely male governments have allowed to fall apart because of their universal preoccupation with war and aggression, and giving priority to the space race over social reconstruction on this earth.

The wider scene

While a synoptic survey of this kind cannot attempt an exercise in comparative education, it is important to recognize the wider thrust for educational change in the achievement of equality for women which is now permeating international debates. In 1976, the Ministers of Education of the nine EEC countries met to discuss common problems in education and training and resolved that

'the achievement of equal opportunity for free access to all forms of education is an essential aim of the education policies of all the member states, and its importance must be stressed in conjunction with other economic and social policies in order to achieve equality of opportunity in society.'
(Resolution of Council of the Commission of the European
Communities, February 19, 1976)

They recommended an action programme which was to include: 'the design and development of specific actions to ensure equal educational opportunities for girls' (December 30, 1976).

There is now movement, research review, and governmental action in many countries. Internationally, UNESCO, along with other organizations of the United Nations, is currently determining what it can do more effectively to promote the advancement of women and their full participation in development. Increasing priority is centred therefore in trying to provide equal access to all types and levels of education. Back in 1966

UNESCO embarked on a long-term programme directed specifically at removing inequalities affecting girls and women in the
field of education, and especially to increase the participation
rate of girls in further education and training as a necessary
prerequisite to the full integration of women into social and
economic development.

In 1975 UNESCO reviewed its programmes and pilot experiments and as a result has shifted emphasis from the simple
if fundamental question of equal access, to the more complex
one of the relationship between *levels* and *types* of education
and recruitment of skilled employment and to higher and
further education.

Latterly, UNESCO's programme has become increasingly concerned with promoting equal education and training opportunities leading to related and higher level employment (UNESCO
1975). Although the main drive of its international programme
has been towards the less developed countries, the principles
underlying the latest experimental projects have clear lessons
for any developed country that still conceals inequalities in a
sophisticated education system. Our own brand of inequality of
access to and quality of education for girls compared with boys
is often lost, for example, in a superficially sophisticated system
of 'relevant' education, used to justify typing and child care for
girls, technical drawing and economics for boys, which has
emerged as a constant pattern across Europe. Relevant for what?
The Oxford definition of the word relevant means simply 'con-
nected with, or pertinent to, the matter in hand', while Jowett
pointed out that 'Many things in a controversy might seem
relevant if we knew to what they were intended to refer'. We
could learn from the UNESCO experiments that the mental,
intellectual, and practical tools which education can most
efficiently provide for women are those that are relevant to
improved employment prospects, financial independence, participation in government and in the economy, as well as to
domestic life.

Similarly the Organisation for Economic Co-operation and
Development (OECD), in its current research into the role of
women in the economy, recognizes the key role of education
and training in the achievement of equal employment policies.
The groundswell of action programmes has accelerated on the
international scene, and many countries are for the first time

ready actively to review their educational practices at governmental level.

Sweden's seminal report to the United Nations in 1968 (Royal Swedish Ministry of Foreign Affairs 1968) for example, recognized the need for reform a decade ago, and has been followed by a good deal of action.

> 'The difficulties confronting adult women on the labour market today are largely attributable to their inferior education compared to that of men. They were not given the same choices in their youth ... Women and girls are still bound to be the victims of "indirect discrimination" [in work] as long as marriage is considered their primary and "natural" source of income.'

Sweden has put into effect many of the recommendations of its 1968 report, and by 1975, for example, all pupils up to Grade 7 (aged about fourteen) studied home economics, textile work, and combined woodwork and metalwork, while basic school curricular principles had been established that:

> 'the school should promote equality between the sexes ... counteracting in its work the traditional attitude to sex roles ... should assume that men and women will play the same role in the future, that preparation for the parental role is just as important for boys as for girls and that girls have reason to be just as interested in careers as boys.
>
> (Sandberg 1975:44)

Ireland's 1972 report to the Minister for Finance of its Commission on the Status of Women made a now standard range of recommendations, from reviewing stereotyped textbooks, equal investment in girls whether or not we expect them to marry (or stay married), effective and new careers guidance, more women Inspectors of Schools, a special programme to increase girls' take-up of mathematics and science, and other familiar areas of concern.

Australia set up a Schools Commission in 1974 to examine 'the underlying causes of, and the extent of underachievement by girls and women in education and its contribution to the inferior status of women', and to recommend special action programmes as a result. The report of their Commission is one of the most fundamental analyses of the Australian education

28

system in print and among its wide-reaching conclusions is one that must ring a loud bell here also:

> 'The Committee believes that, to the extent that schools operate on unexamined assumptions about differences between the sexes, or fail to confront with analysis, sex stereotypes conveyed through mass media and their own curricula and organisation, they limit the options of both boys and girls and assist the processes through which messages of inferiority and dependence are passed to girls because they are female.'
> (Australian Schools Commission 1975:157, para 14.4)

The Commission proposed to set up an advisory committee on the education of girls and women, to accept 'a continuing responsibility to monitor developments', and to develop long-term strategies for change.

One of the conceptual developments that has arisen out of the heightened debates at international level is the growing distinction between the mainly passive state of inequality and the more active structural and conscious practices of discrimination. The growth of anti-discrimination legislation in Europe (following substantial American experience of the last ten years) has been accompanied by increased moves to establish Commissions and Committees to monitor progress and to increase understanding of casual relationships between educational practices and later inequality in achieving equal adult status.

In *Denmark*, for example, the deep personal concern of the Prime Minister for the achievement of equality for women has not only resulted in the establishment of a Danish Council for Equality working direct to the Prime Minister, but the establishment of a Committee on Sex Roles in Education which has begun, in 1977, to review the deeper problems of sexism in education. The *Netherlands* has established its Emancipatie Kommissie, whose early remit includes a focus on educational planning. Here in the United Kingdom, we have appointed an Equal Opportunities Commission, under the provisions of the *Sex Discrimination Act, 1975*, with power to investigate possible areas of discrimination and whose powers include monitoring of education and training – although it ought to be said that the inclusion of education in the *Sex Discrimination Act* and in the remit of the EOC at all, was by no means universally welcomed in the traditionally male-dominated government of education;

and owes its presence to the skilled fight of feminists in the education service, in politics, and in journalism.

Inequality or discrimination?

The antithesis is important if we are to understand the social dimensions of educational planning. Inequality is generally inherited, environmental, and passive, rarely accurately recognized by those who suffer it, while discrimination is active and clearly characterized by those who practise it. Put another way, the former is a state; the latter an action. To confuse the two dimensions in educational debate is to mingle concepts springing from different sets of causes – like Rousseau's natural and his moral and political inequality. Inequality in education has its roots in social history, which records the stereotyping of expected adult roles for men and women and the translation of these into different curricula. The most pervasive inherited unexamined assumption is the alleged inferiority of women, somewhat starkly stated here:

> 'As women therefore, the first thing of importance is to be content to be inferior to men – inferior in mental power, in the same proportion that you are inferior in bodily strength ... woman's strength is in her influence.'   (Mrs Ellis 1842)

The roots of this are buried deep and, like garden mint and couch grass, roots of well established growth are hard to dig out and even harder to remove altogether. New shoots spring up after weeding, many years later.

Inequality itself is two-dimensional, innate on the one hand, and conditioned by outside factors (like human decision on what different groups of people should have and how they should receive it) on the other. The key question is, which kinds of actual inequalities between the sexes are in fact caused by allegedly innate qualities, and which by social conditioning? Dahrendorf makes one kind of distinction:

> 'Four types of inequality emerge ... in relation to the individual there are (a) *natural differences of kind* in features, character and interests, and (b) *natural differences of fact* in intelligence, talent and strength (leaving open the question of whether such differences do in fact exist). Correspondingly,

in relation to society (and in the language of contemporary sociology) there are (c) *social differentiation* of positions essentially equal in rank and (d) *social stratification* based on reputation and wealth and expressed in a rank order of social status.'   (Dahrendorf 1974:19)

In Dahrendorf's terms, his distinction of differences in kind or in fact may be illustrated by the now keenly debated issue of whether girls are or are not born with innately inferior spatial ability; or whether their poorer actual performance in problem arithmetic, mechanical relationships in mathematics and the physical sciences is due to developmental and social conditioning, and an attitude preset by their (mainly women) teachers at primary school that they are unlikely to do well. His rank differentiation and stratification are in my view also interestingly illustrated by the heightened hierarchy of descending academic respectability of the different sectors of education. It would be true to say that public prestige, as distinct from the real value to student and community, gives a rank of descending perceived value to university teaching, grammar school education, advanced further education in polytechnics, other secondary education, primary education, non-advanced further education, day release, and adult education, in that order. That is not only the priority order in which we allocate our resources, but how the value of the education in each sector is presented to boys and girls and to their parents, both by the education service itself and by the perceived public image. Not only are the costs per head heavily weighted towards the academic, the intellectual, and the older pupil or student, but the salary differentials reflect this rank order as well.

This in turn indirectly affects girls' opportunities within those perceived priorities. For not only do girls tend to opt for the 'Cinderella' kinds of education, but when they later train as teachers and lecturers they are to be found in far greater numbers in the less well paid sectors (primary, non-advanced further education, lower secondary). Look, for example, at the following table of costs.

The different actual investment in the education of girls and of boys respectively is sharply illustrated by the fact that boys outnumber girls in the post-sixteen sixth forms, that men outnumber women by two to one in universities (the more costly

31

Table 1(1)   Differential costs of education

average cost per pupil/student (including loan charges)	England and Wales 1972–73
	£
primary	142
secondary (under 16)	232
secondary (over 16)	326
advanced further education*	1,035
non-advanced further education*	421
colleges of (teacher) education	1,238
universities	1,736

(Source: *Social Trends*, 1974:201, Table 189)
* excluding student grants

sectors). By contrast, far more girls are in non-advanced further education and in teacher training. In 1972 the *revenue* costs per head of universities, advanced further education, and teacher training were respectively £1,250, £895, and £565. By any standards, we invest far more in the education of our boys than of our girls.

Tackled another way, Rousseau's two kinds of inequality among the human species,

> 'One which I call natural or physical because it is established by nature and consists in a difference of age, health, bodily strength and the qualities of the mind and the soul, and another, which may be called moral or social inequality, because it depends on a kind of convention, and is established, or at least authorised, by the "consent of men".'
>
> *(Dissertation on the Origins of Inequality)*

both illustrate quite sharply to me the different views on the causes of sex inequalities. Which are caused by alleged differences in natural endowment? Which by moral and social convention, by the consent of the men who dominate the government of education?

It is difficult to say how far the ways in which we organize fourth year options, advise girls about their careers, assess them for discretionary student awards, and plan their housecraft-based curriculum, are a matter of instinctive tradition, prejudice, or conscious priority for boys, which is an indirect form of discrimination. Only by continued analysis and question does a pattern emerge. For example, the greater investment in boys than in girls is not recognized as an active, consciously chauvinistic policy. But it is a disturbing decisive fact with complex causes. In this particular context, there is a useful distinction to be drawn between the words *discriminal* and *discriminatory* to describe educational practices. The former, dating from 1842, means simply 'of the nature of a distinction or division', and is not yet a loaded word. Discriminatory has, however, come to have an adverse and a pejorative meaning, a conscious will to penalize a particular group by giving them deliberately unequal rights and resources. I suggest that discriminal accurately describes those educational practices that aim to distinguish different needs and remedies on firm evidence of innate physical or developmental differences, which (in the view of the educator) can only be dealt with by different means. One good example of this is the education of the physically handicapped. It may be necessary and desirable to give them special and more costly teaching programmes in order to help them to reach the same educational objectives and achievements. A teaching ratio of 1:10 instead of 1:26 for example, special equipment for the blind, electronically controlled typewriters or aids for the spastic, all are forms of positive discrimination based on unalterable differences of capacity at the starting point of their road ahead. Discriminal allocation of a special level, character, and type – of buildings, staff, equipment – are clearly right here. But if one were to translate this into a difference of *what we teach* the handicapped in breadth or depth (for example, leaving out sciences, or languages, or crafts), or to restrict their road to further and higher education, simply because their *method* of travel has to be different, this would be discriminatory, because it presupposes a different actual destination at the end of the road. And there is no reason why, simply because of one sensory or physical difference, the whole aim, education, and future role must necessarily be planned differently for the child concerned.

To translate this into the analogous sex differential, I can find no respect in which the concept of discriminal practices can be validly jusified on educational, as distinct from social, grounds on an assumption that girls have any (relevant) difference in starting point. (The nature/nuture argument is developed in a later chapter.) Yet we have in fact planned consciously separate curricular routes (housecraft; handicraft; pre-apprenticeship courses versus typing) for the two sexes; a practice now open to legal challenge under the *Sex Discrimination Act, 1975*. Because, unlike inequality, discrimination is active rather than passive, its negative characteristic is that it is more often used to deny full opportunity, equal quality and quantity of resources (housing, salary, access to education, social freedom, political enfranchisement), and social esteem to the particular group whom prejudice has classified as a section apart. Its positive quality is that it can only be evident where those who control policy and resources have decided to fix limiting criteria in their rules, practices, and policy decisions which will achieve their deliberately different objectives for the different groups of people for whom they are responsible. Discrimination, once identified, can therefore be attacked at the active source, in the practices of a single, finally accountable group – the employers, the head teachers, or governors, the Committees that authorize rules and practices. If I seem to dwell on this, it is because it will arise frequently as the picture of the education of girls and women in this country unfolds.

Causal relationships

What is implicit in much that is touched upon here, is the strength of the network of causal relationships which are imperfectly understood but which riddle our organizational and curricular practices and which are the principal causes of underachievement. In looking at the education and training of all young people, but especially of girls, those causal relationships are crucial, between the most ordinary school practices and attitudes, organization and limits, achievements and innovations on the one hand, and girls' later lifetime earnings, mobility of employment, ability to follow further and higher education, the achievement of a good educational base for retraining, on the other.

Let me trace back some practical examples. In 1970, there were, in England and Wales, only fifty-two girls taking HND full time in Engineering and Technology as against 7,624 boys. Moreover, there were a mere 132 girls to 20,876 boys taking

HNC in Engineering (the part-time equivalent needing day release by employers).[3] No more girls are likely to be involved in future years unless we attack the two root causes. First, few girls are adequately qualified to enter the courses because they do not tend to take the basic scientific, mathematical, and technical craft subjects necessary at GCE 'O' and 'A' level in any significant numbers. Second, employers are then reluctant to release them to acquire the basic subjects, and local education authorities are reluctant to give girls student grants to make up the basic elements of a deficient secondary education. Of 'O' level candidates in technical drawing and handicraft, 98 per cent are boys; in physics, 78 per cent are boys. At 'A' level, 82 per cent of physics candidates and 60 per cent of mathematics candidates are still boys. Only 10 per cent of girls as against over 40 per cent of boys are given day release and almost all of those are hairdressers or clerks or typists. Until the 13–18 curriculum bias is altered and employers are compelled to release girls in the same measure as boys, the recruitment to advanced technical studies of proportionately more girls is a pious hope. Thus girls will not be able to enter those higher levels of employment that require HND and HNC in technical subjects, until the causes of their under-recruitment are attacked at source. An underlying related cause of girls not opting for (or being encouraged in) technology is also their under-achievement in maths, which springs from adverse conditioning in the primary years[4] and under-achievement in secondary schools.

A second causal example can be given for women employed in, for example, the further education sector. There were in 1973 no women Directors of Polytechnics, only one woman Vice Principal, and only sixteen Heads of Departments in further education, out of a total of 527. Most of the women heads of departments are in traditional 'female' areas, like Catering, Home and Welfare, Liberal Arts, Social Studies, and Crafts and Adult Education. There are, therefore, few likely women candidates from inside the sector eligible to apply for future Directorships. Women in their thirties were girls twenty years ago, when girls studied science and technology even less than today, did not therefore qualify to take science at degree level in any great numbers, have not therefore had the industrial experience or teaching background in technology (or latterly business studies) as young women, and are not therefore offering the kind of experience and qualification sought for these particular top posts. To redress the balance one would need either to alter the criteria for recruitment, or alter the characteristics of women staff in the field by retraining programmes and by special Staff Development Courses. There are even fewer women still in the field of further education at the level of responsibility likely to qualify them to be short-listed for heads of departments, in the first place, leaving aside the top tiers. The top posts tend to be held by holders of technical degrees, the second tier, by graduates in either technical or in business studies. If girls do not study these areas at school or further education college, they do not pursue them at university, polytechnic, or college of advanced further education. They will not then work at the right high level in relevant employment sectors, or teach in the principal departments carrying promotion posts, and hence will not be in the field for leadership.

Girls are often discouraged from mathematical work in their primary years. They therefore dislike it in the secondary years. They therefore drop it at 'O' and 'A' level in far greater numbers than boys. There are therefore fewer women mathematics graduates. As a result, fewer women are employed in industry in posts needing mathematical ability. Very few women accordingly teach maths in polytechnics. As a result, there are frequently no women candidates for relevant top posts in the technical sector.

Women have equally not yet achieved equal pay in hard cash because they are less well qualified than men in factories and industry generally, and have been debarred often from industrial training schemes geared to 'men's' work. This is because fewer girls stay on to take technician and craft training. This in turn is directly due to the secondary schools' obsession with freedom of choice for thirteen- and fourteen-year-old pupils, thus allowing (and encouraging) girls to drop physics, to 'opt' for typing and mothercraft, and to settle for CSE in arts subjects. The imbalance between the subjects studied by girls at eighteen-plus and sixteen-plus is bred at thirteen-plus and in the primary school. It is one major negative determinant of lower later pay.

I have of course somewhat over-simplified the argument in order to sharpen the causal relationships and will reinstate their inter-related complexities later. Many other factors like the married woman's dual role, the attitude of women and men to responsibility, reorganization fever, all have a part to play. But they do not cloud the central causal relationship. If subjects have not been studied at school and college, if attitudes have not been formed earlier, the complete removal of all the social stereotypes and repressions would still not qualify under-qualified women retrospectively to play a role for which they have neither the education nor training.

Between 1·0 per cent and 2·5 per cent of women only, over thirty-five, have had a university education. Only 15 per cent will have achieved substantial GCE or School Certificate Studies. The remaining 85 per cent lack equal pay or complete job mobility because fewer of them compared with men have had a chance to remedy this by later day release, technical training, help from employers, discretionary grants from LEAs. Only positive discrimination will break this causal cycle of deprivation. Other more complex interrelations will emerge, but the point is clearly made and has severe implications for those controlling resources in education.

Underlying all of these themes, and inextricably interwoven with the related but distinct influences of innate or conditioned inequality and subtle or overt discrimination, are the less tangible factors of prejudice, role-conditioning, the whole area of sex-role stereotyping, the influence of inherited assumptions from the (male) leadership of the past and what might be called the 'euthenics' of inequality. That is, the restrictive influence of the practical factors, like the structural sexism of the organization of the school or college, or the methods, formulae, and administrative framework by which resources are allocated differently to different groups for allegedly different needs; the whole translation of theory into practice, in fact.

The headteacher or principal who timetables boys into the one physics laboratory and girls into a converted classroom for biology, is planning on prejudice, not reason, whether he recognizes it or not. The (woman) infant teacher who tells seven-year-old Bobby that 'big boys don't cry' and eight-year-old Jenifer that 'little girls mustn't be bossy' is reacting from inherited prejudice in her attitude to her pupils as sex-groups, and not as individuals. Such influence is inseparable from the question of under-achievement and under-expectation, and a young adolescent of either sex needs above-average poise, self-confidence, motivation, and a good and secure education to overcome its deadening impact.

Prejudice comes from the Latin *praejudicium*, a precedent or judgement based on previous decisions (but not necessarily on evidence). Its present leading characteristic is of judgements and attitudes formed precipitately without reference to logic, to facts, or to evidence; an emotional and unfavourable reaction based on unsupported thoughts. First thoughts or impressions become prejudices when they are not reversible if exposed to new knowledge or first-hand experience. Moreover, stereotypes are essential for the maintenance of prejudice, usually developing from frequently asserted statements or images which are the production of past ideas handed on unexamined. A shrewd comment from one of the earliest and most radical protagonists of women's equality, John Stuart Mill, on the unshakeable tenor of deeply held convictions, has an uncomfortably familiar ring today :

'The difficulty is that which exists in all cases in which there is a mass of feeling to be contended against. So long as an opinion is strongly rooted in the feelings, it gains rather than loses stability by having a preponderating weight of argument against it.'   (J. S. Mill 1974:219)

One more general point should be understood however here. One of the most familiar (and in my view dangerous) characteristics of prejudice is what Allport (1954) describes as 'the device of admitting exceptions'. By excluding a few favoured cases as allegedly untypical, the negative rubric is kept intact for all other cases, as an unsupported generalization. It means in practice that to use the pioneer groups, the one woman Director of an Institute of Education, the two women Chief Education Officers (out of over 120), the minority of women heads of mixed large comprehensive schools, as illustrative examples to encourage the generation following, arouses the immediate response, 'But they are hardly typical'. Every minority woman has met the bland assumption, sooner or later, that she is unusually off-beat, articulate, gifted, divergent, lucky, determined, and totally uncharacteristic of the 'normal' woman. This is worrying in the context of the negative, but irrelevant, image sometimes presented to adolescent girls by careers teachers, of the allegedly 'untypical' minority women ahead of them. Who knows what is typical until a majority have actually tried and achieved it? And yet to talk of majorities is also double-edged, because few boys or girls want to be regarded as deviant, as 'unmasculine' or 'unfeminine' (a theme developed in the next chapter); and divergence carries subconscious psychological strains of implicit guilt at acting 'out of character'. If a norm is based on, say, 64 per cent, as many as 36 per cent are therefore divergent. Why should they carry a label of untypicality? Or be forced into the majority mould?

One effective counter to prejudice (*pace* John Stuart Mill) may well be, first, so to educate the majority of people in objective realization of the real facts that they recognize that the inherited or acquired assumptions on which mindless reactions are based, are unfounded. The clarity with which we expose the illogicality of under-investment in girls when the country needs more skilled labour and more economic productivity will not shake the deeply hostile; but it will almost certainly help to mobilize the more receptive and adaptable, to call the bluff and to monitor what we actually do in schools and colleges to give (and to encourage) real freedom of curricular choice and of aspiration.

It is a long way from Kurt Waldheim's international objective to a Tyneside classroom. Yet it was fifteen-year-old Jennie who summed up for me the hallmark of the adverse conditioning of girls, both by schools and by society, towards inexorable underachievement; their poverty of aspiration. The fifth-year girls were struggling to put together a jigsaw puzzle of new ideas I had been discussing with them in a careers session. 'What, Miss – work till we're sixty?', 'Go with Joe into electrical engineering, instead of the assembly line sorting electronic parts?', 'Of course it pays better – but "it's not right for a girl".' 'Take ONC in business studies at the Tech. instead of a clerk's job at the DHSS at Longbenton?' 'Take charge of the works like Dad instead of helping with school meals like Mum?' 'Stand for Wallsend Council later – you're joking, Miss.' Jennie put her finger on the obvious central malaise they could not quite identify.

'It just don't work like that', she explained, with patient reasonableness. 'I mean, girls are different. I mean, you've got to admit that with jobs short and not enough places at the Tech., and me Mum can't keep us all on, it's got to be Bill, stands to reason. I mean, he's the one who's going to keep a family, not me.'

There spoke generations of conditioning to a role of dependence, of submissiveness to second place in the queue of equal opportunity, of education for marriage, and not the whole adult world; but also of unconscious arrogance and privilege. Women had the right to choose to work after marriage, or not; Bill didn't. Or at least, not in Jennie's eyes. We attacked this. What if Bill didn't marry? What if Jennie and Kim and Liz ended up as the one in five of women now the breadwinner? Is education only so that we can earn money at work anyway? We continued the debate, and the motivation behind this book received a new injection.

Looking at why we educate girls and boys differently (and why this is no longer right) inevitably raises the whole concept of masculinity and femininity, the domestic syndrome of educating girls for marriage as a terminal occupation, boys for work, and neither for freedom of choice of their adult roles. The next chapter traces some origins of present practice and attacks the concept of classification by sex and not by individual ability and aptitude.

TWO

Masculinity, femininity, and marriage

*'Well, Miss Matty, men will be men. Every mother's son
of them wishes to be Samson and Solomon rolled into
one ... My father was a man and I know the sex pretty
well.'*

(MISS POLE *in Cranford*)

'Home is the girl's prison and the woman's workhouse.'

(GEORGE BERNARD SHAW)

We can, I am sure, forgive Miss Pole for generalizing about the
opposite sex on so selective a sample. After all, the government
of education resolutely clings to its right to do so today. The
belief that men and women are immutably different as between
the sexes but are homogeneous within each sex, which we sew
together again each time that the stitches give way before the
ruthless knife of the exposure of illogicality, is one to which

41

society clings with a Panglossian sublimity which Voltaire himself would have conceptually envied.

The nature/nurture argument is developed mainly in the next chapter on the formative years. It is however important for us to look again at the fundamental assumptions that underly masculinity and femininity, because of their influence both on curricular planning and on the advice and encouragement on the one hand or the implicit 'ceilings' of attainment or roles, on the other, which we offer girls and boys respectively in our schools and colleges.

After nearly twenty years of experience of all kinds of educational institutions in England, I am convinced that the woolliness of our definition of educational objectives, and the pervasiveness of the vocational/domestic antithesis of male and female roles in the eyes of head teachers are the two major causes of the under-achievement of many girls and women and their lack of ambition and drive to take advantage even of those facilities that are available to them. In particular, the education service is guilty of doublethink. It alleges widely (and wrongly) that it is not the task of schools to prepare pupils for livelihood (why is work so unrespectable to teachers?) Yet at every point in the school system where choices have to be made between conflicting needs or demands of curricular areas and experiences, teachers do look closely at either vocational needs as specified by employers or training institutions, or qualifications needed for the next stage of education (in itself a tool for economic advancement). And in most cases of such 'choices', teachers tend to perceive an external, work-based role for boys and an internal, home-based role for girls intermittently moderated by exposure to such work as will not interfere with woman's perceived support role to her menfolk and her family.

Head teachers of secondary schools in my original survey area in 1968 (Byrne 1974) were sure (if in my view, wrong) they were not educating for work or industry; but were less sure of any other common goal.

'We educate for life, not livelihood.'

'I want my pupils to grow up happy people.'

'We educate for personal fulfilment.'

'They should leave us as intelligent young thinkers.'

'I educate for leadership in this school.'

'To get them to university or college – the girls will go for teacher training, of course.'

'It's not our job to educate for work.'

'I don't believe in working wives – we educate our girls to be happy family women. Society needs them at home.'

We are reluctant to admit also that the way in which we plan and allocate educational resources is riddled with discriminatory practices weighted in favour of the academic, the older pupil, urban areas and boys, and against the less able, the younger, rural children, and girls. A girl who has the misfortune to be less able, rural, and in the middle years will be quadruply disadvantaged.[1] The overgeneralized statements above by Heads about the purpose and direction of their schools melt away and are replaced by a colder decisiveness when one analyses the timetable and room allocations to explain why the scarcer technical resources are fully used by boys and are regarded as inessential for girls, when rationing is necessary: 'Of course we can't teach physics and technical drawing to the *full* IVth year and we'd never get apprenticeships for our boys without a technical base. After all, they *are* the future breadwinners.'

One's view indeed of the adult roles for which we have traditionally educated girls (and boys) and the frequently unaccountable differences between the education of the two sexes, may well depend on the derivation (conscious or unconscious) of our attitudes. We are likely to be influenced by whether, for example, we believe like Plato that 'there is no function in society which is peculiar to woman as woman or man as man; natural abilities are similarly distributed in each sex and it is natural to share all occupations with men' (*Republic*, Part 6, Book 5); or whether, like Milton, we find reassuring security that discriminatory planning for women's dependence is invested with a Divine right, that 'God's universal law gave to the man despotic power over his female in due awe' (*Samson Agonistes*).

For the fundamental question which appears to have eluded educational planners and curriculum-mongers, government and local education authorities, head teachers and parents alike, is, for what purpose are we educating girls – and boys – in the first place? This is not, let us be clear, a question of the past — vague generalizations about a liberal education, personal fulfilment, non-vocational freedom in an unstructured adult world — these belong with Comenius and Cardinal Newman, with Montaigne and Morant. It is a highly practical question. With what collection of experience, qualifications, knowledge, insight, intellectual growth, practical skills, are we expecting to turn out both girls and boys at sixteen-plus or eighteen-plus; and to fill what adult roles?

I am here, therefore, attacking the whole definition of masculinity and femininity as concepts which could be identified as at all homogeneous or relevant to personal educational development or free choice of adult roles. I place central in importance, the words interchangeability, duality of roles, individuality, diagnosis, in our educational thinking. I would abolish the words 'the girls' and 'the boys' from the vocabulary of all teachers, replacing them with the correct diagnostic identification of changing relevance (the third year, the school leaving group, the stronger or taller, the smaller children, the aggressive, the delicate). To divide up an educational crowd by sex for convenience is intellectually lazy; it is also dangerously pervasive as a conditioning factor to teach both sexes to regard the other as a normative group with expected (and different) patterns of behaviour.

Masculine and feminine?

There is a very real difficulty, of course, in writing of women and education as if either were finitely definable. To generalize about women in a chapter the main purpose of which is to attack the mystique of predetermined 'masculinity' and 'femininity' in the first place, is indeed to sail between a Scylla and Charybdis of controversy. But teachers and planners have generalized for so long about 'boys' and 'girls' as separate species that it has become unavoidable, if we are to look at what is actually happening in our schools and colleges. The rural primary school headmistress who wrote the following, clearly did not think of her children as Jem, Marion, Bobby, or Jean, but as different groups of pupils indelibly stamped by their sex.

'*The boys* dug a hole and made a very satisfactory pond ...

44

a girl brought a jar of water from the football field to show me that it was not fit to drink, although it was always used for the players' tea. Then *the boys* wanted to find out if the rainwater running down the bank contained any debris ...'
(Plowden Committee 1967:para 670)

Here we have a cameo of the end result of the polarization of roles which children are tacitly encouraged to fit, by the praises, criticisms, examples, attitudes of acceptability, expectations of parents and teachers. Physical labour is masculine; so the boys dug the hole, although at nine years old, many girls tend to be heavier and stronger than boys for a short while until the boys catch up and overtake in puberty. But digging in mud is seen as unfeminine. On the other hand, boys were seen to be inquisitive, rational, questioning. Were there no girls curious about the rainwater? And just how had they been taught in this small country school, to have so little curiosity about causes and effects? Behind that quotation whose typical picture I still see in the primary schools I visit today, lies the whole debate about sex roles and sex differences.

Girls grow up to be women in a world which, with the explicit acceptance of one sex and the tacit willingness of the other, until relatively recently, has been male dominated and male oriented. In school, in college and in work, in the home, in the pub, in the street, in the club, both children and adults quietly absorb images of men and women as two different species. But the feminine image carries stigmata which over many hundreds of years have carried an almost universal if unconscious message of inferiority, of lesser importance, of dependence (usually on men), of destiny to a domestic role. The price of rejecting the image has always been and remains a charge of 'unfemininity', an age-old fear of adolescent girls in a world which trains us to value the 'normal' and to reject and shun both the freak and the genius, and those in between whom we do not understand. The unknown is always to be feared.

This chapter deals only briefly with the concepts of masculinity and femininity as they affect the education of girls. I am challenging the whole 'normative' approach which talks about masculine and feminine behaviour and aptitudes as if all girls and women had one, identifiable and constant set of innate qualities, traits, gifts, and characteristics, and all boys and men another. Lester Gelb questions this in an admirable summary of the sex polarization:

> 'Many in the field of psychoanalysis have been guilty of contributing heavily to the excessive institutionalisation of male and female roles which have little to do with sexual identity. Psychoanalysts have contributed to the view of women as weak, inferior, passive, fragile, soft, vacillating, dependent, unreliable, intuitive, rather than rational, castrated and handicapped. Men have been polarised as aggressive, controlling, strong, superior, proud, independent, venturesome, competitive, hard and athletic.'
>
> (Lester Gelb 1973:367)

Banton also summarizes the attributes ascribed to different sex roles as the feminine 'gentleness, piety, compliance, reticence, beauty', and the masculine 'assertiveness, worldliness, management, boldness, competence', and comments that a woman's basic roles tend to be founded on her relationship to the male members of the society while a man's basic roles stress age much more and set less weight on marital status. He recognized that, 'If the norms of behaviour associated with sex and age roles were to be dissolved, the effects on any society would obviously be multitudinous' (Banton 1965:78).

Antithesis

Of the many theories of character stereotyping which psychologists and psychoanalysts have in my view served to reinforce, the intellectual antithesis of man, the logical reasoner, the woman, the intuitive pragmatist, is educationally the most dangerous. Second only to this in the primary sector, in particular during pre-school stage, is the imagery of the mutual exclusiveness of boy and man, the strong unemotional non-paternal; and girl and woman, the weak, tender, maternal, and caring.

Their history lies in a direct long line over centuries, more recently through psychologists and psychoanalysts, to the early theologians of whom Aquinas must have been the most extreme to assert the passive inferiority of women.[2] Perhaps more relevant in influencing teacher training, was the early sway of writers like Havelock Ellis whose 1894 treatise on secondary and tertiary sex characteristics was still popular enough to warrant a reprint in 1934. He held tenaciously to a closely argued view that 'the two halves of the race are compensatory in their unlikeness ... all that we have found in our long course of investigation is in harmony with this primitive and fundamental distinction between the two main spheres of masculine and feminine activity' (Havelock Ellis 1934:vi, 447). He punctiliously and regularly disproves his own case, however, in my view, re-reading his research evidence of, for example, the physical superiority of some college women in America over some college men, of rural women over town women, and of great variations within each sex. This evidence could in fact be used to attack the normative approach. For he quotes the Industrial Fatigue Research Board in England, which established in the 1930s that educated college girls in Glasgow had physical strengths and characteristics superior to factory girls; that the country bred excelled over town bred in physical tests but that college educated girls from both town and country exceeded factory girls. This divergence *within* each sex, is mirrored by our experience today – the National Child Development study of 11,000 seven-year-olds confirmed some greater gaps in achievement and physical performance and intellectual characteristics between manual and non-manual children, than between boys and girls respectively.

It is extraordinary the lengths to which psychologists, writers, teachers have gone, over the years, to prop up these concepts of masculine and feminine extremes by the very exceptions which disprove them as norms of innate characteristics and betray them as socially induced development. Ellis himself quotes Paul Lafitte's *Le Paradoxe de L'Egalité* not in fact to support the ambivalence and the *heterogeneity* of people, men or women, which in my view it does, but the inexorable definition of qualities by sex: 'La Bruyere on more than one side is a feminine genius: Descartes is the type of the masculine genius: the woman's mind is more concrete, the man's more abstract.'

For one who argued that logic was a male attribute the argument is singularly illogical. There is surely a psychological block in refusing to admit that character traits are variously present in all kinds of people, but this has persisted – even Simone de Beauvoir thought that 'woman have no grasp on the world of men because their experience does not teach them to use logic

47

and technique.' (1974:622). Although she is right that some girls' education has tended to lack adequate training in logic, I strongly question the assumption that some of us at least are not born with an innate dose or that we do not acquire or develop some clear thinking along the way.

One early post-war decisive attack on the ideology of the feminine character attempted to draw together in a wide-ranging study the different dimensions of social history, anthropology, psychoanalysis, and philosophy. Viola Klein was in no doubt that although sex is a major factor in shaping personality through social conditioning, individual differences nevertheless prevailed over differences between classified sex groups. She illustrates her thesis in a clear and logical analysis, concluding that:

'Although the present time is a period of transition, and the effects of tradition are still very strong, it is already becoming clear that the more of the masculine functions women fulfil, the more of those traits previously thought 'masculine' they generally develop. It therefore becomes more and more obvious that those traits are not the effect of innate sex characteristics but of the social role, and are changing with it.' (Klein 1946:178)

Not all writers take so clear a view. The purpose behind Evelyn Acworth's scholarly account of women's more dominant role in the historical past (1965) was surely to show that women and government, women and work, and women and politics have not always been strangers, and that some societies have been significantly matriarchal. Her work sheds a good deal of light on the active, decisive, and in traditional terms, 'un-feminine' roles they have played in history. Yet only twelve years ago she could perpetuate the myth that: 'The minds of man and woman are known to function differently: for whereas broadly speaking the masculine mind reaches conclusions through logical processes, the feminine mind does so through instinct and intuition.' And her comment that: 'Man expresses feminine qualities in a masculine way and woman expresses the masculine qualities in a feminine way.' seems to me a totally unhelpful conclusion to draw from an account that in fact portrays women as unusual achieving individuals – the personal fulfilment that should remain the prime objective of education.

I am not of course saying that there are no valid sex differences at all, in challenging the *educational* and *social* usefulness of clinging to outmoded stereotypes of masculinity and femininity. Nor that the normative approach – based on norms of achievement, behaviour, or physical characteristics of certain groups of people – is not useful elsewhere. It is clearly a major tool, for example, in the medical field. It has unquestionably helped us to detect early signs of handicap in young children, to learn more about the 'normal' child and what he or she can be expected to do by various ages and stages of development. But it is in my view a negative, repressive, and wholly inappropriate tool to use as a guide in planning curricula, in encouraging certain behaviour patterns as praiseworthy in boys and unfortunate in girls, and vice versa, and in steering boys and girls towards expected and different adult roles in the society for which schools believe they prepare young people.

The normative approach

Classification by 'labelled' groups, as an educational tool is occasionally helpful but it can be a dangerous influence against real diagnostic work. The leadership of the education service, including teachers and Her Majesty's Inspectors, have long supported the 'normative' approach – one based on alleged sex norms of character traits, innate capabilities, correct or deviant behaviour patterns, superiority or inferiority of potential achievements, which we are told will be different for boys and girls, men and women. After neary twenty years of watching both teachers and children in schools in the conurbation, in small towns, and in rural counties, I find little trace of new thinking, little evidence of knowledge of the new research and seminal writing that has questioned the whole concept of indentifiable *homogeneous* masculinity or femininity in postwar years.

I am tempted, like Zola, to write '*J'accuse*'; in this instance, of neglect, by the education service, to give to the sex-differential debate, the serious attention and respect that our research programmes, conferences, and (influentially) teacher-training programmes have for long awarded the equally important problems of social handicap, racial inequality, multi-cultural factors in learning, and the handicaps of physical and mental disabilities.

That we have far to go on this issue is sadly reflected in the introduction to the collection of valuable new papers published by the British Sociological Association in 1976:

> 'We think we should record the surprise (and even hostility and ribaldry) shown by some sociologists at the prospect of a BSA conference being devoted to sexual divisions and society. As far as we know, nothing similar was expressed about conferences on race and racialism, social stratification or development ... Indeed, we would use any and all the volumes so far published in this series as examples of the virtual absence in sociological discourse of any awareness of gender as an organizing force in society.'
>
> (Barker and Allen 1976:18)

The separation of sex from gender is a useful one – the first representing the mainly reproductive biological differences which distinguish men and women; and the second incorporating the whole trappings of character traits, behaviour patterns, expectation, roles, manners, dress, occupation, status, which we learn to acquire, suppress, or develop by reflecting social attitudes and conditioning.

I believe that educationalists in particular have transposed – perhaps subconsciously – the kind of physiological differences which the early writers publicized as 'masculine' and 'feminine'[3], and ascribed to men and women additional clusters of traits and roles which appeared to match the allegedly physiological antitheses of strong: weak; dominant: dependent; logical: intuitive; cool: emotional; which Lester Gelb's criticism of masculine and feminine polarization so aptly summarizes. I share the view of many that our knowledge is still too imperfect to generalize. I doubt we have advanced as much as we believe since J. S. Mill countered the 'feeble sex' myth of femininity a hundred years ago, which had such a regrettably Royal backing[4] by writing:

> 'standing on the ground of common sense and the constitution of the human mind, I deny that anyone knows, or can know, the nature of the two sexes, *as long as they have only been seen in relation to one another* ... what is called the nature of woman is an eminently artificial thing, the result

of forced repression in some directions, unnatural stimulation in others.'
(J. S. Mill 1869 : 238)

It is precisely because in my view, men as well as women are still encouraged to suppress some characteristics and to develop others, regardless of the delicate and highly personal balance of traits and characteristics which nature gives them from both parents, that they are prevented from developing freely as individual human beings. I am questioning therefore the whole normative approach of typicality and untypicality.

The general argument against using sex norms in thinking about the education of people is mainly the problem of the substantial minority who simply do not conform and are 'untypical'. Children learn fundamentally by praise or blame, by encouragement and approval, or criticism and disfavour. We keep this throughout our lives – the courage to take 'a man's job', to choose to stay single rather than marry for second best, to assert leadership rather than bypass a promotion, does not mean that a girl will any the more welcome the constant implicit social criticism of unfemininity or of non-conformism in so doing. Life becomes a constant bargain of balance – a choice of which issues of conformity to concede, like traditional modes of dress, speech, manners, in order to keep the individuality of more important and radical differences in character, work, role. This, however, is more often seen as a middle-class issue or one for the intellectually able. The less confident average girl from a working-class home, working in a small town or a district with strong regional and traditional attitudes, tends to learn to conform long before leaving school in order to keep the encouragement and praise of the family, teachers, boyfriends who matter to her and whose conditioning is likely to be more traditional.

And yet the more we concede to the traditionality of some symbols, like dress, hairstyle, behaviour, which may at first sight seem trivial, the worse problem we create for those who find these so unacceptable as to reject them – girl or boy alike – and who are then labelled as deviant rather than simply untypical, whatever that means. Standards of male and female dress in school, for example, are still an issue that arouses violent (if different) feelings on the part of both staff and pupils; but schools again are frequently apparently unable to keep up with society's changing convention.

Thirteen years ago, for example, Banton could still write:

'Distinctive forms of dress and of wearing the hair serve to tell people the sex of the person in question and are a much more effective means of conveying such information than verbal communication.' (Banton 1965:69)

If today's apparent unisexuality of dress and long hair seems to contradict this on the surface, look again at how far schools refuse to mirror society. In 1977 a girl was excluded from school and deprived of several months of secondary education because she insisted on wearing to school the trousers which she wears with society's complete approval out of school. Her headmaster, like the head who expels his boys if they refuse to cut their hair, is telling society that he insists on his right to rule what is 'manly' and 'ladylike', regardless of current social conventions outside school. Simultaneously, an Employment Appeals Tribunal has heard a case of a young woman sacked from a leading multiple chemists for wearing trousers on the grounds that they 'needed' their assistants to look 'ladylike'. The Tribunal upheld the employer. It is interesting to note that Simone de Beauvoir was writing as long ago as 1949 that 'woman can be transformed gradually so that her canons of propriety approach those adopted by the males. On the seashore – and elsewhere – trousers have become feminine' (1974:692). Not apparently, in England in 1977. Stereotyped symbols of our expected sex roles cease, moreover, to become trivial when they result in loss of schooling or employment, if rejected.

It is clear that there is no simple answer, no right or wrong. On the contrary, much more research needs to be considered on a wide range of problems, causes, and patterns of existing sex differences and their relevance psychologically or socially. More work on the innate versus conditioning arguments is essential. Jean Baker Miller in introducing *Psychoanalysis and Women* wrote that

'It is remarkable that many people – especially but not only young people – do not seem to know that psychoanalysts who offer alternative ideas did or do exist. This is particularly striking because many of these analysts are highly gifted, some quite prominent in the field.' (Miller 1974:xi)

One message is clear. The education service has also a good deal of homework to do, the first task of which is to raise the debate about sex roles in education to a serious intellectual level, and to vote research funds to relevant and more substantial field-work. We should moreover begin to make socially unacceptable the common attitude of triviality and, occasionally, mockery, which so far has characterized public reaction to the intelligent questioning by a few in the leadership of education, as to why the education of girls should be any different from that of boys; and how solid is the ground for alleged norms of sex differences used to justify different curricula and methods for girls and boys respectively.

The second main argument against speaking of women as an identifiable group is that other variables than character and physique (even if those were constant, which I suggest they are not) are immeasurably more influential than sex.

Social class and the culture and tradition which it carries with it is still a great divider and middle-class girls have, in some important respects, more in common with middle-class boys than with working-class girls – especially those from another region. There are many respects in which rural boys and girls have more in common with each other in attitudes, learning patterns, physique, than rural girls and girls from a great conurbation like London. Parental background is the most influential of all, and that cuts across both class and region.

Indeed, the differences in the educational opportunity, the attitudes, and the conditioning of the middle-class girl and the working-class girl (no one has yet coined a new term for working class, although linguistically it is inaccurate) have been seriously under-researched. One of the more important of the many books which the women's liberation movement and the rise of the new form of feminist activity produced was Sheila Rowbotham's study of the social structures and changes that triggered off the movement – simply because it paints a more real picture of the thoughts and attitudes of the 'non-middle class'. In her view:

'In isolation, the individual woman who passes over into activity is bound to define herself at the expense of other women. This is apparently at the level of class. The freedom of the emancipated upper class woman is simply the other side of the unfreedom of the working class woman who supports her.' (Rowbotham 1973:41)

With some ambivalence, however, in a book rejecting stereotypes she recalls her own reflex image of the women who had educated her:

'When I was seventeen, feminism meant to me, shadowy figures in long old fashioned clothes who were somehow connected with headmistresses who said you shouldn't wear high heels and makeup ... From dim childhood memories I had a stereotype of emancipated women: frightening people in tweed suits and hornrimmed glasses with stern buns at the back of their heads. Feminism was completely asexual.'

(Rowbotham 1973:12)

The implicit gulf of class and the implied rejection of women who did not project the usual 'feminine' image of pretty clothes and hairstyles are in themselves revealing. The most liberated are still conditioned by past reflexes. Schools have much to counteract.

An important gap in this area has been filled by a study of working-class girls in Ealing which forms the central theme of Sue Sharpe's *Just like a Girl* (1976). The relationship between the under-achievement and under-expectation of the girls because careers, high academic work, homework, staying on at school were seen as for boys, as unfeminine, as not part of their mothers' or their own normal patterns, is sensitively told in this readable but well researched book. What comes through very strongly indeed is the need that the girls feel for a feminine identity, for what they see as the security of male domination in marriage even when they believed in equal pay and equal careers. How the girls saw themselves was revealing evidence of their (perhaps conditioned) need for the secure family role which at least was seen by them to be within their grasp.

The 'domestic vocation' of women in education

The perceived antithesis of the sexes is most strongly marked in the educational planning of practical education, especially for the less able. Almost all countries (certainly all European

54

educational systems) divide boys and girls for what are seen as mutually exclusive crafts – domestic and welfare subjects for girls with a gloss of 'extended maternality' incorporating preparation for nursery nursing or child care. Boys are given manually dexterous and work-centred crafts reflecting an aura of future skilled employment. The antithesis of the conditioning of girls' internal and boys' external worlds is aptly summarized by Pascal Lainé, describing what he calls the 'domestic vocation' of women. He points to a further male and female antithesis – the male preoccupation with the *outside* world, the female with the *inward* looking home – which our secondary special fourth- and fifth-year courses reinforce. The casting of woman in a predominantly domestic role is, of course, almost universal:

'The first and the most fundamental division of work ... is between men and women. And it is first a symbolic division of space, which all cultures illustrate. And perhaps this dichotomy between the feminine "inside" and the masculine "outside" is the prototype of a manichean topography constituting social primitive space. Thus the "domestic" vocation of woman seems to be universal, more or less compulsory, only according to the period or the place.' (Pascal 1974:31)

Sadly, this is translated into a subtle permeation of the planning of the education of girls, and is present from the pre-school Wendy House to the now outlawed 'women's courses' in further education.

The whole relationship between marriage, and curricular planning of secondary education for boys and girls and in particular, of careers education, and advice, is riddled with false assumptions, negative and inconsistent thinking, and inherited attitudes traceable directly back to Edwardian and Victorian mother worship. Bertrand Russell once said:

'In the welter of conflicting fanaticisms, one of the few unifying forces is scientific truthfulness, by which I mean the habit of basing our beliefs on observations and inferences as impersonal and as much divested of local and temperamental bias as is possible for human beings.'

(Russell 1961:789)

I know of no fanaticisms so secure and so impervious to evidence to the contrary as the assumption that the *real vocation* of all girls is marriage and looking after children; that of all boys, working in employment with a career leading to advancement and responsibility, and providing for dependent women; and that schools should plan children's education with these different aims in mind.

Socially, of course, marriage has always been the hallmark of the successful woman. Although few today would be as brutally honest as the *Saturday Review*, it is unquestionably still true that adult life in a single state, at however distinguished a level is still somehow regarded as an inferior bargain with life:

> 'Marriage is woman's profession; and to this life her training
> – *that of dependence* – is modelled. Of course, by not getting
> a husband, or losing him, she may find that she is without
> resources. All that can be said of her is, she has failed in
> business and no social reform can prevent such failures.'
> (*The Saturday Review* 1857, quoted in Acworth 1965:125)

The education of women to a supportive role runs right through the nineteenth-century books on women. In another treatise addressed to 'Our Daughters', we are told:

> 'All the arguments which have yet been advanced in favour of
> the higher education of men plead equally strongly in favour
> of the higher education of women. *In all the departments of
> the home*, intelligence will add to woman's usefulness and
> efficiency ... whatever helps to develop latent powers within
> you ... will make you more capable of fulfilling the noble
> mission assigned to you.'   (Mrs G. S. Reaney 1884:214)[5]

Victorian girls were left in no doubt as to their domestic role even if they did not marry – usually housekeeping for other homes. The unmarried daughter's future was still male-dependent, caring for father, brother, the family as a whole, in return for being sheltered and 'kept.'

> 'She is one who is capable of fulfilling her wifely mission,
> inasmuch as she is what God intended she should be – a
> *helpmeet* to her husband. My dear sisters, are you preparing
> yourself for this exalted position in the home ... ? Even
> supposing you are never to become a wife, there is yet every

reason, simply because you are a woman, that you should learn how to make healthy, happy and prosperous homes.'

(Mrs G. S. Reaney 1884:200–1)

The Victorian contempt for the unmarried woman is far from eroded. A hundred years later the handbook used by Swedish secondary schools to teach young people about personal relationships records society's attitude today – unquestionably mirrored in this country:

'There is also a tendency in our society to look down on those who, for various reasons, live without a sex partner. The teacher should combat this sort of superficial and discriminatory attitude, pointing to the self-evident fact that a person can find community, meaning and a content for his or her life, even if he or she is in one sense "alone".'

(Swedish USSU State Commission 1975:5)

We should be clear that women who do not marry, span the entire spectrum from those who lose the opportunity through tragedy, family responsibilities (or like the war generation of women now in their fifties and sixties whose single state is patently due to the war) to women who actively prefer to live alone or to put a career above marriage. They are neither of them 'unfeminine' by the standards that society sets and should be distinguished again from those who are physically and emotionally incapable of marriage, for whatever reason.

Part of the drive to concentrate girls' attention on the domestic skills of life undoubtedly arose from Victorian fears that female labour and longer education for girls led women of 'the poorer classes' to neglect their homes. The Interdepartmental Committee on Physical Deterioration, in interrogating Charles Booth about the causes of poor health in army recruits in 1904 asked how far it was due to poorer food at home and domestic neglect. Booth was sure that female labour was a major cause of neglect of homes and poor cooking; commended the cookery centres of the educational bodies; and strongly opposed the extension of education of girls beyond thirteen. The Committee suggested allowing girls to attend school only half time 'provided they went home for the rest of the day to work with their mothers at domestic work'. Booth supported this idea (Van der Eyken 1973).

The new 1904 Regulations for Secondary Schools (the new grammar schools for girls) of the Board of Education insisted on compulsory 'housewifery' for girls, and the few gifted girls therefore who did manage to achieve a grammar school place in 1904 wasted time on cooking and laundry, while their brothers learned more science. For the Regulations also allowed that: 'In a girls' school in which the total number of hours of instruction is less than 22 per week, the time given to science and mathematics may be reduced to one-third of that total' (*Regulations for Secondary Schools*, Board of Education Cd. 2128, 1904, p. 18).

When state education came to the poor, the polarization of male and female roles was promptly translated into the practical side of the curriculum. Boys did manual crafts, girls learned to launder and cook. Whereas, however, the former was primarily vocational, the latter was partly vocational (with a useful supply of domestic servants) but partly education for homemaking. The London School Board's School Management Code endorsed by the London County Council in 1904 required girls to attend a Domestic Subjects centre for one half day a week after the age of eleven, except for girls in standards seven and eight or taking special examinations. The curriculum of the Higher Elementary Schools in the 1909 Code had as one of two objects the, 'provision of special instruction *bearing on the future occupations of scholars*, whether boys or girls. Manual work for boys and domestic subjects for girls'. The clear assumption was that girls' occupation was domesticity. How different is this from today's obsessive crosstimetabling of housecraft for girls and the more educationally useful metalwork, woodwork, and technical drawing for boys which is an apparently unshakeable pattern of modern secondary school timetabling (and which is now questionable under Section 22 of the *Sex Discrimination Act, 1975*)?

The Code of Regulations for Public Elementary Schools allowed for special grants for vocational courses for senior classes and the sex division is especially interesting in that for the first (but not last) time, cookery for boys is labelled *vocational*: 'For boys – handicraft, gardening and (in schools in seaport towns with the special consent of the Board) cookery. For girls, cookery, laundry work, dairy work and household management' (1904, Cd. 2074).

58

At no time in the history of education has it occurred to the (male) educational planners that cooking for boys is a domestic skill needed to further the freedom of women; only the converse. To this day the assumption persists that the only time boys would or should enter housecraft rooms is if they are going into catering as a career. The pattern has altered little in practice today, even though we have ceased in the UK to have separate 'technical' schools for girls, and we allege a form of open time-tabling. The Newsom Report appeared for example to have moved little from the practices of over 120 years ago, in describing marriage as most girls' vocational aim, although 100 years of women's employment should have dispelled the mythology of universal housewifery. The report is, for example, permeated with assumptions about girls' domestic role:

'For all girls too, there is a group of interests relating to *what many, perhaps most of them, would regard as their most important vocational concern – marriage*. It is true that at the age of 14 or 15, this may appear chiefly as preoccupation with personal appearance and boy friends, but many girls are ready to respond to work relating to the wider aspects of home making and family life and the care and upbringing of children.' (Newsom Committee 1963:para 113, my italics)

It is the word vocational which is objectionable. If this is a legitimate task of the school – and I for one question this when it is at the expense of mathematics, science, sound English language, technical craft skills, civics, education for community life, and participation in some form of leadership (even if only at Parish Council level), then why is it not equally important for boys to prepare for marriage and to be husbands and fathers?

It is significant that the Newsom Report quotes a girls' school in the Midlands whose aim was 'to link their work with their future hope – marriage and mothercraft'. Of thirty-six periods of teaching a week, five were allocated to domestic science and mothercraft, two to embroidery, an excessive four to physical education, and *none whatever* to science, technical crafts, mathematics (arithmetic was taught by budgeting). Even accepting the lower level of ability described and the need to teach by practical methods, the bias is still markedly against providing a basis of breadth and depth for later return to work –

because there is no base for further education or training and little breadth of curriculum. The report confirms this general trend later by recording that:

> 'boys in boys' schools spend on average the equivalent of half a morning a week more in the maths and science field than do the girls in the girls' schools, who in turn spend a correspondingly greater amount of time on the practical subjects ... To some extent these variations are caused by a *differing diagnosis of needs of pupils ...*'
>
> (Newsom Committee 1963:para 627, 629, my italics)

There is now a different pattern in the cycle of women's adult and marital life which is underestimated as a factor for change in educating girls and which is the natural sequence of the 'problem with no name' of which Betty Friedan wrote with such trenchant yet sensitive analysis in the early 1960s (Friedan 1963). She wrote of the increasingly articulate longing of the American housewife for something more than freezer foods for Tom's dinner and new football socks for Joe – for an identity with some purpose and destination other than the supermarket, the clinic, the welfare old people's home, the crematorium. When the children are away or grown up, who is to fill the vacuum?

We have to admit, nevertheless, to having educated the non-academic girls principally for marriage as the terminal occupation to end all, since we first organized a system of schools and colleges to lift women out of domestic illiteracy. How different is the attitude today of the Tyneside schoolgirl, the Birmingham school leaver, the young Londoner, from the arrogant if pathetic rationalization of Victorian dependence?

The concentration on domestic education of girls is of deeper importance than it appears at first sight, partly because it is so universal. Italy, for example, separates technical secondary education for girls into *istituto femminili* with a curriculum almost entirely geared to the domestic crafts or to feminine-dominated employment. Eighty per cent of the girls in secondary 'technical' education in the Netherlands are in *huishoud* schools – domestic science, and preparatory courses for welfare and nursery nursing, etc. Denmark is now phasing out its *husholdningskoler*, equivalent to domestic science schools, and probably will be following the Swedish pattern of insisting that both sexes study the whole range of home and handicrafts at least up to fourteen or fifteen years of age.

The second issue really causes the first – the assumption of woman's economic dependence on man in marriage (or a similar non-formal partnership) and the related 'male breadwinner syndrome'. This is a principle cause of girls' lower motivation to continue in long-term education and training, to strive for the same qualifications, to seek work, advancement, and independence in the same measure as boys. It also relates to a substantial mythology – that women do not work or are unfitted for leadership, which leads teachers to accept implicit lower ceilings of attainment and motivation of their girl school leavers.

Girls' attitudes today

There can too easily be a certain self-selection about the presentation of the rate of change of educational ideologies and reforms, which springs from the fact that it tends to be the most 'progressive' or articulate who attend courses, lecture, train others, visit schools elsewhere, write books, and dogmatize. All education officers have experienced the 'that doesn't happen any longer' syndrome; only to find that it does in 90 per cent of their schools. As a contribution towards self-checking, therefore, I undertook a survey of fifth-form girls from a Northern city comprehensive school in 1975, specifically as a background for this book. Their comments and experiences will appear at intervals throughout, described as 'The fifth form survey'; and illustrate an interesting mix of classic traditional attitudes and newly changing attitudes.

In February 1975, 110 fifth formers from a girls' comprehensive school in a Northern city completed a questionnaire anonymously, to test their attitudes to a number of issues affecting equality of opportunity for girls and women. In particular I was interested in their attitude to femininity as a concept, to different education or careers for boys and girls, and to the adult roles of men and women in marriage and employment. The opportunity was also taken to gather information about their take-up of external examinations, the arts/science split, their parents' education, and a number of other related issues. The school was a 13–18 school admitting a 7–form entry at thirteen plus from a predominantly working-class catchment area, mainly recruiting from council housing estates on the outskirts of the city. It had reorganized in 1972 by merging a grammar school and two secondary modern schools. The 1975 fifth year was made up of about 50 per cent former grammar-school girls and 50 per cent secondary-modern girls transferred in at thirteen plus in 1972. The response and accuracy rate was unusually high, very few questions having a validity rate of below 103 out of 110 and most considerably higher. We attributed this partly to the girls' enthusiasm, partly to the careful preparation by the school, partly to their knowledge that the results would be used in a book, and partly because the questionnaires were completed at one single time in classroom conditions under supervision.

It is not of course possible to say how typical the girls in the Northern girls' comprehensive school are – but there is no reason to assume that they are especially untypical and indeed all of the indications at the school were that its catchment area, intake, and character could be mirrored by any large city with large areas of post-war Council housing. The questionnaire deliberately alternated some questions aimed at a completely open-ended answer with no guidance, and others setting out either specific statements to be approved or rejected, or choices of careers or status to be ranked in order of preference or of personal expectation. By way of background the girls were first asked to present their own view of themselves by filling in a self assessment of personality characteristics on a 7-point scale measuring degrees of opposite traits (for example: rational/emotional; active/passive; weak/strong). The scale went from 'extremely – fairly – slightly – both equal' – to 'neither'.

The girls rated themselves as predominantly working class (17 per cent extremely, 33 per cent fairly, 15 per cent slightly, 2·3 per cent average). Only 11·3 per cent were on the middle-class side of the scale at all. The 'passivity' of the female was rejected – 20 per cent 'extremely active' and a further half to the 'active' side, while half labelled themselves 'energetic'. Temperamentally, however, stereotypes tended to be reasserted – they saw themselves as emotional rather than rational (16 per cent extremely, 39 per cent fairly, 11·9 per cent slightly), while only 4·0 per cent thought they were decidedly rational. Over half veered to 'tender' rather than 'tough' minded; and only

9·0 per cent would admit to being 'unattractive'. Almost all were 'warm' rather than 'cool' (a mere 5 per cent). On the other hand, nearly half thought they were on balance more dominant than submissive. The overall picture which emerged, both during the main exercise and in the selected interviews, was a group of girls with lively minds and down-to-earth common sense, who had been, however, underdeveloped in expectation and over-encouraged in traditional attitudes.

Their views and experiences will recur at intervals. First, however, a synoptic look at the principal causes of stereotyping, which result from the social impact of the normative approach, suggests a fundamental review of teachers' views on marriage, dependence, and paternality.

Re-education for independence, interchange, and paternality

There are several tangled issues whose inter-relationship in the education of girls (and boys) permeate the unwritten assumptions and social reflexes that were characterized by the educational planners I have already criticized. They include the assumption of woman's *dependency* in marriage, especially economically; the myth that women do not work after marriage and therefore do not need – or merit – further education and training; the under-development of mens' paternality; and the need for boys to be educated to expect to share fully in the domestic burden and to further their wives' careers (paid or unpaid) as well as their own.

The mythology of antithesis has, for example, produced its own sub-myths of which the oldest and the longest a-dying is what Alexandra Symonds calls woman's 'declaration of dependence', which in educational terms I suggest has been variously abused to justify denial of day release for girls ('they'll only get married'); restriction of industrial training for women or of student grants and awards for married women; refusal of retraining grants for married women wanting to return to work; and discouragement to look for a career rather than a job, for less able school leavers.

'Many women freely admit their dependency needs and they are not ashamed to say that they are looking forward to marriage so they can quit work and be taken care of ... their

63

opportunity to be dependent without self-criticism ... their declaration of dependence ... Many women, and men too, equate dependence and helplessness with femininity.'

(Symonds 1974:299–330)

One of the most skilful dissections of the extent to which women's opportunities depend on abolishing the mystique of feminine dependence appeared not long after the war. Simone de Beauvoir's classic, *The Second Sex*, covers biological, psycho-analytical, historical, and mythological angles. I read it in its French edition as a fascinated student in Paris in 1955, and the shock to my middle-class, comfortable girls-grammar school assumptions even at that stage, has made me wonder frequently since how its publication in English in 1953 can so have escaped so many allegedly educated teachers who generalize about girls. De Beauvoir observed shrewdly that:

'A woman supported by a man ... is not emancipated from the male because she has a vote ... It is through gainful employment that woman has traversed most of the distance that separated her from the male; and nothing else can guarantee her liberty in practice. *Once she ceases to be a parasite, the system based on her dependence crumbles*; between her and the universe there is no longer any need for a masculine mediator.' (De Beauvoir 1974:692, my italics)

I spoke earlier of the unconsciousness of new thinking which seems still to be widespread. We can of course all find sources to support our theories and there is unquestionably a good deal of further research yet to be done on the social and psycho-logical implications of altering what is currently seen as the more limited paternal role. Both Zillboorg and Gelb are worth reading on paternity and interchangeability of roles (in Miller 1974).

Zillboorg for example defines male feelings in female terms.

'The sense of *paternity* is essentially a feminine attribute ultimately acquired by the human male in his attempt to keep his mastery of the female more secure and less dis-quieting in the light of periodic demonstrations of female superiority by way of having children.'

(Zillboorg 1974:127)

Some may disagree however with Zillboorg's apparent twisting of paternity to a kind of imitated maternity. Each individual in each sex has a unique collection of traits, which cross 'sex norms'. Many women lack what we now see as maternality, and many men have a gentleness with the young, which would not be recognized as masculine. We return to this in the next chapter.

Here, we have to shift ground from the social to the psychological and physiological dimensions. Of course it is true – and right – that the mother can give a baby what no other living person can give, in its earliest years. I remain personally convinced of the desirability for mothers to be full time with their children (that is, not in employment) wherever possible in at least the first two years of childhood unless it is unavoidably otherwise – at least until children are fully weaned and preferably beyond. I believe it to be absolutely right that schools and other sectors of education should help to educate girls – but also boys – in the wide range of knowledge and experience which we have learned in recent years, about how young children grow and what they need. The adult education sector is also particularly well placed to help here. But I simply do *not* believe in the exclusiveness of the woman in this right to know, in her exclusive need to provide for the welfare and development of young children, and in her exclusive capacity to care. We do a very serious injury to boys and men, to educate them to the idea that learning about babies and young children is 'cissy', or that they should not be physically demonstrative with them. We do them wrong to suggest by social norms of masculinity that they have little part to play in bringing up children under the age of seven, except to play a stern Daddy occasionally, to toughen up their sons, pet their daughters, take both to the Zoo, teach their sons cricket and football, but their daughters to play jigsaw puzzles.

This is now changing, and many more fathers (and brothers) are enjoying young children, taking part in shopping and domestic life, and choosing an extended family role rather than an over-rapid promotion (eroding their family time). But so far, the strong impression is that the main progress on this front has been in the middle-class professional sector (academics, teachers, artists). There is little actual evidence of changes of attitude of men in the manual work sector, for example; or indeed of increased recruitment of working-class women to further education, training, or employment as a direct result of any significant sharing of the domestic burden by their husbands. Sweden is in no doubt of the relevance of this to women's full emancipation: 'The analyses hitherto show that no rapid advance of women in employment and the professions, politics, trades union activity etc. is possible as long as men fail to assume that share of the work of the home which falls to them as husbands and fathers' (report by Royal Swedish Ministry of Foreign Affairs on the Status of Women in Sweden to the United Nations, 1968). The United Kingdom is the least prone of nations to record in constitutional terms its changing social policies, but it might well take note of substantial changes in the social and constitutional trends in its European neighbours. For example, an important redefinition has recently taken place in the Federal Republic of West Germany. Paragraph 1356 of the German Civil Law, under the old version, read: 'The housewife leads the household under her own responsibility. She has the right to work for gain as far as this is compatible with her marital and family duties.' The new version of paragraph 1356, however, more accurately reflects the needs of the twenty-first century for which we are today educating our children and, on the arrival of which, today's school leavers will still be under forty-five years of age.

> 'Marital partners settle the management of household after mutual agreement. In the event that the management of the household is left to one of the partners, the latter has to conduct it under his or her responsibility. Both partners have the right to work for gain. When choosing and exercising their activity, they have to take into account in the appropriate way, the interests of the other partner and of the family.'[6]

In Denmark, also, the legislative Acts on marriage are based on the principles that, first, the spouses are independent persons on an equal footing and, second, that both have the same obligation to provide for the support of the family. This is applied to the support of the spouses themselves as well as of the children[7].

Dr Kellmer Pringle, director of the (UK) National Children's Bureau, writing in *The Times* (January 14, 1976) also accepts not only that both public and personal attitudes towards parenthood need to become 'more realistic and deliberate', but that the radical alternative of real equality of the sexes in parenthood is not only possible but perhaps even desirable.

'Those who opt for a lifestyle of shared parenthood will have to choose a like-minded partner. This may well ensure a more durable and satisfying union because the greater interweaving of experiences, both in and outside the home, should foster better mutual understanding. The children would benefit since they would get to know their father on a day to day basis rather than only in the evenings and weekends. Boys and girls would grow up with a more balanced picture of male and female roles and relationships.'

The rotating of the homemaking role, which Dr Kellmer Pringle describes, would deal a decisive blow to the dependence assumption and has obvious implications for men's and women's employment patterns.

The educational relevance of the paternality debate (and thus the breaking of sex norms) is of course of wider influence than the simple question of fatherhood.

I am interested, for example, to see that there were, in 1974 in England and Wales, no male nursery school teachers whatsoever. Moreover, in infant and first schools, only 2,305 out of a total of 50,836 teachers, were men. This is, in my view, simply an extension of the social rejection of paternality; an assumption that it is 'unsuitable' for men to have the care of young children. It seems to me to be wrong on several counts. It deprives children in the formative years of schooling of two contrasting models of human behaviour (which we have labelled masculine and feminine, but both of which include extremes and shades of decisiveness and passiveness, and so on). It gives them a one-sided view of the world – already unbalanced to some extent by their greater knowledge of mother than father. It teaches young children implicitly at the earliest age that society regards teaching and caring for them as women's work, and reinforces their subconscious acceptance of different sex roles. And it deprives men of a rewarding opportunity for work in this field.

Even the Plowden Report, a more far-reaching review and analysis of primary education than most, did not conceive of looking for its extra recommended ancillary assistants from *both* sexes: 'Nursery assistants and teacher's aides will be drawn from the same groups of *girl leavers and older married women* ... we hope to recruit the equivalent of 10,000 older women a year' (Plowden Committee 1966:paras 1205 and 1216). England is not of course alone in this. In 1975, all of France's 50,986 nursery teachers and 150 nursery inspectors were women,[8] while in some other European countries, the actual law of education restricts pre-school education to women. Only Denmark shows a significant degree of progress, with men representing 11 per cent of new entrants to kindergarten teacher training by 1977.

Teachers who still centre their post-Newsom lightweight and shallow 'girls' courses' on what they see as most relevant to the lower qualities of ability – marriage, childcare, and domestic skills – have not caught up with the rapidly changing attitudes of girls and women themselves.

Ten years after the Newsom Report, Audrey Hunt's survey of fifth form girls (Hunt and Rauta 1972:49) showed the beginnings of a new approach in the girls surveyed:

'Most girls expect to marry and have children. Most of them see marriage and motherhood *not as a full-time vocation* but as an interruption of their working lives. On this basis, it should be possible to persuade girls that skills and qualifications obtained early in life will not be wasted.'

Audrey Hunt goes on to reinforce this, accepting that, 'any plans a girl has for a career must be influenced by or influence the extent to which she is prepared to let family commitments interrupt her working life'. But while most of her sample of fifth-form girls wanted or expected to have children, 29 per cent wanted definitely to return to work while bringing up their children and 60 per cent said they probably would. Only 9 per cent wanted to give up work altogether. Hunt's earlier survey of women's employment (1968) showed that nearly three-quarters of girls aged sixteen intended to continue working after marriage and that about three-fifths of mothers with children under sixteen either were working or likely to return to work. 'It is therefore increasingly important to encourage girls to equip themselves with the qualifications and skills needed for satisfactory jobs.'

My own 1975 survey confirmed the expectation that an increasing proportion of girls will intend to work for most of their lives. *Table 2(1)* below shows that over 40 per cent expected to be in a full-time career or job after age twenty-five; and 19 per cent in part-time work at twenty-five but 47 per cent after age thirty. Those expecting to be full-time housewives diminished from 37 per cent at twenty-five to 11 per cent at thirty plus.

Table 2(1) 'What do you actually expect to be doing (whether or not you marry) at the age of 20–25; 25–30; 30–40?' (Fifth-form survey)

	age ranges		
	20–25 %	25–30 %	30–40 %
full-time career	66·0	39·6	34·3
full-time job	15·5	2·0	6·9
part-time career	1·0	14·9	28·4
part-time job	–	5·0	15·6
full-time further education	8·7	–	–
part-time further education	1·9	–	–
housewife	6·8	37·6	11·8

The girls reflected, in fact, mostly traditional attitudes in marriage and work patterns, as these answers show, to the question should girls and boys be educated differently, and if so, why?

'Once married the woman may give up work and have to be supported by the man. If girls are allowed to do the same jobs as men, it is likely that the man will be out of work and unable to support his wife.'

'Boys need an education in electricians etc. (sic) so they can start a family. Girls need an education in cooking, typing, etc.'

'Boys need better education because they work till they retire, women marry and have children then after years go back to a part time job. A woman's place is at home.'

'A boy works to sixty-four years of age and girls get married to be housewives so a boy can have a good career.'

But arguing against the stereotype was fifteen-year-old Liz, who wanted the same education and career, regardless of sex – in her case, repertory acting.

'We are all born with the same brain power and by separate education it seems that girls and boys would be living in separate worlds of ignorance.'

While Jean, a future hotel caterer went even further:

'Because I think that in most jobs women can do as good if not better work than men. There is also no difference in a boy or a girl's intelligence and the old idea of a girl's place being in the home is utter rubbish.'

They looked hard however at the crossing of sex roles in adult life, and *Table 2(2)* shows that 96 per cent approved of marriage, 72 per cent of divorce by consent, 75 per cent of working mothers and 38 per cent of men as housewives if women earned the living. But while 97 per cent approved of women doctors and 94 per cent of male nurses, only 55 per cent approved of male midwives.

Table 2(2) 'Which of the following do you approve of?' (Fifth-form survey)

	approve	don't know	disapprove
marriage	96·3	2·8	0·9
censorship	42·1	28·0	29·9
co-education	59·4	23·0	17·0
divorce by consent	72·5	11·0	16·5
working mothers	75·2	14·7	10·1
women's liberation	33·6	37·4	29·0
equal pay for men and women	87·2	7·3	5·5
men housewives if women earn the living	38·0	10·2	51·9
anti-discrimination legislation	64·2	25·5	10·4
beauty contests	48·6	23·9	27·5
male nurses	94·5	0·9	4·6
women doctors	97·2	0·9	1·8
male midwives	55·0	16·5	28·4
a woman Prime Minister	87·2	9·2	3·7

When pressed to look at alternative extremes of the marriage/work conflict, the overall picture seems ambivalent – as one would expect given the sudden injection of new ideas against five years of traditional teaching and attitudes. Below the girls' answers to a question testing thirteen statements concerning home, work, and marriage are extracted.

	agree %	don't know %	disagree %
careers are fine, but real fulfilment is in a home with children	36·1	26·9	37·0
Careers are important and you can be a good wife and mother as well	68·5	9·3	22·2
A career is just as important as a family even if they seem to conflict	33·3	21·3	45·4

The ambivalence which the three results expose was discussed with those interviewed, whose main reaction was that the very fact of working through a questionnaire, which needed thought before a real answer could be given, had partly changed their attitudes. The school had, of course, under a dynamic new head, taken advantage of the survey to begin to restructure its careers education and had organized extra background activity on the same wavelength.

'You've made me think.'
'I've talked to David about it.' (fiancé)
'I'll have to think it all out again.'
'When you think of it, we do take a lot for granted.'

These were typical comments. Does it take much really to arouse girls to question tradition – its costs and its benefits?

A brief look at the real facts relating to marriage and work may be revealing to any readers not familiar with the factors for change which have drastically altered social trends in the last ten years. Between 1951 and 1971, for example, the percentage of women in work in this country who were married rose from 40 per cent to 64 per cent. The economic activity rate of married women from forty-five to fifty-nine years of age (i.e. whose children are no longer likely to be dependent) has also risen from 22 per cent to 54 per cent (Britton 1975). The middle-aged married woman is now the most important element of women at work – not the young single woman as so many assume. Britton argues that the decline in interval between leaving full-time education and marriage, the longer span of full-time education for girls, and the steady reduction in the period of work before increasingly early marriage, will reduce the availability of single women for the labour market and by definition increase the demand for compensatory recruitment of married women. This will be only variably true, however, according to how far there is competitive male labour for the same jobs. In the open market, the stereotyped attitude towards a married woman's 'dependency' still gives preference to men (alias society's view of the breadwinner). The rate of return to work after six years of marriage increased proportionately more in the decade 1961–71 than in the preceding decade.

Women's proportion of the civilian labour force in fact is also steadily increasing. In 1977 women in the United Kingdom were 38·8 per cent of the civilian labour force, 42 per cent in Denmark, 38 per cent in West Germany, 37 per cent in France, (but only 28 per cent in Italy) (*Eurostat 1977* Basic Statistics of the Community, Table 7).

The argument indeed that women's education is wasted because she does not work after marriage has to be modified not only because it is demonstrably not true (nearly a fifth of all women are the breadwinners) but because of a wide variation in 'wastage' rates between occupations. And before married, non-employed readers raise an eyebrow at such a concentration on the employment aspect, let us reiterate the obvious: the higher the education and the deeper the personal development, the better a woman will be in every other role she plays – wife, mother, community worker, citizen. Her right to the best and widest education is not the less because she does not use it in (paid) employment.

It has long been established, however, that the higher the qualifications a woman has achieved the more likely she is in fact to return quickly to work, to remain at work, or even not to interrupt her employment pattern at all. This is not only true for England; Evelyne Sullerot's scholarly work on her special enquiry into French women at work confirms this for France also:

> 'The influence of the level of education achieved (certificates obtained) has a particularly striking effect on the continuity or discontinuity of working life, regardless of the family situation of the woman. Women without qualifications or those with only a primary leaving certificate are proportionately more numerous in breaking their working career, than those who have attained a qualification equivalent to or higher than the secondary technical or vocational certificate. The more educated the woman, the less likely to interrupt her career.'
> (Sullerot 1973:85)

Of her sample, only 19 per cent of those with higher education, 12 per cent with higher technical education, and 14 per cent of graduates broke their working life. But 28 per cent of the unqualified did so; and 27 per cent of those with the minimum leaving certificate of education (Sullerot 1973:86, Table 19).

We should distinguish between 'educating girls for marriage', that is, with marriage as the principal occupation in mind, and educating all young people to the responsibilities of parenthood and of good and sensitive personal relationships both within and outside marriage. The former is placing marriage as an objective in itself; the latter should place it – for both sexes – into a context where it is only one element of adult life, and not necessarily the preoccupying one in the context of educational preparation. Equally, are we aware of what a double standard we apply to academic and less able girls? Grammar school girls are not sidetracked by cookery, laundrywork, child care, or how to keep a husband happy, at the expense of sound language, maths, science, and creative work which is their foundation for further and higher education. That these may be more difficult to teach to the average young girl is perfectly true – but that is no justification for a secondary timetable for 40 per cent of our girls that gives eight hours a week to a collection of personal and domestic educational areas of study at the expense of more solid intellectual study needed as a basis for non-advanced further education. Girls who are not high flyers are not, by any means, all deprived of intellect, of ambition, or of the need for breadth of interest. Nor should their horizons be limited to a surban semi-detached. Equally unfounded is the current facile belief that the only way to arouse the interest of a less able fourteen-year-old girl in school is with curtain materials and cribs, a visit to Heals, the science of cosmetics, the tools for a successful marriage, or the making of summer dresses.

It is not necessarily to criticize the value – indeed the necessity, perhaps – for schools to educate young people towards a greater understanding of the demands of marriage and what both partners can give and receive in personal fulfilment, to suggest that in using the 'normative' context to do so, those girls who do not marry (or are unable to remain married) may be particularly ill equipped to cope with the social problems, domestic demands, psychological pressures of life alone. They have not been educated to choice; but to an idea of normal and abnormal social behaviour. Careers teachers also tell me constantly of girls in co-educational schools who deliberately underachieve in subjects in which they are gifted, in order not to outshine their boy friends – for fear of losing them. Girls hoping to marry at an early age will frequently drop a training course in midstream on marriage, for fear of jeopardizing its early harmony, and are then defenceless as unqualified women on a diminishing job market if later left on their own through widowhood or desertion. Working-class girls have been more especially susceptible in the past to the tradition set by their mothers and grandmothers that marriage was the principal way out of weary labour in the mill, in the factory; and set it as their principal goal in the short term. Whether they achieve a return to work will depend on whether we succeed in eroding the conception of men's work and women's work, opening up the industrial training sphere to women, and persuading industry that if women can do a job satisfactorily, they have the same right to it, breadwinner or no, married or single. We do not pay wages and salaries in practice differentially according to employees' dependents. Why then do we allow employment practices to restrict the right of women to work as well as man, not in order to support others but for their own financial independence and personal satisfaction as well as contributing usefully to the economy?

I write against a background not only of continued educational under-achievement by girls and women, but in a time of – in some respects – diminishing educational opportunity for them, whatever theory of open access we hold. One great weakness in educational planning over the last three decades is that the main thrust of development has been increasingly male dominated, with progressively fewer women in the leadership of education, a theme to which we shall return. Equally disturbing is that wherever there has been expansion – in sixth forms, polytechnics, advanced further education, craft, and technician training – it is principally boys and men who have taken advantage of expanding opportunity and indeed in many sectors and subject areas, so far from narrowing the gap of under-achievement, girls and women are falling even further behind. I am personally convinced that one main cause of women's under-expectation is the whole interrelationship between the stereotyping of masculine and feminine roles, the domestic syndrome that leaves women with either half a role or two, depending on whether they continue to (or return to) work after marriage or not, and the mythology of woman the dependent, with the right to be kept by a man if she can find one; and man the provider and breadwinner. These strands interweave to affect curriculum planning (even in the primary years and notably in fourth and fifth secondary years), careers guidance, choice of (or access to) employment, and the planning of further education.

I should perhaps make it clear that I am in no way suggesting that we attempt to abolish marriage, dependence or the present lifestyle which men and women now follow, in its entirety. There is no need for us to stamp boys and girls into just another set of moulds which this generation may like better than the ones they inherited. For some women, it may always be that their future happiness is principally bound up with marriage, husband, and children, and there is neither need nor power to reject this entirely. What is essential is that boys' and girls' horizons are widened to consider the place of home-making as that of men as well as women, and that girls need to see themselves as contributing directly to the economic and productive life of the country – not just its reproductive life. In the short term, many girls may still settle for the easiest instant happiness of the domestic idyll which the media and the women's magazines paint (so unfaithfully to real life). But so many generations of women are now finding in young middle age that this is not enough, and that living like the Lady of Shallott in a mirrored world is inadequate, that we do not have the right to set the problem aside. The gradual restructuring of men's and women's roles so that men take a full share of domestic burdens and women of economic responsibility, is a vital task in which schools have a major part to play. The next chapter therefore looks at the beginning of the road – the primary schools.

THREE

Pre-school and primary – in the formative years

'It is only by a wide comparison of the facts that the wisest full grown man can distinguish well-rolled barrels from more supernal thunder.'

The Mill on the Floss (GEORGE ELIOT)

'Give me a child until he is seven and I will give you the man.'

JESUIT TEACHERS

It was September 1940. My father's fighter plane swept up over the village school, leading his squadron out to the North Sea, and leaving three children faced with our sixteenth change of school since the age of two.

Nervous, shy, a very small six, I nevertheless looked stubbornly at the glowering headmaster of the little village school

77

into which we had been unceremoniously dumped after a happy succession of lively RAF and town schools all over England. I had never been disbelieved before: I was shocked. 'Of course I can read,' I said defiantly. 'Everyone can read.' We both reacted from reflex, from our (different) norms of expected behaviour. No child in his limited experience had ever read *Reynard the Fox, Book 10*, at six years old; therefore I was lying or boasting. Everyone I knew had read fluently for so long, we had forgotten any time when we could not; therefore he was just being stupid. Neither of us altered a succession of reflex judgements, until I thankfully left the school in 1945. On the following day, although I could read *Tales from Blackwood* fluently, my arithmetic was found to be wanting – predictably, since most parents can underpin reading skills but few can teach numbers, and too many school changes deprive children of consistency in acquiring difficult number rules and logic. For the wrong sums I was ruthlessly caned. Outraged and frightened, I walked home two miles in the hot sun to inform a disconcerted mother that she had made a mistake, this was a silly school, and please to find another. Returned there under an armed truce, I nevertheless completely blocked for four years on all number work, on any work with the headmaster at all, and on any group activity except singing. I read everything in sight avidly, I did nothing else whatever, except write up projects set by an intelligent mother. It was wartime. I was bright. They left me alone until incredibly I passed the scholarship for one of three places at the city grammar school, neither able to multiply nor divide at all, and only very imperfectly able to add and subtract (deduction from experience when shopping). It took my pastorally-oriented grammar school five patient years of special coaching to get my maths to the matriculation standard then required for university entrance. They never overcame my number block. It took the motivation of a PhD to do that.

I tell this story to illustrate several points although it is of course (one hopes) both extreme and nearly forty years out of date. The primary years are formative years. We carry over from them not only our learning patterns, but our attitudes to other children, to adults, to different subject areas, to perseverance and failure. It took years before I could work properly with a group or to any form of timetable; and I only really succeeded when I finally got to university.

This anecdote however also illustrates the inequality of social chance and the crucial role played by parents.

If I had not had a family that could cope with extra teaching at home by less orthodox methods (George Bernard Shaw with the ironing; projects on railways based at the public library; feudal anecdotes at breakfast) to make up what I missed at school, I would have left the village elementary school at fourteen like the others. I doubt if I would have even passed the eleven plus in those competitive days, despite a reading age of fourteen at ten years of age, so totally incompetent at numbers and the kind of general knowledge examiners liked, if I had not also been middle class and well mannered at interview. Would my grammar school have worked so hard for a child of only average ability, or with a less supportive home, whose ultimate success was more risky? My experience over twenty years convinces me that we still unconsciously favour the academic misfit over the child of average ability who has the courage to be different (or who does not know s/he is different). When I finally made the freedom of university, I was one of 0·65 per cent of girls from that rural county who got there. What happened to those who didn't?

Girls (and indeed boys) who are most vulnerable to the good or bad influences of the primary school are those of average ability; those from insecure, unconfident social backgrounds; children of merit and gifts of character with practical rather than academic brains, who are unfortunate enough not to fit the stereotype of the others in the little pocket of life in which they find themselves. Set a norm, and you condemn those who find that they do not fit.

In 1945, a second shock changed my world and my outlook. Startlingly, I had passed the scholarship. My father, still my legal guardian although he did not have custody of us, flatly refused to sign the necessary forms to allow my sister or I to take up our grammar places – 'a waste of time educating the girls,' he said. And in those days, rules were rules. I owe to my mother's private education, her determination, her poise in adversity, and her red-tape-cutting with two Directors of Education, my extended secondary education which has been the key to an exciting later life. But just down the little country road ten-year-old June, so much cleverer than I and mathematically very gifted, listened to her mother. 'I'm right sorry, love, but your Dad just won't let you go.' An inarticulate family with an unexpected swan, they gave in to conditioning which gave her brother Jem his City school place over his sister; and she left at fifteen to go into a factory.

In theory, today things are different. Yet I see modern Junes leaving school too soon, giving up too soon, conforming too soon. There is little difference in grammar school take-up (where they still exist) and comprehensive education is removing one sex barrier. But if we set different standards *within* schools, even if not between schools, so that girls achieve differently from boys because 'it doesn't matter so much for a girl', or because 'girls are different', we are whitewashing over the inequalities of 1945 with a superficial modern gloss of individual fulfilment lost in group differences. A shrewd look at primary school practice and its early influence is perhaps still timely, after all.

It is difficult to disentangle the chicken and egg relationship of possible innate sex differences, early conditioning to under-achievement, and what boys and girls actually do in school. It is arguable where to begin. I propose to look at the actual achievements of girls and work backwards to causes. What does a modern primary school look like?

We take perhaps too much for granted that it is totally unlike a secondary school. It will be co-educational – of over 23,000 maintained primary schools in England and Wales in 1974, only 105 were single sex. Very little of a girl's day in the primary years will be formally timetabled – which is why activities that are in fact timetabled acquire an especial importance to a child, inevitably. It is worrying therefore that most of the activities that are timetabled are sex linked. Despite the strictures of the Plowden Report (1966:para 681) a substantial number of schools still separate boys and girls for crafts. It is a commonplace to visit a school and find the boys playing football and the girls doing needlework, the boys building an engine or hutches for pets, and the girls cooking buns on a Baby Belling.

Co-education came much sooner to the primary-school child. Gone are the days of the old Board School, three deckers with their girls' and boys' departments, separate entrances, and distinctive playgrounds. By 1927, for example, the old London County Council had relatively few single-sex infant and junior departments of its elementary schools, although it kept very strongly to the old tradition that teaching young children was women's work[1]. In rural areas, of course, village schools have always been mixed, for obvious reasons. No village could support two departments; it was hard enough to keep a school open at all.

Probably the most fundamental shift in emphasis in teaching younger children came from the new drive following the (second) Hadow Report on primary education in 1931. The committee endorsed the previous Hadow Committee's proposed split of elementary schools into primary and senior departments, but it is most remembered for the now-famous keynote of its report: 'We are of the opinion that the curriculum of the primary school is to be thought of in terms of activity and experience, rather than of knowledge to be acquired and facts to be stored' (Hadow Committee 1931 : rec. 30). Yet the Committee found *no* important educational consequences of the differences between the sexes except for physical education and (not unusually in 1931) an implicit assumption that girls needed more 'sheltering' – hence the preservation of girls' and boys' playgrounds (an urban phenomenon; rural children knock about in totally mixed play and always have).

There is always a danger in generalizing. To describe an 'average' school (if such a one can be found) is to do an injustice to the pioneers, the initiators, the many teachers and schools who are rethinking unceasingly how they should or can alter methods, emphases, environment, to reflect the community in which they are set, and the changing needs of children as well as those that will remain constant. Yet to quote exclusively from 'good' practice is to bury our head in the sand and forget that if 10 per cent of teachers, say, are outstanding, and 20 per cent coping only with difficulty, there remain 70 per cent of average to good teachers in the middle whose capacity for and interest in change will remain slower and more limited.

Because children are taught in a co-educational class in a less structured and untimetabled day, it is tempting to assume that they are taught always in the same way. Teachers will be convinced that they treat girls and boys alike. A shrewd observer will see differences in our attitudes towards girls which are translated into the way we plan what they do, the way girls are handled, the way they are stretched or discouraged in their work. Any school that makes great play of 'interest-based' activities and lacks a programme of educational objectives based

81

on *needs* and not pre-conditioned interests, will also be planning a 'hidden curriculum' which is subtly and pervasively different for girls because of the different interests that parents, nursery school teachers, relatives have encouraged them to regard as 'feminine' and acceptable and praiseworthy. Social behaviour spills over into classroom activity.

It is difficult to tease out the interrelated questions of sex differences (genetic or conditioned ?), of classroom practice, and of children's achievement. I want to start with attitudes and behaviour problems and work back to the origins of what we do with small girls (and small boys) and its implications for later education.

Teacher attitudes are almost certainly the dominant influence on how children develop in school; they may well be more accountable than they realize for the persistence of different interests, activities, and levels of achievement in girls and boys.

One of the findings of the National Child Development Study, which will surprise few, is that more girls than boys were anxious for adult approval and more boys than girls for peer group approval. Nearly three times more boys than girls showed 'anxiety for acceptance by other children' with no social class difference. More girls than boys were 'anxious for adult acceptance' and more working-class girls than middle-class girls; but there was no class difference for boys. The largest individual difference was for inconsequential behaviour (i.e. with no regard for consequences of actions). For every one middle-class girl there were four working-class girls, six middle-class boys, and ten working-class boys (Davie, Butler and Goldstein 1972: 147–8).

These are important issues because they are likely to mean that neither sex will develop freely until the conditioning of attitudes by adults and by peer groups is altered. Parents have the major role but the school can exert considerable influence. Teachers' attitudes to girls' behaviour will condition them more quickly and readily to feminine stereotypes, which they are then less likely to reject, and to argue for different activities or, in the secondary years, subjects.

How do girls behave? And why?

The pre-school and infant years are of crucial importance, and

82

there is an urgent need to collect together in sponsored research the growing evidence of the subtle sexism of childrearing, of the conditioned environment of playgroups and nurseries, of (unconscious) parental differences of attitudes. Re-education through adult education programmes, maternity and child welfare clinics, pre-school playgroups, and the teachers and pre-school leaders, would teach all who have the care and education of young children, first, the implications of their behaviour models, and second, how better to encourage children to be individuals first and not girls or boys in preset moulds.

Elena Belotti's seminal work on the social conditioning of the feminine role in early childhood is perhaps one of the most thorough and sensitive existing analyses of the subtle influences of different behaviour patterns on small girls. She observed, for example, a characteristic practice in Italian nursery schools of girls actively being taught to look after boys, to tidy up after them, to help to maintain peace and order, while a tolerant Nelsonic eye was turned to male disorder and rowdy games (Belotti 1973 : 205–8). Her work is particularly penetrating on the subtle familial influence of differential parental behaviour to sons and daughters – the latter often being 'failed boys' when the long-awaited and desired son does not materialize. Here again, more research is needed into different behaviour patterns between not only different social classes, but urban and rural environments, children with siblings of both sexes and those in families of all girls or all boys. As peripatetic Royal Air Force children in the chaotic 1930s, we seemed to clump into natural cross-sexed groups, crawling in and out of the cockpits of our fathers' frail planes, identifying with the mechanics and truck drivers who ferried us about, with no thought of dividing up girls from boys. Rural girls more often climb trees and race around – but on farms they may revert to shadowing the 'farmer's wife' role. The playgrounds I frequented as an education officer in the slums of a cobbled-streeted Northern mill town had more sociometric groups that crossed the sexes – mixed unstructured active games and no skipping ropes – than the neatly 'nice' schools of Hampstead and Chelsea from my London days.

A child will learn to behave following the praise or criticism of parent, teacher, other children. Girls are praised for being quiet, clean, tidy, helpful; and criticized for being muddy, rough,

83

noisy, lazy, untidy. Listen to typical primary school teachers.

'Why, Maureen, you've had your hair cut, you look quite a young lady. I'm afraid Ella is growing bossy, she'll have to watch it. Never mind Jennie, you have a good cry and you'll feel better.'

'There's a good girl, to help teacher. Such a helpful child, she always offers to put the toys away. A little boisterous for a girl, but she's quieting down as she settles into the class. Jill is such a nice, polite little girl. (She's growing almost pretty.) Alison, you won't grow up pretty if you scowl like that. Emma, little girls don't fight like that, leave Jackie alone. Gillian, do you *really* want to go out in all that mud – why don't you help me tidy away the crayons? Lou, Jimmy's barked his knee again, go and get the first aid box. Tracey, what a pretty new dress!'

On the other hand, boys are praised for toughness, for strength, for leadership, for organization, for adult behaviour, for initiative and originality. They are criticized for weakness, for 'cissy' behaviour, for rudeness, but not for noise as such.

'There's a brave boy, Bobby, real boys don't cry. *Big* boys don't show when they're afraid. Well done, Ian (he's a born leader, you know, always has his team ready first). John will go far, he's so good at organizing. Look at him with the others round that model. Jackie, show Caroline how to manage her lever on the model. Kim, can you carry those boxes to the stockroom – there's a strong boy. Alex, could you be very grown up and take this over to the junior school to Mr Jones? Very carefully now, (he's a real little boy, you know, quite a tearaway at playtime). Bobby, *not* in trouble again (he's still a bit tearful but the junior school will toughen him up). Boys, not so much noise *inside*, go and be noisy in the playground, if you must.'

One could elaborate, but most teachers and parents will recognize the drift. What foundation in physical or psychological differences justifies these different attitudes, these two discernably different standards? It is not surprising that well before secondary school, girls have learned to like sedentary occupations, to be biddable and helpful and domesticated, and to identify with adults more than boys; and that boys have learned to be assertive, to fight (adult approved as preliminary toughening for future rugger pitches), to show initiative, and to hide their emotions and stifle even the healthier of their fears. They learn that Brownies are for girls and Cubs for boys, with all that that implies.

This has serious implications for children of either sex who do not fit. The National Child Development Study (Davie, Butler and Goldstein 1972) confirmed the general view that boys are more accident-prone than girls. How many were tempted beyond their capacity through fear of being called a coward? More boys had a history of inguinal hernia. Is this the conditioning to carry heavy weights for teacher or a more robust girl friend? In my village school it was always the small boys who struggled with milk crates at playbreak. I still see this in our primary schools today. A manly activity?

Lovell (1963:228) suggests that boys' doubling of physical and manual strength from five to eleven and from eleven to sixteen, while partly natural, is highly likely to be partly dependent on the cultural conditions that give boys frequent vigorous muscular activity and discourage it in girls in the crucial developmental years.

How far, I wonder, does the curbing of the natural exuberance of girls turn their vigour into nervousness? How far is their energy not used up in the sedentary occupations which they quickly learn will win them praise and implicit approval not only from parents and teachers, but from boys with whom they play, who reflect the attitude of their parents and older brothers? Where aggression and physical energy in girls is inhibited by social pressures it may lead to increased fearfulness, worrying, disturbance, thus reinforcing the feminine stereotype. It is almost certainly reinforced by parental attitudes of discipline – a father's smack once for all for a grubby son who breaks the tea things in horseplay; a longer withdrawal of approval, a verbal 'telling off', an atmosphere of mother's disappointment in a daughter who fails to measure up to standard. Does this increase the dependency of girls and the independence of boys?

It is perhaps possible that the greater interest of girls in mothering dolls, and the greater thrust of boys towards aggressive, assertive behaviour, are due to physical influence to some extent (for example, endocrine glands) and it may well be that further research will clarify this. Meanwhile it is surely important for schools to counteract these imbalances. It is above all in these primary years that it would be possible to create an atmosphere of acceptability for small boys to work out their dormant paternality, the finer feeling which unquestionably is present in the male as well as the female, by making sure that boys as well as girls work out role playing games with all the trappings of home life. I am not only talking of the Wendy House syndrome, but the care of younger children in the school. There is no reason why a gentler older boy should not help with small children in the reception class at playtime or when they arrive, as many older girls do (apparently by instinct) – except for fear of being called 'cissy'. Teachers have a responsibility discreetly to set new standards of social behaviour which enable children to be themselves, and to show other children that for boys to be peacemakers, gentle, and domesticated is no more incompatible with efficient self defence, strength, and the world of work then it should be for girls. Similarly girls should be taught sensible self defence and to learn to be independent and courageous (but not, surely, necessarily aggressive?).

The conditioning of behaviour and attitude is likely to be endorsed, however, by the books, pictures, and teaching materials that fill our primary schools still.

Primary schools are today very different, of course, from those of the 1940s. Classrooms are full of practical equipment – *Cuisenaire*, Katherine Stern, Colour-Factor, Dienes apparatus, Fletcher maths, have replaced the multiplication tables of my heathland village school. Four or five reading schemes will be scattered through the classrooms of the more affluent; others, caught by the recession, will be able to plough through only one – perhaps *Breakthrough to Literacy*; *Janet and John*; *Nippers*; *Ladybird* – much as we did through *Reynard the Fox*. One thing in which the books will differ: almost all of our books were totally irrelevant to the world of 1940 – because they were fantasy readers, a stylized world of fiction. Today's books reflect today's world – or do they? Only, I suggest, a small part of it, mainly comfortable, well-to-do, well furnished suburban homes with a domesticated non-working mother rarely free of an apron, and a professional-type, white-collar father, with a slightly out-of-date car which Johnny (not Mary) helps him to clean. Whatever happened to the tenements, the housing estates, the large families in terraced streets like Eve Garnett's *Family from One-End Street*, in which it is interestingly Kate and not the boys, who wins the scholarship to grammar school.

Sexism in children's books

There is little point in duplicating the now growing literature on sex-role stereotyping in children's books, but it is essential that we realize how harmful this stylized and one-sided presentation of society to our children, and especially to girls, must be in both educational and social development. All reading schemes currently used in our schools show the most traditional male/female domestic roles. You will look in vain for a single picture of, or story about, the millions of working wives and mothers, the husbands who shop in the supermarket, the wives who drive cars, women who put up shelves and put plugs on electrical appliances, male nurses and female doctors, women digging gardens, and men cooking Sunday lunch, none of which is particularly uncommon. Whatever happened to the 1970s? Where are the women of the mill towns, the men who are unemployed and home making, the dual-role families?

Basically, what has happened is that we have simply endorsed the stylized pretty pictures of the past. Only very recently has anyone questioned where past images are still sensibly relevant. I do not suggest that we should attempt to force children into patterns to which they are ill suited. But ignorance, lack of opportunity, negative guidance against trying new activities or new aspirations for size cannot be said to give a really free choice. And conditioning through educational media is an important element in this. The Swedish National Sex Role Project have compiled a check list for the guidance of educational publishers[2] and are steadily monitoring publications in use in their schools. In our own country the Bullock Report on reading and language confirms how essential it is that reading schemes should be reviewed and made more realistic because of their decisive influence in the impressionable years. In view of the importance of the Bullock Committee's report to primary schools, I quote in full:

'The words and pictures should complement each other in such a way that the child needs to examine both with equal care. The printed word must be critical for any understanding of the action. Another important aspect of content is the effect on children's attitudes, to which far less attention has been given in the past. *Any reading scheme should stand up to questions about how parental roles, sex roles, attitudes to authority etc. are represented* ... Researchers have reported that the contents of primers display 'a striking divergence from the realities of community, family and child life, and from what is known about child development'. We do not suggest that reading schemes should be passed through an ideological or ethical scanner. But we do believe that children's experience should not be confined to a restricted range of reading matter presenting a narrow range of attitudes. It is particularly important to avoid this in the impressionable years, for it is never too soon to start thinking about the ways in which attitudes may be influenced by reading.'

(Bullock Committee 1975:104–5)

The importance of reading schemes and children's literature must indeed be obvious to all. The Swedish National Board of Education's Sex Role Project aims at studying all aspects of schools and teaching from different standpoints causing sex differentiation and pinpointing current deficiencies as well as developmental possibilities. As part of its work it is reviewing textbooks and readers (monitoring, *not* directing) for undesirable sex-typing in schoolbooks and has sponsored a general textbook *Boy, Girl – Does It Matter?* (Centerwall and Strömdahl 1974). While there is no law in Sweden prohibiting discrimination in teaching materials, the Board of Education has laid down a national guideline that teaching materials should not include texts or illustrations of a sexually discriminatory nature.

Belotti (1973) refers to the work of an American feminist group at New Jersey University who analysed fifteen collections of children's books and 144 reading schemes, showing more starkly than most the dominance of boys and the passivity of girls. In all 144 reading schemes, mothers were in their kitchens, although 40 per cent of American mothers go out to work. The American committee which resulted from this initiative, after a further survey of 1000 books, sent out a blacklist naming 800 of them as 'irredeemably male chauvinist' to libraries, schools, and parents' associations (Belotti 1973:135–7). Glenys Lobban (1974) has similarly reviewed British children's readers from the stand-point of a practising primary school teacher and found a depres-singly familiar patronization of the weak, submissive, passive, and home-based image of small girls and their mothers which I criticized in the last chapter in the context of 'normative' social and psychological thinking. Most serious is the adventurous, initiatory image of males and the dependent 'waiting to be rescued' image of females – shades of modernized medieval chivalry.

Some excellent work has been done in the United Kingdom by one voluntary group, CISSY (Campaign to Impede Sex Stereotyping in the Young), to raise consciousness among teachers and librarians, by analysing children's literature and readers to show how stereotyped and sexist most readers are. The group has presented papers to publishers and librarians analysing the onesidedness of roles, but their work and that of the Writers and Readers' Publishing Cooperative (Children's Rights Workshop 1976) appear to have fallen on singularly deaf ears in educational circles. We should be clear that this is not a discussion of possible control of textbooks and readers; but a condemnation of constant publication of existing stereotypes of unadventurous, timid, vacuous, lifeless girls and decisive, courageous, strong and imaginative boys, as illustrative models for children in real life. *Breakthrough to Literacy* (Mackay, Thompson, and Schnaub 1970) has some excellent stories show-ing interchangeable roles, and is perhaps the best on the current market from this point of view.

It may be argued that children realize that stories in books are not real. This is specious, I would have thought. First, school readers *purport* to be real. But reading schemes do not just teach reading. They mirror the non-school world; they put a seal of approval on patterns of behaviour. It is arguable that children may regard library books as separate from the stamp of adult approval (hence the one-time popularity of the *Just William* books, hardly an acceptable model of behaviour in school terms) but it is inconceivable that a young child who is handed a reader by a teacher will not take the images and ideas in it as 'school-officially-approved'. Conformists will con-form. And they do.

In 1975 I examined the science books being used in the pri-mary and middle schools in the area which I administered. In all but one, every illustration showed boys in the active experimental situation and girls standing admiringly, handing over a test tube or being shown what to do. Why? Six months ago the (newly) interested proprietor of a toy shop went through his stock with me to check the illustrations on the lid of every game. Only three out of 270 games had a picture of a *girl* showing a boy how to play it. The remainder showed a *boy* (often younger) showing a sweetly pretty *girl* how difficult it was to play everything from Ludo through war games to a more sophisticated version of Monopoly. Only one out of seventeen chemistry sets showed a girl at all; a small sister watching with fearful respect as big brother bubbled an alchemist's brew. Most of the games were currently available in schools for 'activity' periods. Have teachers complained to manufacturers? What feedback has there been?

What in fact have teachers done? The pressure for review and for 'break-in' strategies to persuade (not direct) publishers and manufacturers to listen, learn, and shift emphasis has come primarily from voluntary groups, parents, Women's Institute working parties, journalists, academic research workers. Surely teachers cannot still be totally unaware of the unreality of it all in 1977? There is one ray of hope. The National Union of Teachers at its annual conference in 1976 at Scarborough resolved that:

'At national level, the Union should undertake, in cooperation with leading publishers, an examination of currently available reading matter for children, with a view to the elimination of the portrayal of traditional concepts concerning sex based roles;

and

At local level, associations and reading centres (where they exist) should be encouraged to pursue a similar investigation of reading matter available for local schools within the local authority's area.' (National Union of Teachers 1976:17)

Perhaps some reader will be encouraged to press for an early report of the NUT's national survey, and for its matching by a governmental and local authority initiative.

One such rather gentle and so far imperfectly known initiative has at least 'broken the duck'. In 1975, HM Inspectorate published the first report on curricular differences between the sexes in England and Wales since the Board of Education's secondary report in 1923 – a time lag which in itself reveals a lack of consciousness of the scale of sexlinked curricular differences based on practices of doubtful educational validity. The Inspectorate visited a sample of primary, middle, and secondary schools to examine differences in the programmes followed by girls and boys, but also drew on their evidence from visits made for other purposes.

The Inspectorate found a familiar pattern in the primary sector (including 8–12 middle schools). A predominantly female staff looks for ways of interesting boys in mechanical toys, activities, projects, because these are rightly thought to hold their attention; but teachers make less effort not only to encourage girls to be interested in constructional, three dimensional work, 'but even to respond to the attention given to them by girls'. The Inspectorate confirm that the lack of three dimensional experience in the early years may so underdevelop some children's interest and energy as to hold back the later sound development of spatial concepts in maths and some of the basic principles of science. Girls, of course, are less likely to top this up out of school because they are encouraged at school as well as at home, to spend lots of time in 'domestic' kinds of activities. Boys are more likely to be encouraged to help Daddy in the home workshop, which underpins their measuring and spatial development. But precisely because girls mature earlier than boys in the pre-school years, it is all the more crucial that parents and teachers give them construction toys, encourage them to build, measure, count, actually to enjoy playing with numbers, and to look at craft play (even if it is messy or noisy) as natural and fun. The label 'it's for boys' is stuck on far too many activities in girls' minds well before the age of five; and is endorsed by far too many infant teachers in early school days.

HM Inspectorate implicitly criticize the widespread practice of encouraging children to play out traditional male/female domestic roles, so often a major feature of creative play materials and equipment. I am sometimes tempted to test the ingenuity of infant teachers by suggesting the removal of every Wendy House from schools; but experience teaches me that both teachers and children will only make one from cardboard if we do! It could be used, however, as a potential positive help in breaking down the stereotype of 'little mother', if used to encourage and praise boys for learning to tidy it up and work out a domestic *father's* role to take shares with Mummy. It would be their first introduction to the idea that Mummies work outside the home as well as Daddies, so both have to bath the children, wash up, clean, etc.

Play is a very important aspect of the infant school, in particular, but also of junior schools. The subtle influence of adult approval and of 'felt' criticism will shape different standards for girls and boys which will in turn strengthen or weaken innate tendencies. The gentle guidance or leadership of an adult sensitive to this in 'directed play' will help to develop group feelings in children in the transitional years from the individualism of the nursery school child to the 'team', gang or social groups of the older primary children. It will also help each sex gradually to absorb new standards of socially acceptable behaviour. That teacher attitudes do affect the behaviour and attainment of children is unquestionable. HM Inspectorate again comment that:

'In many instances, schools begin to formalize their different expectations of boys and girls when the children enter the junior classes at about 7 years of age, and this becomes widespread for the 9–11 year olds.'   (1975:3)

The further experience of boys in modelling and using tools helps their development of a sense of geometric relationships and the nature and properties of materials. Girls' needlework – as I have seen it taught in an average school – has little transfer value in mechanical spatial terms. Even primary school science tends to be taught by the few male staff, embedding its 'masculine' flavour even more firmly in children's minds.

Equally important in my view is the teachers' unaccountable insistence that physical activities should be separate, as if there were no robust girls and no slender boys who hate football and getting muddy, or even working in a team. It is not just a physical problem. Boys' physical activities are centred on teamwork, leadership, decisive activity (football, camping, outdoor pursuits, building a hut together). Girls' netball is very much a minor sport and most other organized activities are culturally based rather than in the mainstream of the modern world. (Folk dancing is fun, but cannot compare with the identification with male adults that boys have when Wembley comes round every year.)

If women are to work and run a home later, they need physical stamina, quick adaptability, an ability to cope with socially mixed 'difficult' situations, an outwardlooking personality. Do primary schools lay the foundations for this in timetabling 'girls' activities of a gentler, more ladylike, inward-centred, homebased kind?

Some of the more useful evidence of the actual difference in boys' and girls' attainments comes from the National Child Development Study, a research analysis of the abilities, attainments, behaviour, physical development, health, and home environment of the 16,000 children born in one week of March 1968, 11,000 of whom were studied seven years later. The longitudinal character of the study makes it particularly valuable but it must be stressed that the findings must be used with caution, dealing as they do with a particular sample – a genuine cross section across Great Britain – and do not necessarily provide evidence of the causal relationships which lie behind the inequalities and differences which emerge. Second, somewhat inevitably, the judgements involved in rating the children were often subjective ratings by teachers: 'As rated by their teachers, the girls showed better 'oral ability' and more 'creativity' than the boys. On the other hand, the boys were judged by their teachers to have more knowledge of the world around' (Davie, Butler and Goldstein 1972:20).

One of the most important lessons for teachers to learn is that nine tenths of what psychologists and teachers measure is attainment and achievement following what we have trained children to do socially and mentally and is not measurement of true potential at birth, at five, or at seven years old. To assess achievement is useful; to diagnose needs essential; to rationalize differences as genetically caused (post hoc, ergo propter hoc) is specious without very substantial, large-scale, objective research.

This study goes a long way to confirm that differences in social class outrank and cross sex differences. Readers should go back to the source for the full picture, not least for the hidden comments on 'induced' behaviour. Boys' poorer performance in reading is confirmed, with a question: 'Perhaps this is because reading is to a large extent a passive occupation, more suited to the female role in our society, with which girls will identify' (Davie, Butler and Goldstein 1972:111). In reverse, boys' superiority in arithmetic may be because: 'Arithmetic skills in our society are more closely associated with the male role than the female; boys are therefore likely to be more highly motivated in this area than girls' (Davie, Butler and Goldstein 1972:114).

There is no point in summarizing the varied findings here – the report is succinct and readable. It confirms decided differences in attainment and behaviour between the sexes but, to me, endorses the extent to which these are substantially affected by parental and teacher attitudes. The next step is surely research to test how different techniques of play, classroom activity, social education from current practice can narrow the sex gaps to the benefit of both sexes. Of these, spatial ability seems to me to be the crucial area for 'break in' strategies.

Sex-linked activities – why?

One immediate step for teachers is to cease separating children for craft and project activities. The Plowden Report in 1966 rejected this as undesirable – although its own illustrations are almost entirely typecast. It is small boys who are pictured building an engine with packing cases (Plate 8), a boy grappling with measurement and geometric design (Plate 29), while girls below play with a thermometer and beaker (Plate 30). A small girl concentrates heavily on a saucepan on a cooker (Plate 35). Two small boys struggle with a weight, pulley, and car tyre to work out leverage (Plate 38) although at their age, girls are (temporarily) heavier and stronger. The caption, that differences between arts and crafts between the sexes are disappearing, shows a group with extremely traditional easel painting which has always been common to both (Plate 40)! Over the page, two boys are building a wall (Plate 41). 'Inventiveness with materials' shows a small boy standing with an Emmet-like construction while a girl looks on passively, neatly seated at her tidy desk full of number blocks. Only in the library and the orchestra are the photographs really illustrating mixed activity.

Yet the report alleges progress and denounces separate activities and criticizes schools which had moved little from the 1930s (para. 1966 : 680).

> Craft in the elementary school was traditionally separated from art. For the boys it meant woodwork, cardboard models and geometrical drawing, and for the girls, needlework and knitting. Certain other crafts, notably basket-making, book-binding, weaving, block printing and occasionally pottery became common in the thirties, but the primary schools were not much affected. Latterly a much greater variety of crafts, including wood-carving, clay-modelling, dyeing and block-cutting, have come into the primary schools, and *the distinction between what is done by boys and girls has partly disappeared. Except possibly for the oldest children*, it is quite artificial and unhelpful : boys enjoy stitchery and girls can benefit from work in wood and metal.'
>
> (Plowden Committee 1966 : para 681)

(I personally question the validity of distinguishing even for older children.)

What have HM Inspectorate advisers and teachers done since then to analyse how the differences illustrated in Plowden arise through teacher-guided classroom patterns; and to counteract them? In 1974–5, a large proportion of the primary schools in the area that I administered mirrored these patterns. Progress is barely traceable.

Documentation on what is sometimes called 'the hidden curriculum' is also growing. Frazier and Sadker (1973) suggest, probably rightly, that school uniform is partly a vehicle to suggest to girls how they should behave (the implicit constraint of skirts against the greater freedom of trousers and jeans). The nursery and primary school have become immeasurably freer now than the secondary sector in this – any typical classroom of 1978 will have many, perhaps most, girls in trousers, trews, and ski-pants, especially in winter. The American examples of indirectly restrictive behaviour patterns, however, are still also more commonplace here; discouragement of girls from climbing trees, being rowdy. Evidence is growing that the sextyping of curricular choices at secondary level have their roots in the primary years – particularly girls' rejection of study areas perceived as 'masculine' (mathematics, physical science) and boys' rejection of modern languages and natural sciences[3].

Sex differences – real, illusory, relevant, or incidental?

The psychologists and geneticists have much to answer for. Despite conflicting views and contradictory research evidence they have dogmatized to the layman and teacher about sex differences, many of which are either socially induced or irrelevant to learning, as if they were as immutable as the law of gravity. Some shibboleths bite the dust yearly; others endure. It is difficult to disentangle the genetic, social, developmental dimensions, but these underlie so much that happens in later years that it is not possible to bypass them completely, and the section that follows is implicitly as relevant to later chapters as to this.

Sex norms – use or hindrance?

In the last chapter I questioned the possible misuse of a normative approach out of context. It is sometimes of course extremely useful to establish the extent and character of an educational problem by analysing large-scale samples and extracting factors that appear to be common to particular groups. It has without any doubt, for example, helped teachers, administrators, and politicians to argue for more and special resources for the socially deprived, for those in overcrowded homes, or schools in areas dominated by social classes IV and V, and so on, when strengthened by evidence of correlations between lower social-class groupings and educational under-achievement, especially in reading. The danger arises when we argue that because a majority or a significant number behave in a certain way, all children or people in the group, class, or category which we have selected to look at will necessarily either show the same characteristics or produce the same problem. Not all children from social classes IV and V are deprived. Not all immigrants have language difficulties. Not all children with IQs below, say, 90 will present acute learning difficulties. Other factors like temperament, motivation, parental background, early childhood experience, wealth or poverty, health, will alter the situation favourably or unfavourably. Yet the establishment of 'norms' or of correlations does serve to highlight risk factors. It warns us of likely problems (or gifts). We therefore are likely to screen more carefully to see what special needs we must meet in teaching.

If we then think we have established a recurrent pattern of different ability, achievement, behaviour between different groups of children, how do we select our classification (by age? all seven-year-olds?; by class? all in social class V?; by region? those in the North?; by sex? boys or girls?). The only safe step is to *test* children against our expectation – to diagnose whether they are or are not showing the signs we have been taught to look for. There is still a danger that we will in fact see what we are looking for, because we expect to see it. We are no longer likely, I suggest, to be objective observers because we are by then preconditioned.

It is perhaps at this point that I become most sceptical about using sex differences as an automatic basis for different teaching approaches, different adult attitudes towards girls and boys, and different assumptions of girls' and boys' alleged 'natural' interests. Educationalists have now been largely trained out of the 19th century assumption that all children of the poor are incapable of advanced (or even secondary) education. In 1970 we ceased to believe the fiction that all children whom a psychologist designated as having an IQ below 75 were 'ineducable'. Yet articles and books abound in which generalized assertions are made that boys (by implication or by explicit statement, all boys) are innately superior in spatial ability to girls; and girls (implicitly all girls) are innately superior in verbal ability to boys. I do not think that the evidence is substantial enough to prove that these sex differences in *achievement* (which is what we are measuring) transcend the other major variables of individual intelligence, temperament, type of mind, social class, home background, type of school, type of early teaching, and learning *within* each sex. And if they do not, the whole normative approach comes into question for the education of girls, unless it is used only to highlight risk factors. There is every point in looking further diagnostically at boys and at girls in our schools against *possible* causes of verbal and mathematical under-achievement. But do teachers not do this already? What has happened otherwise to the education by 'age, ability and aptitude' which Section 8 of the *Education Act, 1944* makes it our duty to provide? What happened to the individual personal fulfilment which teachers claim is the major educational objective? Educational diagnosis of individual children, not of 'girls' labelled as a group, is the only way in which we can justify our claim to provide the right education for every girl.

There is a quite practical and organizational angle to this. If any teacher agrees with the preceding paragraph, she or he cannot then justify splitting 'the boys' and 'the girls' for any classroom activity, and especially for the crafts, for constructional work, or – in my view even in the primary years – for physical activities.

There are of course several dimensions to the 'innate sex differences' debate. How general are the differences: total, most, just over half? If we are tempted to use a norm to direct how we handle a whole group of children, the scale of normal difference (and therefore of divergence) is important. Should teaching attitudes be based on different sex interests: or counteract them? Should they be irrelevant to basic core education? Valentine (1963) supports the view that there are greater individual variations between different children of the same age than differences between the average for the different ages 2–5. It was this overlap that the Bullock Committee will have had partly in mind when arguing for more sophisticated and *individual* methods in diagnosing children's language needs and their standards of achievement. In nearly 600 pages and over 330 recommendations, the Committee discuss throughout children as individuals, as groups with identifiable common needs (the gifted, the slow learner), and in terms of individual readiness to read, visual perception, hearing, and previous exposure to discursive rather than functional language.

'In our view, there is no advantage in mass testing and centrally stored data unless the outcome is individualised help directed precisely at the children who need it. As a general principle we prefer that systematised observation should be followed by selective diagnostic testing of those pupils about whom detailed and specific information is required.'

(Bullock Committee 1975:rec. 199)

A marked contrast to the traditional approach of classifying children by IQ, by social class, or by 'type' whatever that meant to the psychologists and the Spens and Norwood Committees, were the theories of Piaget, which had a substantial impact in the 1950s and early 1960s. I am personally sorry that Piaget is no longer read with the same thoroughness because he has 'gone out of fashion'. His approach, which rejects entirely 'normative' guides, tends to explain a child's intellectual life as a result of his or her own actions, and of his or her own internal reflection and consideration for others, rather than as the training of an inherited ability. Piagetian teaching will develop the 'caring' instinct in all girls *and* boys; the leadership approach in all children in whom it is inherent; the logical deductive approach in all, even the intuitive; and an understanding of social behaviour in individual children – not in boys and in girls differently. Essentially a *diagnostician*, Piaget breaks down into elements how a child thinks, and was in no doubt that the formation of sound mathematical concepts depends on the whole previous experience and development – planned organized teaching of preceding logical steps. Nowhere in eight massive volumes of case records have I found in Piaget's work any facile classification of boys or girls as such. He writes of Iea, Bez, Nil, Vila, Stie, Cel, Gis, Schmei, Far, as individual children, not as boys and girls in the way in which the village school-headmistress did in the previous chapter.

If Piaget was right, and the world of the child from 2–7 is represented by signs, symbols, and images, by a reorganization of the picture of our world through imaginative play, speech, and questioning, then the nursery and infant teachers have an overwhelming importance on the development of small girls, second only to parents. And if the geneticists are right and girls are in fact born with a missing cog where the little boxes in our computer-brains are labelled 'difficult problems' or 'internal combustion engines' or 'coefficients of correlation', then the nursery and infant schools have a direct responsibility to encourage girls to play with, for example, Dienes apparatus or construction sets with an enquiring mind instead of cutting out, pasting, and gluing paper dresses for dolls.

Genetic differences?

The genetic distribution of XX and XY chromosomes which determines sex is not basically in question. Few of us may want to argue with the physiological view, for example, that the alteration in the early months after conception of the hypothalamus, which regulates glands and part of the nervous system, produces the sex of the unborn child. What I want to know is, what has that to do with a less well supported but widely held view that the different *reproductive* processes on which physio-logical sex differences mostly depend, carry with them (immut-ably) a typical female, intuitive, illogical, unreasoning mind, deficient in perceptual faculties; and a typical masculine logical, reasonable mind, deficient in imaginative ways and sensitivity? I doubt if Professor Tolkien, a fine imaginative writer and the father of a family, would have been impressed with a label of 'unmasculine' on the somewhat specious grounds that *The Lord of the Rings* combines elfin imagery, delicate language, and finely painted scenarios along with some aggressively warlike themes.

And yet there is too much and too regularly repeated evidence of actual and fairly constant sex differences in the way in which boys and girls learn and work in school for us to ignore the vital question, how much is nature and how much is due to the earliest differences in parental attitude to sons and daughters? It is surely time this was argued thoroughly and nationally in a major debate and the ghosts laid.

The argument is not of course new. Giving evidence to the Board of Education's Consultative Committee in 1923 on the secondary age range, Cyril Burt saw little justification for cur-ricular sex differences based on psychological premises:

'There are important physical differences (between boys and girls), there are also important differences in temperament and emotion; there are too fairly broad differences due to training and tradition. But in the higher intellectual levels, at any rate before adolescence is completed, inherent sex differences seem undoubtedly small. *The bearing of psycho-logical conclusions upon sex differentiation in the curriculum is thus comparatively slight.* Whether the training offered in Secondary Schools to girls should differ from that given to boys is a question to be decided *on other than psychological considerations,* by our views both as to the ideals to be aimed at in all education and to the parts which men or women should (or in practice will) play in a civilized community.'

(Board of Education 1923:90, my italics)

Terman, one of the early pioneers of IQ testing could equally see no differences in the average intelligence of women and girls and men and boys, (1919:68). Unlike Wechsler (1958) who asserted not only that the distribution of male and female intelligences was different, but that 'our findings do confirm ... that men do not only behave but think differently from women'.

In 1925, the London County Council tested 2,000 children at seven years old and found, among other things, that girls were superior to boys in every respect including the written and oral arithmetic (Havelock Ellis 1934:388). Havelock Ellis however held that girls tended to reproduce material rather than reason, were microscopic rather than telescopic in outlook; that boys were more inventive and original and stronger in judging phenomena and in reasoning.

A latter day Havelock Ellis, Dr Corinne Hutt (1973) writes in a popular and readable, but, in my view, pervasively stereotyped analysis of males and females, that almost everything from verbal and spatial activity to children's behaviour at nursery school is a 'natural' extension of 'natural' proclivities. The laconic nature of her references makes it difficult to test how solid they are, or how relevant or large the samples quoted. She makes the same mental jump that is only too common among psychologists. Typical co-operative activity quoted is older girl buttoning shoe of small girl; but two bouncing toddler boys trying to join in an active game with older boys. That this is familiar is not in doubt; that it is *socially* induced is, to me, certain. Typical interaction between nursery boys and girls is shown as mingled groups of boys with enquiring faces looking at pond fish, and two tall girls with skipping ropes – hardly nursery activities[4]. Even as infant/junior examples they are as likely to spring from teacher-directed school activities or induced behaviour attitudes than from unfettered choice. Many primary schools can illustrate lively groups of both sexes out at the gravel pits; and playground patterns (especially in downtown areas) of totally mixed ball or chasing games. Her case for biological bases for psychological sex differences must be better documented to be credible: the relevance of a biological base spelled out before we accept it as a determinant factor to reinforce children's sex roles. My criticism is not of the factual findings of research (for example that boys may excel in certain kinds of reasoning and girls in verbal fluency) but the deductions made from this. The *formative* influences of early play, of parental attitude, of teaching techniques, which reinforce what children show that they do well at three, five, seven years old, obviously is going to be cumulative and the sex differences will widen – without counteraction.

I ought to make it clear again that I am not denying all sex differences as they are at present demonstrated; but their origins, and their relevance to schools. Nor do I wish to see a unisex world in which people are indistinguishable and the relations between the sexes made meaningless. I am questioning – not defining theories to replace theories.

While Brierley, an HMI writing in 1975, accepts, for example, that even concentration on the genetic dimension does not alter the overlap between the sexes (which I am suggesting is more generally substantial than is alleged and therefore invalidates use of norms as guides), he somewhat oddly implies *no* overlap in spread of intelligence:

> 'Variations in the gene-outfits of all forty sex chromosomes ... prevent sharp male-female differences to give an overlap between the sexes in secondary sexual characteristics, temperament and *probably* intelligence.'
>
> (Brierley 1975:18–19, my italics)

Why 'probably' intelligence? Is Brierley suggesting that there is a masculine and feminine temperament and intelligence? Or that there is *no* overlap (or a doubtful one) in patterns and types of intelligence between the sexes? Surely not. There is not enough evidence to prove that sex chromosomes alter our intelligence or temperament on a consistent sex-linked basis – otherwise there would be no spread of variation within each sex; and there clearly is. Is this a Freudian slip betraying how hard it is to kill the myth of masculine and feminine minds, and the 'inferiority' of the feminine mind? Brierley himself indeed warns against the dangers of using overgeneralized evidence of some sex differences to mask individual differences between boys and boys and girls and girls. There is no doubt that more research is needed into the whole question of genetically and socially induced patterns of girls' and boys' achievements and behaviour.

> 'Are such differences due to our specific culture? We shall not be able to answer this question adequately until women have had strictly equal vocational, social and educational opportunities for many generations ...

Research findings, at present tentative, will need to give us firmer clues to the intellectual and emotional differences between boys and girls, before we can judge whether differences are due to upbringing and tradition. Careful analysis of the achievement of groups of boys and girls in various subjects of the curriculum is necessary too ...

It is crucially important to recognize that, although there are average differences between men and women, *we ignore the uniqueness of the individual, man or woman, to our great loss*. Research effort needs to be stepped up which will help to pinpoint individual talent and provide teaching material to enhance it. Society will profit by attention to individual differences because there are obvious benefits to be gained from fitting the job to the individual instead of the individual to the job,' (Brierley 1975 : 18–19)

The Board of Education recommended such research in 1923. Fifty years later we are still waiting for it. I wonder whether it is because it is girls and not boys who have been most disadvantaged?

Arithmetic, mathematics, spatial ability?

Much is made in particular of the sex difference in the primary years in understanding relationships between space, number, and logic – mechanical and spatial competence. The allegedly innate inferiority of girls has been taken for granted with an assurance that is daunting when one looks at the pattern of classroom behaviour that results in the regular unwillingness of girls to look at arithmetic, measurement, maths, as acceptable 'feminine' activities. In Susan Isaac's classic on teacher training, still a standard in 1963 when many teachers now in schools were trained, she takes as certain boys' superiority in their understanding of mechanical relations, which is surely the result of teaching, rather than of innate gift, although she recognizes the influence of suggestion:

'Take for instance one of the few already clearly established sex differences in ability, the difference between boys and girls in mechanical understanding. That the majority of boys are superior to the majority of girls in the understanding of machines and of mechanical relations is certain. It is however thought by many psychologists that this is not a strictly innate difference in ability but one that develops chiefly as a direction of their interests. And this difference in interest is itself partly the effect of suggestion and environmental pressure, although in part it does seem to be spontaneous and inherent.'

(Isaacs 1963:68–9)

In 1965, student teachers were still being told laconically that there were sex differences of physique, interests and attitudes, which their teaching methods '*must take into account*' – but with no such evidence or qualification. No wonder teachers' judgements are often reflex (Cohen and Garner 1965).

It is now widely believed that early experience with constructional toys, building materials, measuring apparatus, practical games, help to underpin spatial ability which in turn helps later mathematical understanding. So does exploratory experience, which boys appear to enjoy more than girls (part of the acceptability of noisy, dirty, or energetic activity which playing with old car engines, visiting the railway will involve). Boys in the National Child Development Survey were rated by their teachers as 'more interested in the world around'. How much is this due to teacher-set patterns of activity and behaviour? Six primary schools in a rural county surveyed by me in 1975 took boys and girls on different educational visits – a man teacher took *boys* to the engineering works and the Land Survey Unit, for example. Why segregate? 'Boys are interested.' It is difficult to see how girls will become interested if not exposed to new experiences.

Max Coltheart argues that visuo-spatial tests show no social class differences as such in test scores (unlike IQ and verbal test scores where there is a correlation) but suggests that large sex differences are always found when spatial tests are administered to males and females. Male and female scores admittedly overlap, but he claims that the average male score (exceeded by about 50 per cent of males) is exceeded by only 20–25 per cent of women (Coltheart 1975). He questions whether male visuo-spatial superiority may be inherited like *recessive* characteristics such as colourblindness or haemophilia (i.e. males inherit from mother only, but a female needs to inherit from both father and mother to display the trait). The weakness of this argument seems to me to be that if most girls are weak in this ability in the first place, they are surely unlikely to pass on a dominant trait to their sons? Whereas, moreover, colourblindness is a purely genetic factor unaltered by environment, visuospatial ability can clearly be improved (or held back) by environmental factors, whatever its baseline.

Supposing Coltheart, Corinne Hutt, and others to be right in their addiction to innate spatial inferiority of girls – what steps are HM Inspectorate and the nursery and infant schools taking to build in pre-school experience and classroom activity, to counteract it? What advice are we giving to young mothers at clinics on helpful early play techniques, toys, and games which counteract the deficiency? Why have we avoided remedial activities parallel to the special language help we give to slow readers (of either sex)? That teaching method can influence levels of achievement is illustrated by a recent Irish survey from the Drumcondra Educational Research Centre (Irish Department of Education 1977), which tested secondary pupil achievement in the different processes of mathematics using a team of fifty-six school inspectors, tests, questionnaires, and a sample of nearly 4,000 children in 145 classes. Highest *overall* mastery was achieved in operations with whole numbers, charts and graphs, whole number structure, and fractional structures; lowest overall mastery with decimals and percentages, operations with fractions, and arithmetical problems. But importantly in our current context;

'Throughout the test, the answering of the girls was superior to that of the boys. In no objective did the boys answer more successfully, and in certain instances there were marked differences ... The tendency for girls to score better than boys ... is still in evidence.'

(Irish Department of Education 1977: 11–13)

Contrary to previous research findings, these girls were superior at *problem solving*, not merely in rote learning. The research team is looking further into the sex differences.

I have deliberately postponed discussing the influence of the pattern of teacher employment in the early years until a later chapter; but clearly it is an extended integration of the stereotyping of a child's early environment. Proposals for change are included in the final chapter which draws together the threads that interweave the different sectors. Meanwhile it is small wonder that girls (and boys) associate leadership, authority, responsibility, and ambition with men and boys, when traditional roles are played out in the environment of the formative years. That the primary years are influential in terms of adult identification is illustrated by Barker Lunn's primary survey (1970:186–91) which showed that 13 per cent of fourth-year girls, but only 2 per cent of fourth-year boys, already wanted to be teachers when they grew up. Girls had already declared for nursing and hairdressing and boys to be footballers and sportsmen. We saw too in the previous chapter how Plowden based its planning of increased use of teachers' aides and ancillary assistants on female recruitment ('suitable' because of the maternal young children syndrome and the more practical issues of the availability of a pool of part-timers waiting for employment). Is it too radical to suggest the recruitment of more men to ancillary work, even making one full-time post from two part-time assignments aggregated? What are the real, as distinct from conditioned, objections? Would not some unemployed schoolboy leavers be better training for nursery nursing work than waiting for non-existent jobs in the North East? Are there no boys who have abilities to care for others, look after the younger and more defenceless, learn to be creative and not destructive? If not, one might ask, what has our secondary system made of them?

It is, however, even more the secondary years that account for the patterns of women's under-achievement and under-ambition. Perhaps we should move on to see how girls become women.

FOUR

Secondary education – through route or cul-de-sac ?

'*The modern world is full of artillery; and we turn out our children to do battle in it, equipped with the shield and sword of the ancient gladiator.*'

(T. H. HUXLEY, speaking to teachers
at South Kensington, 1861)

'*I am not yet so lost in the lexicography as to forget that words are the daughters of earth and that things are the sons of heaven.*'

(DR. JOHNSON, preface to the *Dictionary
of the English Language*)

September 1949, and the first generation of 'the Butler Act children' we were facing our most important educational hurdle. For me the last stages of a battle of passive resistance were won,

107

science had bitten the dust after the fourth year's incoherence of four successive science teachers; and I started my School Certificate year with an unbalanced but then happy combination of three languages, three humanities, two creative arts (and maths fortunately limping reluctantly along behind, under the baleful reflection of university entrance). Five miles away, up on the heathland, the children I had left behind at the all-age village school had all left school at Easter or summer at fifteen, with an elementary education of arithmetic (no maths), botany, but no other science (no specialist rooms), no modern languages, no technical crafts (except the school garden's annual village prize), and a smattering of history and geography from a visiting teacher. (They had, however, won every musical festival cup in their class every year.) June, the small girl who passed the eleven plus with me – but did not come – also left school with them at fifteen plus. There wasn't even a secondary modern school for her.

Things, you will say, are different now. We have extended courses in secondary modern schools, comprehensive education is widespread, curriculum planning is more enlightened, attitudes have softened. Look at the achievements in external examinations, at technological advances in teaching methods, at new pastoral and organizational approaches to children growing through adolescence. Look at the £600 million pounds we spend on education compared with the stark rationing of teachers, buildings, even paper and pencils of the first post war decade[1]. Look especially at the growth in opportunity for girls. Latter day 'Junes' are provided for now. Or are they?

One obvious but often overlooked complication in dealing with the education of groups rather than of individuals is their variety and unpredictability of previous experience and development.

The girls who enter the secondary schools of today will vary as dramatically in their physical growth, their maturity and outlook, and their social background as they do (like their brothers) in intellectual ability and in cast and type of mind. Some have already reached puberty and 'womanhood' and are beginning to think like young women rather than small girls; others will not develop fully until fourteen or so. Some have left small rural primary schools for a mixed area comprehensive school, a single-sex grammar school, a mixed secondary modern with no sixth form. Others have grown up in the hurly-burly and rough and tumble of a large urban primary school in the inner city where the accent is on education by peer groups for survival as much as on class-centred learning. Some will have seen only the sedate respectability and traditional behaviour of the new primary school of the middle-class commuter village or residential area. Many will come from areas that mix almost all of these elements.

Their attitudes will have been conditioned by their primary school teachers as well as parents. Will they have been under the care of a latter day Miss Read[2] or a Glenys Lobban whose excellent work on sexism in primary schools makes her class-room an unusually unfettered environment for the active enquiring girl and the dreamy sensitive boy as well as the quiet girl readers and the noisy boy modelmakers to be seen in traditional groups elsewhere (Lobban 1974).

It is easy to look at the surface of our secondary schools and see good intentions of open access, positive efforts to encourage both girls and boys to develop individually and to stretch themselves, imaginative new approaches to learning, and steady improvement of educational achievement. We can also see the reverse. Moreover, the evidence of HM Inspectorate is that most curricular differences spring from custom and tradition and not from educational philosophy.

'Of the 98% of mixed schools in which the sexes are separated for some aspects of their work, only a very small proportion of heads give educational considerations as major reasons for such separation ... separation of boys and girls for certain subjects is convenient for purposes of organisation.'
(1975:21)

We will look at the inspectorate's findings a little later, but register here that the survey established a scale of difference between girls' and boys' access to subjects and their take-up of different disciplines, and between patterns of school organization, which is totally unacceptable.

'The prevailing picture is one of traditional assumptions being worked out through the curricular patterns of secondary schools ... it is more likely that a society that needs to develop to the full the talents of its people will find the (striking differences and) discrepancies disturbing.'   (1975:24)

What has really happened is that many problems have simply gone to ground, hidden in a sophisticated beadpattern of school timetabling and in discriminatory planning of the glass palaces that have replaced the pitch-roofed, bell-towered, cramped old elementary school with its iron-frame desks and high windows. Hidden, too, is the curriculum, in a mass of 'bias courses', of integrated programmes, of school organization in tutorial year groups, of extra-curricular activities, and of pre-emptive choices of different study and behaviour patterns for girls and for boys.

The curriculum, as I see it, includes not only the clearly defined teaching of subjects, areas of study, and overt and structured learning activities, but this 'hidden curriculum', which transmits to young people a collection of messages about the status and character of individuals and social groups. It works through school organization, through attitudes, and through omissions – what we do not teach, highlight, or illuminate, is often more influential as a factor for bias than what we do. Much of what girls learn and experience in the secondary years will condition their attitudes to husbands, colleagues, workmates, their acceptance or questioning of governmental systems, their psychological mobility between the roles of economic provider, homemaker, worker, voter, citizen.

Hidden, indeed, also are the inequalities not only between the sexes, but within each sex; between girls of different regions, different classes, different backgrounds. Crossing like a matrix are cumulative dimensions of priority for the academically able, priority of resources for the older (sixth former or student) against the younger (nursery child, secondary fourteen-year-old), priority of esteem and investment for the traditional and academically respectable (universities, sixth forms, advanced higher education) over the highly efficient and industrially relevant but politically non-U and (for educational planners) 'nouveaux-riches' colleges of technology and further education.

The effect of this matrix of twin dimensions of inequality is that wherever the matrices interrelate, a compound of inequality occurs. Girls who are in the less favoured educational sectors are doubly, triply deprived. Social problems abound for them, too. It is daughters, not sons, who tend to be kept home to look after younger brothers and sisters; and miss school for domestic crises; to take some of the daily burden from their working mother; and to shop after school and on Saturdays when their brothers are learning the seeds of later group dynamics through the pores of their skin in gangs, clubs, football teams, competitive activities, and skilled leisure pursuits which develop the additional physical coordination and muscular strength that will later be used to assert a male job priority in certain fields of work.

Before looking at differences both in achievement of girls and boys, and in the way we educate them in secondary schools, I want to reinforce what I set out decisively in Chapter 2 on the objectives of education. I in no way underestimate the wider value of a liberal education, nor the outstanding work of our best secondary schools in using our rather freer curriculum than that of our European colleagues, to develop personality, maturity, culture and intellect, social responsibility. Both the aims and the achievements of education can be measured against almost any yardstick we choose and be seen to be partly successful. But I am unrepentant in saying that any school that turns out its girl school leavers without the qualifications that the outside world demands – rightly or wrongly, and in my view, rightly – and ill-equipped for the world of work, is failing its pupils completely in the twentieth century – and the twenty-first, which today's school leavers will enter at the relatively young age of forty. To turn out well adjusted, happy, generally knowledgeable sixteen-year-olds who have been allowed to spend all of their last two years almost exclusively on what they like and not on what they need – because frankly it is easier to teach children who are interested in and like what one is teaching – is to embroider round the hem of a garment without checking that its material, cut, style, and fit are right. I have passionately defended elsewhere the place of music, art, dance, and ballet, creative crafts, drama, in the central curriculum and not on the fringe, as part of a balanced education for life and not livelihood (although for some gifted children it should be possible to do both). All the schools that I have planned and designed have been built with dignified and special provision for the arts. But it should not be at the expense of a common core, to which I shall return later, of the basic academic and tool subjects which are essential to all future adult roles, and most of all for career advancement. The essence of balance is the rejection of mutual exclusiveness. I was therefore reassured to read in the Prime Minister's speech at Ruskin College (October 18, 1976), which launched the current national debate on education, his view that:

'The goals of our education from nursery school through to adult education, are clear enough. They are to equip children to the best of their ability for a lively, constructive place in society, and also to fit them to do a job of work. Not one or the other, but both. For many years, the accent was simply on fitting a so-called inferior group of children with just enough learning to earn their living in the factory ... There is now widespread recognition of the need to cater for a child's personality, to let it flower in the fullest possible way. The balance was wrong in the past. We have a responsibility to see that we do not get it wrong in the other direction. There is no virtue in producing socially well adjusted members of society who are unemployed because they do not have the skills. Nor at the other extreme must they be technically efficient robots. Both of the basic purposes of education require the same essential tools.'

Many of us have been arguing for this for years, only to meet with, from many, an unaccountable rejection of society's demands for a common core of basic education. I shall later be arguing for this for both the 60 per cent who now attempt GCE and CSE and for the 40 per cent who do not. Meanwhile, it would be well to recall what a balanced education once was.

I referred earlier particularly to personal individual fulfilment as the principal and over-riding of educational aims, in spelling out what I see as the main objectives of education. I can, however, see no incompatibility whatever between a liberal education in the sense that (unlike the early trade and technical schools) it does not teach skills for a particular trade (lace making, carpentry, laundrywork), on the one hand, and an education that recognizes that certain subjects, areas of knowledge, skills, and experiences are essential for every school leaver, male or female, able or slow learner in order to fit them for free access to and choice in the world of work, their principal activity on leaving school.

The finest definition of a balanced education that I have yet seen is the well known but still relevant definition of a liberal education which T. H. Huxley delivered in his address to the Working Men's College a hundred years ago:

'That man, I think, has had a liberal education who has been so trained in youth that his body is the ready servant of his will, and does with ease and pleasure all the work that, as a mechanism, it is capable of; whose intellect is a clear cold logic engine, with all its parts of equal strength, and in smooth working order; ready, like a steam engine, to be turned to any kind of work, and spin the gossamers as well as forge the anchors of the mind; whose mind is stored with a knowledge of the great and fundamental truths of Nature and of the laws of her operations; one who, no stunted ascetic, is full of life and fire, but whose passions are trained to come to heel by a vigorous will, the servant of a tender conscience; who has learned to love all beauty, whether of Nature or of art, to hate all vileness, and to respect others as himself.'

(Bibby 1972:62–3)

For Huxley, balance was a mind 'with all its parts of equal strength'. I suggest that 'personal fulfilment' in adult life in 1978 (and in the future for which today's school leavers are being educated) cannot exclude an understanding of the predominantly scientific and technical community in which we live. Literacy still remains the key to all other learning and to fiscal, civic, and adult freedom. The 'gossamers' of Huxley's metaphor may surely include music, drama, ballet, and creative. arts as well as sport; but we have provided the latter as a compulsory activity at the expense of the former, for which we provide neither purpose designed accommodation nor enough staff for pupils to opt. His 'anchors of the mind' are forged by reasoning and logic, training in objective analysis and spatial relationships, as well as by understanding human and political relationships, and the past through history as well as the social present. But the former is regarded still as predominantly a male need. Unlike today's educational planners, Huxley wrote the cheque for his beliefs. True, he fought for physical and natural sciences to become a compulsory part of the then classics-dominated secondary curriculum. But he also took on the London School Board, of which he was a prominent member, almost single-handed to fight for the right of elementary school-children in the slums of the East End to be taught music (singing in those days); and for art education and the teaching of beauty, as well as of logic and scientific method.

Today's fifth formers are clearly less traditional about this than their teachers. Sixty-eight per cent of my northern girls thought that different careers for girls and boys were wrong and 87 per cent were opposed to a different secondary education. How far the education service has progressed towards an exactly like education for girls and for boys since Huxley slated his contemporaries, is debatable.

'With few significant exceptions, girls have been educated either to be drudges, or toys, beneath men; or a sort of angels above them ... The possibility that the ideal of womankind lies neither in the fair saint nor in the fair sinner ... that women are meant neither to be men's guides nor their play-things, but their comrades, their fellows, and their equals, so far as Nature puts no bar on that equality, does not seem to have entered the minds of those who have had the conduct of the education of girls.' (Bibby 1972:59)

He would be disinclined to alter his criticism if he were to see the fourth- and fifth-year timetables of many of our modern schools, one feels.

Asked what he would do about it. Huxley was equally un-equivocal. Educate people; not 'women' as such.

'We reply, emancipate women. Recognise the fact that they share the same senses, perceptions, feelings, reasoning powers, emotions of boys, and that the mind of the average girl is less different from that of the average boy, than the mind of one boy is from that of another; so that whatever argument justifies a given education for boys, justifies its application to girls as well. So far from imposing artificial restraints upon the acquirement of knowledge by women, throw every facility in their way ... Let us have "sweet girl graduates" by all means. They will be none the less sweet for their wisdom; and the "golden hair" will not curl less gracefully outside the head by reason of there being brains within.' (Bibby 1972:59)

He had little in common with Ruskin, who, writing in 1865, while arguing for sound intellectual education for girls, clung tenaciously to the different character of their needs:

'I believe then, with this exception, that a girl's education should be nearly, in its course and material of study, the same as a boy's; but quite differently directed. A woman, in any rank of life, ought to know whatever her husband is likely to know, but to know it in a different way. His command of it should be foundational and progressive; hers, general and accomplished for daily and helpful use.'

('Of Queen's Gardens', in *Sesame and Lilies*)

This kind of thinking was widely current even in the 1960s, when the Newsom Committee justified the greater time spent by boys on maths and science and by girls on practical subjects, as 'caused by a differing diagnosis of the needs of pupils' (1960: para. 629). I reject the different needs much as I question that anyone has dignified their timetabling practices with 'diagnosis' and not reflex.

Access to a full curriculum?

I have indeed listened with fascination over nearly twenty years of living in and out of schools and colleges to heads and teachers who appear firmly to believe that they really do offer all of their girls and boys a full choice of subjects or study areas; that all pupils at fourteen plus have the real possibility of a completely free option; and even that they do in fact have a common core education up to school-leaving age. I am frequently told that boys and girls are in fact taught together in co-educational schools, that schools regard them all as individual young people and that practical matters like resources and school organization never determine childrens' educational diet. I simply do not believe it. My eyes see otherwise wherever I visit schools.

From 1968–69, I looked at secondary education in considerable depth in three Local Education Authority areas. Six years later, I was fortunate enough to be able to spend a full year looking, first, at the education of girls in primary and secondary schools, and later, at problems of rural deprivation in education[3]. What follows here draws from time to time on all three studies, and was guided substantially by my growing recognition that what I was told as a staffroom visitor in no way seemed to match what I actually saw in the schools, nor the timetabling practices, differential achievements of girls and boys, and regional and national patterns which have been well documented elsewhere. I believe it, therefore, to be essential that we start from a basis of facts and not of hypothesis, and of diagnosis and not of assumptions.

Girls are admitted in equal numbers to boys to secondary schools, at eleven plus. They are therefore in theory, starting out on the same fast motorway or slower country road to their destination, as their brothers. But whereas we teach boys the intricacy of the Spaghetti Junctions of curricular routes at fourteen plus and sixteen plus, I contend that we leave our girls on single tracks or at best, dual carriageways, with very few side turnings, junctions, or crossroads. The traditional arts/sciences split dies hard. Before we look at the character and ethos of the schools, the scale of actual differences between the sexes should be recognized.

Table 4(1) 'Do you think boys and girls should have a different education? If so, why?' (Fifth-form survey)

	%	
	Yes	No
Do you think girls should have a different secondary education from boys	13·1	86·9
Do you think girls should have different careers from boys?	31·5	68·5

'Can you give a reason for your view?'	%
There should be equal opportunity for both sexes	48·2
No difference in intelligence between girls and boys	17·6
Girls and boys do have different natural capabilities	9·4
Girls and boys do have different natural preferences	4·7
Girls and boys don't have natural differences in aptitudes	2·4
Different destinies – career not so important for a girl	8·2
Broad education is necessary for both	4·7
Co-education means they can help each other	4·7

The northern fifth formers were asked about the purpose and objectives of their education as they saw it, and in particular, whether they thought girls and boys should have a different education; and why, if so. Perhaps teachers should listen to their pupils more, if *Table 4(1)* is typical of girls in 1978. I spoke earlier also of the evasiveness of educationalists on the subject of examinations and qualifications. The fifth form girls were more realistic, as the table below shows:–

Table 4(2) 'Why (in your *own* opinion) are you taking public examinations?' (Fifth-form survey)

opinion	%
need the qualifications	41·4
helps get a good job	38·4
have to – compelled	8·1
test of ability	3·0
something to show for time at school	5·1
other	4·0

Inside secondary schools

At eleven (or twelve or thirteen in some three-tier systems) girls are leaving primary or middle schools having learned with a minimum of timetabling, in a school day of which less than a third is sex divided. They have learned the unwritten laws that 'ladies don't play football' (see Reyersbach 1974), that boys are expected to be stronger; they are afraid that girls are not very good at maths or arithmetic, they know they are expected to look after visitors and make coffee, and help with tea at the PTA while the boys move the hall chairs. They have learned a kind of needlework which is usually domestically oriented; they know it is not feminine to crawl over the sawn-off engine in the yard getting oily. They are keen for the approval of teachers; they know what kind of behaviour will win it.

On the other hand, if they have come from a good, lively, sensible school – and there are many such – they will have learned healthy competition with others (whoever, not girls or boys as such), how to work in a team on a project, how to live together in camp for a week, as well as how to organize their work. They will know that although some are still struggling with the newer approaches of the Schools Mathematics Project, many girls find number work fun; they can outshine their brothers in essay or poem writing. Their drawings win praise (although a keen observer will see that more girls tend to concentrate on people, gardens, scenery, and more boys on drawing things, models, engines, diagrams, circuits). The more fortunate will have done some primary science – mostly with male teachers. Latterday Miss Reads, some very evident in two of the rural counties I looked at in 1975, may have taken the 'natural' interest of girls in living things and encouraged them to spend more time looking at botany and natural history rather than at electrical kits, albeit to good purpose if it arouses their spirit of curiosity and grasp of cause and effect. It need not be to the exclusion of an introduction to some basic principles of the physical sciences, of course.

The secondary school day by contrast is heavily timetabled. From the moment that Jennie and Cathy walk into their old three decker or the new glass palace, they learn that every period of the day is earmarked and that boys and girls begin now to divide as such. The physical design of the school, in some aspects necessarily because of the different physical development of older children, regularly tells them they are different as they hang up coats, divide for games, are cross-set for subjects taught as integrated in the primary years. Most of all, the adults are sex-typed – male caretakers, female secretaries and school nurses, meals helpers. Whereas visitors to the primary school are often women (advisers of infant and primary education, other head-mistresses), visitors to secondary schools are mostly male – nine-tenths of all senior education office staff, two-thirds of secondary advisers (except for housecraft and languages).

School organization and choice

A minority of schools is beginning to tackle new approaches to school organization, which break down artificially slanted groupings. A fundamental constraint is that we do not have enough specialist rooms, teachers, or periods in a thirty-five or forty period week to teach everyone everything and we have no national yardstick of minimum central or optional fringes. One key is timetabling. A school of 1,600 pupils may have over 2,500 spaces to be slotted into a typical timetable, over a hundred staff, perhaps 600 actual subdivisions of classes. Many large schools are now timetabling by computer (although this is only as sound as the programmes we feed in), but even with this practical help, there will be conflict between pupils' choices or career needs, and the staff's wishes to teach alternative subjects or different year groups, classes, or courses. There is a genuine problem.

The curricular philosophy of the head and senior staff may produce a certain pattern in the first three years of either defined subject links or of integrated curricular areas. When the larger classes or half classes of lower school subdivide into a proliferation of small groups, career needs inevitably assert themselves (if the school has a careers education programme at all, that is) and conflict between 'interest-based' courses and basic educational and vocational needs begins to develop.

It is in one sense as unhelpful to talk about girls' education as a single identifiable question as to talk about women as a homogeneous (feminageneous?) group in the first place. It is frankly arguable and perhaps arbitrary, whether we can usefully divide children into academic and non academic, or motivated and unstimulated, potential stayers and leavers, and so on. For ease of discussion, I can however see no alternative but to look separately at some aspects of secondary planning, simply because that is what schools do – plan separately for what they see as different groups of children. The separation of one aspect of what may be seen as 'academic' work should not, therefore, be seen as necessarily approving a rigid split of attitude, or of curricular planning. Indeed, part of my later case is that many of the principles of balanced education, which we apply to the 40 per cent more able, ought to apply to the no less important average girls who have other gifts than the heightened intellectual speed and analysis (which is not, being realistic, everyone's gift), and other needs than the unskilled labour market or the kitchen sink.

Nor do I see how one can avoid making certain assumptions about the curriculum. This is dangerous, but crucial, ground. As this goes to press, teachers, parents, industry, politicians, planners, are hotly debating what the curriculum does, and what it should, mean. Well trod paths are being rehammered; familiar paces of the old education minuets are being danced in fashionable ritual, as what is becoming known as 'The Great

Debate' develops momentum. I want therefore to spell out certain curricular principles in relation to the decisive objectives for the education of girls as well as boys which I outlined in Chapter 2. The argument that follows hinges on this.

It is not to overlook the needs of the less able girls, the 20 per cent (65,220 in 1974) who enter employment with neither GCE nor CSE passes, and the further 20 per cent who achieve fewer than five passes above grade 3, to start looking at external examination objectives and girls' achievements in them. Nor would I argue for a balanced curriculum with some compulsory elements of both science and humanities, creative as well as technical arts, solely because of training, job, or career needs. But these are paramount and overriding. One can achieve personality, fulfilment, interest, social adjustment by almost any esoteric combination of the 250 GCE/CSE subjects now on offer. For training and for employment, a specific, defined core however has become essential. Any girl who does not want to end up on the unskilled labour market must achieve at least five 'O' levels in a central group of essential subjects. An analysis of the Regional Advisory Councils' Directory of Further Education courses reveals two interesting if predictable facts. First, nine tenths of all further education courses above craft level are labelled with minimum entry requirements, starting with four or five GCE 'O' level passes. Second, the compulsory subjects listed for recruitment to two-thirds of the further education courses are chosen from a very limited range of 250 subjects. The central five are maths and English, physics and chemistry, and a technical craft, and the remaining 'respectable' subjects specified tend to be limited to history, geography, modern languages, biology, and English literature. Subjects like housecraft, design for living, pottery, are often specifically excluded from the 'eligible' list.

The pattern changes for advanced courses of education and training. A distinction which is not generally appreciated is that while the standard two 'A' levels will gain entry to Higher National Diploma courses, to teacher training, and to intermediate levels of training, three (in relevant subjects) have become essential in practice for most degree courses at university, for many CNAA degrees, for the more demanding professional training (medicine, law, most architectural schools)[4]. Girls who are discouraged from aiming at three or four 'A' levels and settling for two only are in fact being denied one whole area of further education opportunities.

The secondary school cannot reject, I think, its inescapable task of providing girls as well as boys with the right qualifications for their future career or job, with the right basis for further training or further and higher education, as well as the less tangible experiences which will help them grow in leadership and personal and general management. Counter arguments are already emerging in the national debate, and run something like this.

> Examinations aren't everything. GCE is no longer so vital now that CSE has developed. GCE does not necessarily test ability or competence, so it doesn't matter if pupils don't achieve it. One can't assume that GCE English means one can write or spell competently. GCE maths doesn't mean one is numerate. Able school leavers can be well educated even if they leave without successful Grade 1 CSEs or the statuory 5 GCE 'O' levels. Those who concentrate on these ambiguous forms of measurement are Philistines, unconscious of the *real* aims and purposes of education. Examinations are a straitjacket. Young people should be allowed to develop freely.

The northern fifth formers disagreed with this evasive approach. They were in no doubt at all as the direct relationship of public examinations to the world of work. Asked why they thought they were taking public exams, 41 per cent said they needed the qualifications and 38 per cent thought they helped to get a good job. Only 3·0 per cent thought they were useful to test ability. Asked to rank their GCE/CSE subjects as most and least useful and then to say why (an open-ended question with no preset list) 75 per cent ranked their subjects 'useful' because necessary for a job, and 60 per cent ranked certain subjects as least useful because they were not needed for or helpful to a job. Asked which reasons most influenced their choice of which subjects to study, the girls were given nine reasons to rank in order of relative importance. Forty-nine per cent gave as the first reason that they were necessary for the chosen job or career on leaving school, and 39 per cent 'because I am good at them'.

There are of course two separate but related angles to curricular inequalities. The first is actual access in the first place;

the second is the character, type, and quality of what is offered. All of the evidence points to considerable differences of access between girls and boys. Differences of type and quality are, after all, irrelevant to those who cannot study a topic at all. To debate whether flats, maisonettes, or houses are better, still seems academic to those without any hope of a roof over their head at all. Communities without enough food in the Third World would regard as frivolous a debate on whether rice, bread, or pasta were the better staple, or whether butter or margarine is better for our health. Similarly, the first basic problem that girls face at all is how to achieve the same education as boys from the quite simple question of basic access. This of course raises again why we teach which subjects to whom.

The curricular route

Access is of course first a fundamental question of providing the same resources, and by no means all single sex schools still have the full range of staff or specialist rooms, for example, for both areas of science and technology — physical and natural, industrial and environmental.

We have built, designed, and staffed many schools for half a curriculum and now we lack teachers and capital money to level them up. Single-sex schools will leave out altogether one whole area of the curriculum (unless they are very unusual) in that girls' schools have been deliberately designed without technical craft facilities and boys' without the domestic crafts. The deprivation of technical drawing, metalwork, and woodwork is far more disadvantageous to girls than the reverse, because it does three things. It labels technical work, machines, tools, draughtsmanship as 'masculine' with all the implications that that carries with it — especially for adolescent, boy-conscious girls. They are even less likely to opt for technical training if they risk being regarded as unfeminine in a development stage in which their own instincts and conditioning combine to make them accept the triviality of the media messages as serious warnings that they will end up on the shelf if they do not assert their femininity. Girls who do not perceive themselves in the classic media images may in fact have a hidden advantage. Fifteen-year-old, eleven-stone Janice in my northern sample was determined to make Oxbridge and get a good degree 'because I know

I'm not attractive – I'm going to *have* to earn my living'. Since she had an attractive personality, she will probably find later she has marriage as well – but she will be qualified.

The second main relevance of technical crafts is that they underpin mechanical and spatial understanding and provide a practical motivation to continue with maths involving, as they do, mensuration, accuracy, and causal relationships. If girls really are deficient in spatial ability, why do teachers not provide us with the very educational experiences that will develop it?

Third, the practical crafts are an excellent base for later leisure pursuits and for non-vocational skills which are essential in our personal lives. I have moved house – alone – four times. The steady growth of my still limited expertise with screwdriver and hammer, drill and measuring tape, was born of midnight desperation, surrounded by unfitted shelves and cabinets and kitchen wall fitments. But I confess that it is to three male colleagues that I owe an expert wall of bookshelving for my 2,000 books. No future housewife should leave school without a competent grasp of woodwork, strains and stresses, electrical circuits, how plumbing and heating systems work. For these girls' schools need workshops to add to their physics laboratories (and many are deficient in these also). Women have driven cars since World War One. Understanding how they work is an essential tool of adult life for all – and can save expensive mistakes. Metalwork shops in boys' schools spawn redundant car engines used for projects and demonstrations. What of the future girl drivers in girls' schools? At least in co-educational schools the physical facilities are there for those teachers to use, who recognize girls as living in the world of twentieth-century transport and not of nineteenth-century carriages and pairs (or pedestrian cobbles). Boys will not of course consider their parallel lack of housecraft room as equivalent deprivation. Why should they? Their first task on leaving school will be to find the nearest suitable female to wash, cook, launder for, and organize them. But I believe it is as essential to insist on all boys' schools offering housecraft and home economics, as the reverse. My argument in Chapter 2 recurs – education for their *shared* domestic role, is essential to woman's later freedom and mobility. Using facilities at a girls' school will not do – the activity would keep its 'feminine' label – and only the integration of this area of family study into the normal curriculum, will make it respectable for boys.

Has co-education and its implicit free access in fact made any difference, however? If we look at the growth of CSE, taken by the middle ability girls most likely to aim at craft employment, taking the practical subjects as an example in the early years of the examination, we find little changing impact of either sex on non-traditional areas over the years.

Table 4(3)   CSE entries 1967 and 1972

	1967		1972	
	B	G	B	G
metalwork and woodwork	35,554	54	63,233	213
domestic subjects	365	31,994	1,901	66,161
technical drawing	34,527	227	55,356	593

Source: DES *Statistics of Education.*

By 1972, two-thirds of all secondary schools were mixed. The theory of open access was however blocked because the subjects have all been labelled for boys only and girls only and *cross-timetabled*. It would therefore be impossible for a pupil to opt for both areas of study, or for the reverse area.

In 1975, HM Inspectorate found that the heads justified this on grounds of timetabling convenience. 'Relatively few schools offer craft subjects on a rotating basis in the first two years to enable boys and girls to have reasonable experience of the whole range of possibilities' (1975:7).

There is an added hidden danger in timetabling restrictions – pre-emptive patterns.

'Some of the patterns of curriculum developed in the first three years ... produce, either purposely or by accident, restrictions on what appears to be a free choice of options for the fourth year stage ... In the fourth form, technical drawing is introduced as a supposedly free choice for boys and girls. The craft department in line with contemporary practice and thinking is unwilling to teach technical drawing in isolation and insists it must be linked with metalwork. Only those pupils who have previously taken metalwork are allowed to study technical drawing.'   (1975:7)

And by 1974, predictably, girls accounted for a mere 1,919 out of 122,000 entries in technical drawing in GCE and CSE. This is a deplorable record, bearing in mind that draughtswomanship, cartography, tracing are highly suitable skilled employment outlets for girls of average rather than high academic ability. Technical drawing is clean work, demands no special physical attributes, calls for the qualities of neatness, dexterity, attention to detail for which girls are said to be noted (hence their prevalence as assembly-line checkers).

Southampton Technical College in 1972 pioneered special courses for trainee draughtswomen on day release to top up their maths, science, and technical drawing in 'determined efforts to prove that once young women can be attracted to technical studies they are capable of equalling and often surpassing the results of their male contemporaries'. The aim was to qualify them for Ordinary National Certificate and the college has encouraged girls to career advancement in shipbuilding, mechanical, electrical, and architectural draughting. The success stories of pioneer girls are told in *On Course* (DES, No. 24, Autumn 1972). Many have gone on to attain higher qualifications.

Similarly, fewer than 1,100 girls take woodwork, or metalwork, against about 111,200 boys. Head teachers are ambivalent as to why we teach handicraft in schools, against the constant allegation that it is not the schools' job to prepare pupils for specific jobs. The handicrafts are clearly vocationally linked for many less able boys; but not all. Not all boys go into engineering craft apprenticeships. Many enjoy the pure creativity of craftmanship – study the essence of non-vocational education. If the justification for the most expensive specialist facilities in the school is, as I believe, the general transfer value of skilled and scientifically based craftwork, there can be no validity in depriving girls of this essential educational experience. Relatively fewer of the 124,000 girls entering for domestic crafts and needlecrafts (only 500 or so boys) use their vocational outlets, than boys use handicraft. The standing of metalwork in particular is generally greater in employer's eyes, than housecraft – rightly since it has a greater transfer value.

We have to search deeper into pupils' motivations and into teacher attitudes and practices to explain why even when girls are in a school with the fullest facilities and a staff sensitive to role changing and modern social pressures, girls still opt for traditional subjects. In Sweden, too, despite the compulsory foundation work for all pupils of home economics, textile work, and combined wood and metalwork up to Grade Six (thirteen years), when pupils are allowed to opt from Grade Seven, 94 per cent of boys choose wood and metalwork while 88 per cent of girls choose textile work. Similarly, the Swedish work experience schemes in the fifth year, see boys opting for industrial or trade productions and girls for nursing and service occupations. Girls, as in England, dominate in liberal arts and social sciences; boys in technology and natural sciences. The girls' options are reported to 'afford poorer outlooks for employment after graduation than many other curricula'. (Sandberg 1975:40–1).

It is essential that we illustrate and in a lively acceptable manner whenever we write, publish, or talk, both sexes in *interchangeable* roles. Even Tyrell Burgess's *Inside Comprehensive Schools* (1970) has a block of entirely sex-typed illustrations. Boys are modelling a feudal farm; girls are drawing needlework patterns. Girls are typing and cooking. A boy works a lathe. Boys are being adventurous in the gym; learning judo; potting up plants in the greenhouse (more girls do natural sciences). Girls are dissecting in biology. How do we induce teachers to see interchangeable roles for young people if even government publications reinforce the traditional? As the book is aimed principally at parents it is doubly regrettable to have missed an opportunity to encourage new parental attitudes and approaches by giving a strong lead.

Physical education is perhaps the most marked curricular example with social connotations. It looms larger in our school organization than in any other comparable country. Its indirect influence on sex stereotypes is perhaps disproportionate to what I regard as its dispensability after about the age of thirteen. The issue is more important than it seems, for untypical boys as well as for girls. When children arrive at secondary school at eleven plus, the pattern of polarity (football v. netball) is already established; so is the primacy of the former and the inferiority of the latter both in league terms and in the public eye. (When will 'Match of the Day' show hockey or netball?) Lovell[5] recognizes that excellence in sport has become especially necessary for boys' peer group acceptance, while Hallworth found that girls rated good looks and attractiveness highly even within girls themselves; but rated prowess in sport much lower than boys did (Valentine 1963).

The artificial split for physical education at secondary level, first, endorses in girls' eyes the exclusive masculinity of the prestige sports which is a generally harmful and an unnecessary sex message. It is possible perhaps that girls might be embarrassed in a football scrum, but there seems no real reason why, in a mixed school, cricket should not be optionally as mixed as tennis; hockey and lacrosse as mixed as rounders is in a primary school; or swimming as mixed as the changing facilities allow (and most are designed like mixed public baths). Head teachers split PE for sheer timetabling convenience in most schools. One result is that from early childhood, girls' muscles and physical stamina develop differently. If they underwent as much as their physique allows (as women do in some Aboriginal tribes) their physical co-ordination and skill would be more similar to that of average men. (Look at nurses who are trained to handle heavy patients who are unable to help themselves.) By no means all boys are taller, stronger, heavier – myopic and astigmatic boys will have the same difficulty in ball games as girls with eye defects. Mixing more games would enable teams to be grouped diagnostically according to real skills, weight, and agility and not by sex. The more delicate boy would not be bullied on to rugger pitches and cross country runs by mockery and scorn and the robust girl would be free to use up her excess energy. The hidden curriculum comes into play in extra curricular activities – sex-linked sport and PE will be replicated out of school and reinforce the adolescent sociometric 'cleavage' at thirteen plus and fourteen plus when girls see boys as rough and boys see girls as soft (social friendships spring from grouped leisure pursuits). Once past about fourteen years, I can equally see no justification for *compulsory* PE in the fourth and fifth year (other than convenience of timetabling, an invalid criterion), when the thirty-five period week allegedly does not allow for common core of tool subjects for all.

This polarization has a longer-term effect in adult years. I am strictly speaking criticizing the godlike status of organized sport more than creative physical activity. The serious introduction of ballet and modern dance, for example, for both sexes, into primary and secondary schools as an equal option to be encouraged, would give lasting pleasure to many future adults otherwise deprived of an interest through lack of knowledge (or acceptability). Dance can be quite as demanding as athletics and gymnastics and properly taught can link well with drama. The antitheses of masculine virility and feminine 'cissyness' would gradually be eroded with a ricochet benefit on individual personal development of both sexes – Huxley's 'gossamers' as well as 'anchors'.

The qualifications route

While it is essential that we do not concentrate only on the subject angle of the curriculum – and the increasing subdivisions of each discipline which specialization necessarily brings[6] – we cannot focus an educational debate on education for life, for leisure, for government, for adjustment to work, without looking at the subject 'funnels', through which we pour the stream of educational knowledge, experiences, skills, attitudes, and achievements which make up what we call the curriculum. One of the well-worn paths which is being trod in the Great Debate is the simultaneous decrying of subject disciplines and examination patterns on the one hand, and defence of GCE and CSE subjects on the other. But as long as we have sixteen plus examinations, and as long as employers, training bodies, further education colleges, and higher education institutions demand not only minimum recruitment *levels* of attainment (five 'O' levels, three 'A' levels, success in OND or HND) but minimum *areas of study* (maths, science, English, technical crafts), so long do we have an obligation to make sure that girls as well as boys leave school with the measurable educational equipment that they need for work, study, or governmental or community life. If examinations are unnecessary or irrelevant for girls, we cannot justify priority of staffing and curricular resources for them for boys. And if boys need certain subject patterns for open career advancement, so do girls.

Even a brief look at the subject demands of some forms of vocational training that offer particularly suitable new opportunities for girls will illustrate the need for all pupils to study a common core to sixteen plus. Recruits for assistant scientific officers in meteorology need four 'O' levels, of which English, maths, and physics or general science are compulsory. For housing management[7] the training base is five 'O' levels including

English language and maths or a science *other than biology*. Future dieticians will need five 'O' levels including English, maths, and chemistry. Computer and data processing require five 'O' levels, with compulsory maths and English. Training for a Company Secretary means maths, English, and a science among the statutory five, while even future cartographers must choose their three to four 'O' levels from maths, English, science, art or technical drawing, modern language. Pharmacy technicians, dental auxiliaries, architectural technicians, chiropodists, air traffic controllers, landscape architects, quantity surveyors – all fields well suited to girls (no nonsense about physical strength or masculine attributes) – all require five GCE 'O' or 'A' levels which include maths, English, and most of which require a science.

Nor is CSE generally acceptable except at grade 1. Indeed only a very small minority of candidates achieve grade 1 passes in more than one subject.

How have girls fared in achieving the right basis for a completely free and unconditioned choice of job or training, at sixteen plus?

Table 4(4)   Sex imbalance and growth rates of GCE take-up

	percentage of relevant age group	
passes	*boys*	*girls*
5 'O' levels		
1953	11·13	10·27
1962	15·60	15·17
1973*	22·7	23·3
2 Advanced levels		
1953	5·44	2·79
1962	8·78	5·38
1973	4·1	4·4
3 Advanced levels		
1953	3·77	1·62
1962	6·15	3·26
1973	9·2	6·6

(Source: DES *Statistics of Education 1962* Part III, Table 18 *1974*, Vol. 2, Table 22.)
*Note: This 1973 figure includes CSE above Grade 5.

First, they have narrowed the gap at GCE 'O' level in achieving the minimum *number* of passes for recruitment to some career-based training. In 1962, 16·5 per cent of boys and 15·2 per cent of girls achieved five 'O' level passes. By 1973 the girls had overtaken – 23·3 per cent against 22·8 per cent of boys – minimal differences in either year. But *Table 4(4)* shows a disturbing shift of unequal achievement – upwards. Superficially, all looks well. The 1953 gap in achievement of two 'A' levels had vanished by 1973 (4·0 per cent of both sexes). But the gap remains – for boys and girls achieving three 'A' levels – 9·2 per cent of boys but only 6·6 per cent of girls. And this is the level of qualification needed for completely free movement in the *higher* education sector. Most universities and CNAA degree courses require a three 'A' level entry; and almost all the major professions. The traditional lower ceiling of the girls (teacher training with five 'O' levels or up to two 'A' levels) will leave them with no equivalent alternative as the teacher education cuts (see Chapter 7) remove the traditional major career opportunity for girls competing for diminishing places at colleges of education.

The poverty of aspiration bites deep. It also varies in intensity in different regions. *Table 4(5)* gives the more substantial of the regional variations from which it will be seen that girls in the South East consistently achieve above the national average and that girls in the North under-achieve. But throughout, the principle inequality gap occurs at Advanced level. Twice as many Southern boys as Northern girls achieve two or more 'A' levels.

I spoke earlier of cumulative factors of under-achievement. Westergaard and Little (1965) discuss the compounding of inequality between the social classes and illustrate a marked disparity between boys and girls of different classes in their achievement of the 2 'A' level passes needed for higher education. In their analysis boys of semi-skilled and manual workers fall behind the top groups in ratios of 39:53 and 41:53. But the girls' gap is much wider: whereas 39 per cent of 'semi-skilled' boys achieved two 'A' levels as against 53 per cent of social class one, only 41 per cent of girls from *professional* homes achieved this. Only 24 per cent of 'semi-skilled' girls as against 41 per cent of similar boys, achieved the two 'A' levels needed for advancement.

Table 4(5) School leavers' GCE/CSE achievements – England and Wales 1974 – regional variations

	boys %	girls %
(a) With neither GCE passes nor CSE of Grade 5 or better		
National average	22·1	19·9
South East (excluding Greater London)	16·5	14·5
South West	18·2	16.6
West Midlands	25·0	22·0
Wales	31·9	31·3
(b) With at least 5 'O' level passes and/or at least 1 'A' level		
National average	24·1	24·5
South East	29·0	28·9
South West	26·9	27·1
West Midlands	21·1	21·0
North	19·9	21·1
(c) With 2 or more 'A' level passes		
National average	13·3	11·0
South East	16·5	12·9
South West	14·3	11·7
North	10·1	8·3
West Midlands	11·4	9·6

In each case, the regions with the two highest and the two lowest levels of take-up have been selected. The Outer London South East and the South West are constantly above the national average for this kind of academic achievement (as distinct from further education).

Source: DES *Statistics of Education 1974*, Vol. 2, Table 27.

I believe that the 1973 three 'A' level gap correlates highly with the proportion of boys and of girls who reach universities. It is of considerable significance that the further education figures in *Table 4(6)* below show a steady improvement proportionately as well as numerically on FE courses for which five 'O' levels or one or two 'A' levels are adequate entry qualifications. The gap mentioned above of 9 per cent of boys but 6 per cent of girls attaining *three 'A' levels* (as against 4 per cent of each sex with two) is replicated in the 1973 university entrance figures – 9·3 per cent of boys and 6·2 per cent of girls.

Table 4(6)   School leavers' destinations

	university		teacher training		further education	
	boys %	girls %	boys %	girls %	boys %	girls %
1925	0·67	0·46	0·46	1·42	0·70	1·46
1937	1·05	0·51	0·35	1·39	0·94	2·58
1950	2·67	1·23	0·28	2·21	2·08	5·20
1960	4·2	2·1	0·86	3·12	5·52	8·64
1973	9·3	6·2	1·9	7·3	13·4	21·3

Source: DES *Statistics of Education 1973*, Vol. 2, Table B. (converted to percentages).

I am not of course saying that university entrance is necessarily always a better career qualification – although graduate status is still the major base for a good deal of career-based further professional and managerial training, leading to top jobs. It remains a major route to advancement. Moreover, the fact that most girls read arts subjects at Advanced level means that they are less qualified for the science and technology based advanced further education which is the main vocational alternative to teaching, nursing, or administration. The upper range of diploma courses of the new Technical Education Council tend to acquire Advanced Level qualifications in scientific and technical subjects at GCE 'A' Level – and are the entry route to a wide band of skilled, and therefore better paid, job opportunities.

Single sex or mixed?

The single sex and co-educational controversy is one of the most difficult issues facing us today. Steady reorganization of secondary education non-selectively is involving increasing co-education. Is this better? By what yardstick? Ten years ago I argued as strongly as any for more mixed schools, partly to help the development of social education, partly to widen access to subject areas not available in single-sex schools, and partly in the hope that the presence of girls would add a slightly civilizing element to boys and that the presence of boys would act as a spur and an incentive to the girls. It hasn't really worked like that at all, and it may well be that now we need a major national debate specifically on co-education or single sex – the antithesis of the two points of view put by Sheila Egan and Sheila Wood in 1973. The former opposed single sex schools on the grounds that they reinforce stereotypes of an already biased system and encourage girls to take less difficult and more limited options by well-meant kindness, while Sheila Wood's view that 'in all co-educational schools almost without exception girls will see a community where responsibilities are held by men. We think too many schools are boys' schools with girls in them' (*The Times*, April 25, 1973) is very much borne out by later events and the steady decline of women in top posts in schools. How important is the issue?

Here I must declare a partisan position and offer a subdued apology to the private sector. My argument centres on state schools for two clear reasons, but therefore leaves out two aspects of 'discriminatory planning' relevant to private schools. The first is that there is a considerable provision of preparatory, day, and boarding schools for boys and a relative dearth of private provision for girls. Sociologically, I personally regard this as a female advantage since it obliges girls to come to terms with the real world as lived by the 95 per cent of the rest of us, at a much earlier age. But I recognize that if parents do in fact sacrifice to send sons (but not daughters) to schools regarded *ipso facto* in their eyes as better, by whatever criteria, it reinforces what Belotti and others describe as the enhanced perceived male status of boys in early childhood. Second, although girls' direct grant and independent schools are catching up slowly, there is past evidence that industry and the wealth producers have steadily endowed and modernized the boys' schools with new scientific and technical facilities to the almost total exclusion of girls' schools. Notwithstanding, any girl who is a potential candidate for private education is likely to have certain advantages, such as a supportive home, a secure social or financial background, and a culture-oriented family. She is not, therefore, a first candidate for my concern, compared with

133

the cumulative depressed potential achievement of the remaining 95 per cent.

The actual distribution of single sex and co-educational schools in England and Wales is widely misquoted and the facts are important. *Table 4(7)* gives the present distribution of

Table 4(7) State-maintained single sex and co-educational schools – England and Wales 1975

	boys only	girls only	mixed
nursery	–	–	612
infants	–	–	4,744
first	–	–	2,098
junior with infant	1	1	11,129
first and middle	–	–	331
junior	55	48	4,271
middle deemed primary	–	–	578
subtotal (primary)	56	49	23,363
middle deemed secondary	9	8	456
modern	156	169	1,216
grammar	206	213	147
technical	10	9	10
comprehensive	193	187	2,216
other	37	28	90
subtotal (secondary)	611	614	4,135
total (primary and secondary)	667	663	27,498

Source: DES *Statistics of Education 1975*, Vol. 1. Schools

maintained single sex and co-educational schools. In 1975, over 77 per cent of all secondary schools were co-educational. But the total figures are misleading. Over half of all secondary schools (excluding middle schools) are now comprehensive, and of these, 87 per cent were mixed. A third of all secondary schools are still secondary modern – and 78 per cent of these were mixed. On the other hand, grammar schools now account for only 12 per cent of the state sector, but 74 per cent of these were single sex, and of 174 direct grant grammar schools, all but three are single sex. Together they account for nearly a fifth of all secondary schools, but nearly half of all single-sex schools. Educating your daughter separately is therefore in practice limited mainly (outside the Inner London Education Authority) to either those who can afford direct grant school fees, or whose children are of grammar school ability and live in unreorganized areas.

My principal concern with this controversy is the achievement of 'equal means the same' which is unattainable while girls' schools offer housecraft etc. but no metalwork/woodwork and technical studies; and boys' schools the converse. The cost of extending the practical accommodation of all 1,300 single-sex state schools to cover the full range (which should be compulsory in my view if they continue in being), even if estimated at a modest £100,000 per school would greatly exceed the capital resources of the education building programme, if added to those needed for the normal reorganization process. It is regrettable, although in the light of this basic arithmetic, politically understandable, that single-sex schools were exempted from the *Sex Discrimination Act* and no parent can therefore demand woodwork for girls at a single sex school. This whole question needs a further enquiry nationally. There is a genuine dilemma, because it must also be said that there is growing evidence of girls' greater personal motivation and achievement from single sex schools, and of greater curricular freedom within the range of subjects on offer.

The findings of the HMI Report already quoted, (and the annual DES statistics bear these out) suggest that 'girls are more likely to choose a science and boys a language in a single sex school, though in a mixed school a higher percentage of pupils may be offered these subjects' and this raises an important question – why? One needs to look at the two dimensions I raised earlier, both access and choice.

An analysis of *Tables 4(8)* and *(9)* below show that both sexes have slightly greater access to non-traditional core subjects in single-sex schools but that sex differences are still extremely marked.

The pattern of curricular differences shapes a quite distinct education for girls and for boys. HM Inspectorate found in 1975 that boys and girls were not offered equal access to what I am personally designating as the main common core subjects:

Against this must be set the actual patterns of girls' and boys' decisions. Their choices do not necessarily correlate with the difference in availability. What is significant, and disturbing, is how much wider the sex difference is in the final subjects taken, and the marked difference between the mixed and single sex schools.

Table 4(8) Percentages of pupils being offered access to subject

subjects	single-sex schools		mixed schools	
	boys	girls	boys	girls
Physics	85	62	91	75
Chemistry	81	75	79	78
Biology	79	96	91	96
French	75	92	87	90
German	33	44	21	18
Geography	91	72	61	61
History	92	69	57	61
Art	97	98	98	98
Music	55	94	75	81

Sources: DES *Education Survey 21*, Table 7: p. 13.

Table 4(9) Percentages of pupils actually taking a subject

subjects	single-sex schools		mixed schools	
	boys	girls	boys	girls
Physics	51	14	47	11
Chemistry	29	20	28	17
Biology	31	47	27	51
French	28	45	24	39
German	7	8	4	8
Geography	50	38	33	28
History	41	32	23	29
Art	35	38	37	36
Music	6	15	10	13

Sources: DES *Education Survey 21*, Table 7: p. 13.

This has extremely serious implications for the career choices of both sexes. Far fewer girls had the chance of even opting for physics and chemistry – essential for most technical and scientific further education and training. Biology, especially on its own, has a very limited value as a base qualification. On the other hand, boys have much less chance of studying languages than girls (surely equally serious now that we are in the EEC?).

In 1968, of the 30 per cent sample of secondary schools in my three survey areas, all but two of the mixed schools split boys and girls for up to a third of the curriculum for organizational reasons (Byrne 1974: Chapter 10 and Appendix C). In 1975, looking at rural schools, I found hidden splits – within rural science for example, girls were concentrating on pets and horticulture and boys on agricultural science. More revealing were the differences in expectation in the rural schools, where few girls below the top 15 per cent had horizons beyond the solicitor's secretary in the nearby market town, or a bank counter in the county town. Although many were highly intelligent and from middle-class homes, they mirrored what Sue Sharpe has since described in her Ealing girls who saw 'male' jobs as beyond them.

'I don't think I could face it as a girl, but a boy is less squeamish.' (vet)

'I think this job would be too complicated for a girl.' (computer science)   (Sharpe 1976:75)

But the rural leavers had had their career patterns set by the school's insistence on planning not only science but vocational subjects by sex. Economics was restricted to boys in three schools; typing to girls in all.

Ernest Bevin once spoke of the 'poverty of aspiration'. Nowhere is this more true than of girls' expectations in aiming at jobs or (rarely) careers after leaving school. Secondary school may well be guilty of pre-empting the future careers choice of girls by 'persuading' them by direct or indirect means to 'choose' subjects that are a less useful or relevant foundation for future adult (working) roles than those followed by boys. Equally repressive is the feminine stereotype of non-aggression, compliant behaviour, what Alice Rossi (1964) calls the 'lid phenomenon', causing ambitious girls to repress any strong desire to stretch their talents fully because of a 'ceiling' implicitly accepted. Fifteen-year-old Jackie from the North doubts her ability to argue with the head of science to do both physics and chemistry as she wished. 'I'd never have the nerve to argue – that's why I'm doing just chemistry.'

Not only, moreover, is the level of girls' achievements

different but its character is even more markedly different than the HMI access tables show. Concentrating on the central subjects only (others are taken in relatively small numbers although they may be even more sharply sex typed) by no means all boys and girls capable of maths and English at GCE or CSE level actually achieve and pass these. Boys outnumber girls in maths, while the reverse is still (though less) true for English. The published statistics are unadjusted for school leavers and include further education candidates and adults. It is therefore impossible to work out a proportion of the age group by sex but even if all of the candidates in the sciences, languages, and humanities were school leavers, we are still not actually achieving the balance of the old matriculation or the balance on which employers and colleges insist. It is incredible in a sophisticated western democracy that the mother tongue and basic numbers are not *compulsorily* examinable up to the school leaving age for all pupils capable of entering for what is now a graded examination. It is the more so, when the major acknowledged sex difference is identified as numbers versus language.

The northern fifth formers (also in a single-sex school) were asked what subjects they were taking in both GCE and CSE and the computer analysis split these to show arts, science, and number of subjects. Fifty per cent of the year group were from the former grammar school, 50 per cent from former secondary modern schools. *Table 4(10)* has, for me, some disturbing implications. About half of the girls entering took no sciences at all. Indeed, half of the year group did not enter for any external examination. Those more able girls who took five or more subjects were as heavily weighted on the arts side as my own unbalanced matriculation. (It has been a severe career disadvantage. Only by basic re-education in the rudiments of maths, science, and technical principles, have I survived in a world centred on building programmes, technology in education, and intermittent interdisciplinary work with technologists and technicians.) These northern fifth formers will not have a balanced basic core suitable for later retraining.

There is a wider, quasi-social, or developmental question on the single sex/mixed issue. R. R. Dale's work on single sex and co-educational schools is now widely known but is, in my view, over-estimated. On balance he declares for co-education, producing some evidence of girls' preferences for and adapta-

Table 4(10) 'What subjects are you taking at "O" level or CSE?'
(Fifth-form survey)

| number of subjects | percentage taking: | | | |
	science 'O' level	science CSE	arts 'O' level	arts CSE
none	52·7	43·7	20·0	57·3
one	21·8	28·2	2·7	15·5
two	15·5	22·7	6·4	11·8
three	10·0	5·5	8·2	8·2
four			13·6	4·5
five			17·3	2·7
six			24·5	
seven			6·4	
eight			0·9	

tion to men teachers (surely only an extension of the media's encouragement to them to hero-worship the male, from pop stars to the current boy friend) but warns against too facile an interpretation. His samples are naturally small; of them, moreover, over half thought it 'depends on the teacher' (Dale 1969). His conclusions, which are nevertheless well worth study, may however be put into question if his attitudes are as sex-linked as the following quotation implies. It is important in validating or otherwise the objectivity of his sight of girls' real as distinct from assumed attitudes.

> 'To do their best to ensure good administration of tests, the researcher and his assistant travelled to each school in 1964 and 1966 to administer the tests in person, *the researcher taking the boys and his assistant the girls.* This was designed to ensure standardisation of the testing of each sex, but unfortunately the woman assistant had to leave after a year and was succeeded by a man, *thus breaking the standardisation of the girls* ... it could possibly have made it somewhat harder for the single sex educated girls to admit to their troubles etc. when a man was present ...'
>
> (Dale 1969:12, my italics)

I find it inexplicable and very disturbing that an entire re-

139

search project should be based on the stereotype of girls reacting fully only to women, and boys to men. They may well do, as long as they are implicitly told that that is what is expected. It would have been more valuable deliberately to have crossed say half of the interviews to see if attitudes did change. My own view is that young people react to personality, clarity, enthusiasm, intelligence, relevance and not to sex of interviewer, in a structured research project.

Dale's findings predate most of the now more secure comprehensive reorganization and must be set in period. He does suggest that sociometrically there are more advantages than disadvantages to co-education. We need to see, however, I suggest, more research into the possible influence of the structure, organization, and ethics of secondary schools on girls' attitudes to different subject areas before we have ground for a decisive national policy. On balance it seems wiser to attack stereotyping within mixed schools, by in-service training courses, research, and control, than to restrict girls' curricular and social opportunities in 'half a school' simply because co-educational schools do not yet all have the mix right.

One must, moreover, be wary of arguing too much from the more favourable curricular and achievement statistics from the single sex sector. They are weighted by the 171 direct grant schools' results, and these are clearly favourably placed with a motivated and mainly middle-class recruitment. It is only to be expected that their girls would over-achieve by comparison with the partly 'first generation grammar' pupils in maintained schools or the more mixed social class intake of comprehensives. I stress again that we cannot find answers from single dimensional analyses. We are still defining these. Central government should authorize more research and comparative analysis within and between sectors – private and maintained, single sex and co-educational, selective and non-selective.

There is little question that schools push boys much harder than girls generally and offer more demanding work to the former. The Crowther Committee found far more premature specialization in boys' schools than girls and criticized the lack of practical aesthetic subjects for able pupils, and inadequate time for English; and the prevalence of general, less demanding courses in the sixth for girls, and their rarity for boys, required, in the Committee's view, justification. Hornsby-Smith and

Newberg in turn update the picture in their survey of 200 grant award holders.

'Differences in the wishes of male and female respondents add support to the interpretation given earlier that there are culturally defined rigidities in school subject choices. Thus one girl in five would like to have studied more physical science compared to one boy in 13, and one boy in three would like to have studied French or German longer compared to one girl in five ... A higher proportion of girls than boys wished they had studied the biological sciences longer, but whereas nearly all the girls had studied them for a time at school, at least half the boys had never done so.'

(Hornsby-Smith and Newberg 1972:56)

The girls in my own Northern fifth-form sample were asked whether they thought they had to specialize too early, and if so, what subjects they would have preferred to take. 75·7 per cent said no; but 24·3 per cent thought they had specialized too soon. The subject preferences are entirely predictable. Nine per cent more would have wished to do modern languages, 14 per cent sciences, a further 14 per cent biology specifically, and 27 per cent 'vocational subjects', which mostly meant typing. Eighteen per cent wanted to take domestic science but could not.

Asked why the 'missing' subjects were preferable, the answers (open ended) reflected the realism of at least half who saw education as relevant to work.

Table 4(11) 'Why are the subjects preferable?' (Fifth-form survey)

reasons given	percentage
useful for proposed job	55·0
useful in marriage or later in life	30·0
useful for travel	10·0
needed for further education	5·0

Reasons why choice is limited vary from esoteric ideologies about suitable options for girls to highly practical limitations of rooms, laboratories, and staff – although any true education-alist should be adamant that rationing should be on grounds of educational capacity and not inherited hormones. One obvious constraint (increasing with the teacher recession) is of specialist staff. A later chapter discusses teachers, but the specialist angle is perhaps most relevant here.

The staff for the job

One immediately practical limitation is that of the availability of staff to teach GCE 'O' and 'A' level. The actual availability of graduate specialist teachers in the secondary sector in no way matches the basic establishment of common curricular prin-ciples. I recognize that many will reject my continued use of subject names and argue that a curriculum described solely in this way cannot be regarded as suitable for, or relevant to, to-day's schools. I am not sure that we cannot retain them as *disciplines* rather than subjects. By all means label history 'social and economic studies' or various aspects of geography, 'environ-mental studies'. The batch of knowledge, experience, skills, and of dimensions (linguistic deduction and application, sense of chronology, scientific laws, political and social principles) never-theless falls clearly into one or other of the major subject dis-ciplines and it is evasive, not to say intellectually dishonest, not to admit this. Analysis of the GCE/CSE proportionate split of entries between traditional and 'new' areas of study shows indeed that whatever schools say, they do in fact vote with their feet towards identified subject areas. Moreover, the esoteric form of timetabling, of course structure, does not alter the fact that areas of study can only be effectively taught by a teacher who has herself (or himself) covered them in some depth. Anyone who questions that curricular responsibility for major curricular areas does not rest overwhelmingly with honours graduates is invited to take me to schools where Burnham has not been used to give Scale 4 almost exclusively to them. A language and literature based French and Latin degree may for example give the capacity to lecture on France, classical Rome, and European developments as well as on French language and literature.

Against this background, look at the actual availability of men and women graduate teachers in the secondary sector. It is widely alleged that we teach maths and English to all pupils. 'In the fourth and fifth years the fixed points in the curriculum in current practice are likely to be more than four: English, Mathematics, Religious Education and Physical Education' (DES 1977 : para 2.9). 'English and Mathematics are almost invariably part of the common core' (HM Inspectorate 1975 : 12).

But of graduate teachers of these subjects, the imbalance is both one of sex and of literacy versus numeracy.

Secondary only graduate teachers, 1975

	men	women	total
maths	6,728	2,727	9,005
English	7,212	7,725	14,937

If we need 14,000 specialists to cover English for all, we presumably need 14,000 maths specialists, and 50 per cent should be women. We do not have them.

Let us assume that the curriculum debate defines science as part of a future common core. In the sciences it is clear that to cover even *half of the same age range* as in maths and English we have a shortfall which is even more marked.

Graduate teachers, 1975

	men	women	total
physics	5,538	1,134	6,672
chemistry	5,211	1,441	6,652
biology	3,097	2,879	5,976
other science	4,392	1,145	5,537

Clearly the main shortfall is in women teachers – with whom girls still identify.

Even with the addition of non-graduate teachers, we clearly have to ration access to these subjects for reasons other than curricular.

The arts fare slightly better.

Graduate teachers, 1975

	men	women	total
history	8,437	4,938	13,375
geography	5,588	2,841	8,429
economics	3,322	791	4,113
French	5,065	5,474	10,539
other modern languages	4,275	3,206	7,481
music	772	565	1,337

The point I am making is that recruitment depends on the accident of what earlier students have previously studied at university, not on planning principles as against defined principles of curricular need. If we establish that, say, maths, English, history, geography, one language and one creative subject should be taught equally to say 50 per cent (or 75 per cent?) of the age range (not necessarily to GCE, but to examinable standards), we would need proportionately the same balance of staff as for maths and English, not twice as many French teachers as scientists, half as many chemists as historians. And we are not over-provided. Considerably fewer than 40 per cent of pupils achieve 'O' level or Grade I CSE French, a result which Europe and Scandinavia put to shame. Languages are an essential modern business tool as well as a social pleasure. To achieve a defined policy we need to define the resources we need, with a manpower/womanpower programme to attract special kinds of graduates for teaching. The much vaunted 'surplus' of teachers is singularly missing here.

To concentrate overmuch on graduate teachers would be unjustly to underestimate the contribution of the college-trained teachers, and the above should be read strictly against the point that I am making about adequate staffing – of both sexes – to offer a full curriculum of specialist subjects. I shall be touching on the question of part-time teachers in a later chapter. In the same way that the Emergency Training Scheme produced many outstanding teachers, the colleges of education have exported some outstanding educationalists. It must however be said that the way in which they have developed in isolation from polytechnics, tertiary colleges, industry and commerce, has left many college leavers with an imperfect grasp of the world about them.

From the sixth form to a residential college, often set in small market towns or rural areas, back to the secondary school, is not a recipe for shattering traditions and replacing them with dynamism. The added predominance of young women in the colleges may well have acted to create an artificially sheltered environment in which to prepare to deal with young people. Schools often reflect this sheltering from the noise, conflict, and ambivalence of the world outside.

Masculine schools, masculine thinking

Women are after all in a tiny minority in the government of education. The main thrust of planning is in the hands of men. As a result one sees a pervasive atmosphere of masculine terminology, assertions, labels, boy centred organizations. I do not believe this to be as trivial as may be thought. Constantly to refer to boys, he, men, male patterns of behaviour, will make girls feel they are being allowed into the 'male club' rather than entering an open mixed environment with a new ethos. Freud was right to link our unconscious involuntary modes of speech now popularly labelled 'Freudian Slips' to what we really think and want. Male pervasiveness impresses a male norm, boys as the pattern to be followed, the exclusive right to which girls are exceptionally added. It is the more effective because so totally unconscious.

The Crowther Report is a major example. Generally better than many in punctiliously writing of 'boys and girls' Crowther still regularly drops into male descriptions on all key issues – technical training, career advancement – 'he' throughout, 'the *boy* looks for a job'. The whole section on education for industry (paras 550–6) refers exclusively to boys and men.

After one sentence of lip service to girls' need of day release, a substantial section on craft and technicians speaks only of boys' needs and men at work.

More seriously the research which is a major influence on the report is almost exclusively male based. True, the Social Survey of school leavers includes 1,767 boys and 1,499 girls, but the remainder is based on a National Services sample of 8,850 Army and RAF boy recruits and 17,000 *male* technical college students. Whatever induced the Committee to exclude totally comparable samples of girls (first-year nurses, further education students, 6,000 secretaries)? Women who were girls or leavers in the late 1950s must look back on this male dominance in educational diagnosis as quite unacceptable. I believe it to show in the whole slant of the report and its endorsement of sextyped vocational education which belies its words elsewhere. After all, if the needs of boys and girls were in fact held to be the same, Crowther could not justify defining them differently throughout; and if they were different, research should have been based on an equal sample of girls.

Four years later, the Newsom Report (1963) produced models of school organization and bias courses for the less able which have been the most harmful influence against equal (because the same) educational opportunity since School Boards invented laundry classes. The main recommendations endorse the concept of 'relevance' for different adult roles; and the polarity between technical, industrial, career-slanted courses for boys and catering, nursing, commerce, and distribution courses for girls, with a domestically slanted core, received an official accolade.

One revealing and almost startlingly biased study, even in this context, is David Boyd's study of eight elite groups (1973) manifesting characteristics of high occupational position, high status, group consciousness and cohesion, exclusiveness, functional responsibility and power, which is wholly male centred. Halls' introduction talks of mass academic education 'throwing up new men' to exercise leadership roles, and the correlation between elite fathers and elite sons. No mothers and daughters? Or indeed fathers and daughters? Boyd studies the Civil Service, the Foreign Service, the Judiciary, the Armed Services, the Church of England, the banks. Unquestionably, these are male-dominated, if not sacred preserves. The study could, I suggest, have identified elite women with relative ease – but the message of women's achievements and courses is as under-exposed as woman's role in history (decidedly not her story) as at present taught. The Boyd approach is woven through the whole slant and curricular contents of most of the history, social studies, civics, humanities courses now on offer in schools.

The masculine phraseology and subconscious aura persists today. I am reminded of the national conference in 1975 at which I was, as usual, one of three women among 270 male colleagues. We were addressed throughout the day as 'gentle-

146

men' by the public school educated Chairman. We have never quite worked out whether despite our peacock apparel compared with the dark mufti of our male colleagues, he simply had not learned to tell the difference yet; or whether he was paying us the supreme compliment of having graduated finally to professional manhood. In an otherwise excellent collection of articles in the *Guardian* (June 29, 1976), head teachers writing an open letter to a parent about the needs of what is defined as a bright 'child', confirm the non-existence of girls in co-education. Goodall, head of an 1,800 *co-educational* comprehensive, writes of 'your son' and 'he' throughout his welcome to the school. Hattersley of Whitgift talks of wider opportunities for his 13–18 boys and girls but (six months after the *Sex Discrimination Act, 1975* made curricular discrimination unlawful) writes of 'boys' and girls' crafts' and ends by offering 'your son' a well-stocked library. I do not believe that men who talk only of boys think seriously of either girls or of young people as a whole. And I believe the subconscious message transmits itself daily to any girls and women staff who are in schools dominated by male-descriptive men.

For obvious reasons, there is more evidence on the examination achievements of girls than of the educational menu offered to the lower two quartiles of ability. Yet these are in the greatest need of a solid, work-oriented, serious education which will help them up the ladder from the unskilled labour market. In this group are also the missing women shop stewards, women trade unionists, women organizers of voluntary groups and services in inner cities and on housing estates. Yet the curricula I see in the schools I visit are still too often centred on a patronizingly trivial collection of domestic skills and consumer material based on their future homes, ambiguously labelled 'Design for Living' or 'Child and Home'. Or alternatively typing, which I would remove compulsorily from the secondary sector and replace with education for community participation at relevant levels. The place for typing and commercial skills is in further education. Recommendations for major reform are mainly deferred to the last chapter, but there are some immediate steps relevant to primary and secondary education which might be noted here, before we go on to look at careers education and the tertiary sector.

Remedial action

Diagnosis is an empty tool without remedy – and that means governmental action, redeployment of resources, and retraining. There is now more than adequate research into social class problems of under-achievement in education and that particular debate now hangs on political agreement on different forms of interventionist programmes (the EPA principle, only a token answer to quieten those faced with crisis conditions; the vicissitudes of urban programmes and inner cities versus rural poverty). The government's own HMI report acknowledges an educational problem in the sex inequality debate. We need now to write the cheque for our beliefs – a five-point programme for immediate action:

(a) National funding of research into the organization and teaching methods in the primary and secondary sectors with a view to eliminating sexism and the early production of national guidelines of good practice.
(b) Compulsory injection of material from known research and case studies into all initial and in-service education and training courses for teachers, to counteract sex-role stereotyping.
(c) A national annual programme of local and residential re-education programmes for teachers, starting with heads and deputy heads, from 1979–85. This should be organized at three levels, as part of the DES/Regional programmes; by university training institutions; and by local education authorities, on the lines of previous 'crash' programmes for multiracial education, for mixed ability teaching, and for school reorganization.
(d) Establishment of a National Board to monitor (not control) teaching materials for sex-role stereotyping or sexism, which would be independent of central and local government (but including assessors from each sector). Such a board should not have powers of direction, but should be given funds for publication of guidelines of good and bad practice, and an initial research budget to develop pilot non-sexist materials for experimental use.
(e) The recall of the Central Advisory Council for England and Wales (mandatory under Section 4 of the *Education Act*,

1944) – with extended terms of reference to include Scotland if need be) to look at the whole set of causal relationships in the education of girls and women across primary, second-ary, and tertiary education. The CAC has not met since 1967, and it is arguable that successive Secretaries of State are in default, since the CACs for England and Wales are em-powered to advise the Secretary of State 'on matters con-nected with educational theory and practice as they think fit', which they clearly cannot do if they are not recon-stituted. We have had major enquiries into every sector, at the end of which it is conceded that girls are still disadvan-taged. There can be no question but that 'Half Our Future' is still under-investigated : the female half.

Meanwhile, the re-education process must include girls them-selves, and career education can do much to counteract defici-encies in school attitudes.

FIVE

Education for a career – the right to choose

'If you want to slip into a round hole, you must make a ball of yourself – that's where it is.'

GEORGE ELIOT, *The Mill on the Floss*

'Happiness is the exercise of our vital functions in accordance with virtue.'

ARISTOTLE.

After 2,000 years, however, no one is yet agreed what are in fact the vital functions of men and women,* nor whether and why they are really so different? Into what kind of round holes do we need to curl ourselves? Certainly on a frosty January morning in 1950, a term after the September day which opened

* This chapter should be read against the earlier arguments of Chapter 2.

Chapter 4, I was left in no doubt by the teacher who had acquired 'careers' as some acquire the chess club or Saturday games (and as she worked her way through ninety vague but biddable fifth formers), an academic career was my lot. 'Languages', she said briskly (with my disastrous maths and no science, it seemed Hobson's choice, somehow). But no question of topping up at 'The Tech' like the boys from the secondary modern down the road; or of social and industrial economics at an emergent College of Advance Technology; nor even commercial management and on-the-job training. Clever girls went to (prestigious) universities to read for arts degrees; not so clever went to (safe) nursing or teacher training; the rest were offered the (respectable) outlets of bank, building society, commercial college (as far as statistics go, they still are). The odd deviant or two pounded a defiant and non-U way to (relatively) higher wages at the few factories in a low-wage rural county, to pay for what they saw as the security of an attractive future home with their city-school-educated boy friends. (In those days we actually got engaged before marriage and 'saved up'.) But none of us thought out the conflicts and interlocking needs and demands of marriage, work, home, non-marriage (by choice, not as an accident of fate), or *alternating* patterns of each lifestyle. The unwritten rules were really very clear. College or professional training away from the city–but not domesticity. A local marriage and a good steady job for the time being. Careers talks meant a local job, or which university, or do you *really* want to be a vet?

Nearly thirty years later the daughters and sons of my college friends now beat a regular path to us for advice on not only jobs but how to handle Mum, what to do about a flat, will they forfeit their grant if they marry before finishing college – and how to argue with the Council for a crèche at the polytechnic. Times and issues change – but young people do not, beneath the surface. For most young women today, despite the apparently sophisticated gloss of the post-Beatles era, the triple burden of domestic commitments, an eleven-month-old baby, and a half finished Diploma in speech therapy, laboratory technician's certificate, or ONC in business studies still leads to strain and tension and – 'shall I just give up and go back later?'. It is not Tim nor John who so worry; only Alison and Jackie.

But for the 80 per cent of girls who do not make further or

higher education at all at any very advanced level, the issues are even more basic. The less able they are, the more likely girls are to limit their horizons to *local* opportunities. They are less adventurous and less confident. Leaving at sixteen plus, they are too young to go away to a strange big city. They already have strong local ties and local boy friends. They accept the domestic demands of their own family and younger siblings more readily than their brothers or the able intellectual, who combines realism with a tiny touch of justified ruthlessness ('I've my own life to lead'). They seek the security and immediacy of local employment – and its limits, refusing to travel from Lincoln to Nottingham, Morpeth to Newcastle, Tiverton to Taunton, for the wider, more challenging training, employment, a career base. They seek the comfort and approbation of conformism – still.

To sit and talk with a group of today's fifteen-year-old girls, many ready to leave school, is moreover really to be part of a mixed community ranging from immature girls still with the attitudes of older children hidden in the outer poised shell of the modern adolescent, to the maturity of young women already planning a home; and every shade in between. The fifth-form room of a direct grant girls' grammar school has little that one would recognize in the atmosphere of the fifth-year common room of a ten-form entry inner city comprehensive school. The last year of a quiet rural secondary modern school may often have created a different cast of young people, with distinctively different ideas of society, from that of the multiracial, fast-moving, large London schools. We should not therefore talk of girl leavers as a group. But one trait seems still common to all but a very small minority. They seek 'a nice job for a girl' and one which they can tailor to fit child rearing and looking after Ted.

By the time that girls reach the hurdle of adolescence, after a Grand National obstacle race through the earlier stages of education (with a Beecher's Brook at every stage of educational 'choice') they have exchanged the clear irrefutability of natural child-centred logic for this subconscious growing inner conflict of their own social and emotional domestic roles, educational purposes, instant desires for work and pay, and dawning recognition of longer term needs. They do not know where they are going – and their post-school roads often seem as unrelated as between marriage, full-time study, and work, as the fast and straight M1 is from the equally straight but leisured, tree-lined, pheasant-paced 'Seven Mile Straight' from rural Horncastle to Boston. They neither interlock nor recognize each other; and are used by quite different clienteles.

What is a career?

Careers education from thirteen years onwards should teach girls (and boys) how to use any or all of the routes available to suit different destinations, which are in fact rarely mutually exclusive, which will lead to a career through life – paid or unpaid, permanent or intermittent. *Career* need not of course merely mean work. The Shorter Oxford Dictionary defines it variously as 'a racecourse (1751); a swift running course (1534); a person's course or progress through life (17th century); a profession affording opportunities for advancement (1803)'. The latter had been seen to be only narrowly relevant to an academically gifted minority, but should be extended to encourage all girls to seek advancement by planned steps, of which marriage is only either an intermission or an incidental. The first three seem to me to be better combined for the majority of girls leaving school expecting to pour energy and motivation concurrently into marriage, motherhood, study or work, and community involvement. For the purpose of this chapter, I am defining career in two ways – progression in *employment*; participation, achievement, and progression in *government*: what is clear is that education for a career implies an external world, not the internal limitations which Pascal Lainé and Belotti defined as perceived by women.

Education for work

Despite the enlightened work of some careers officers and teachers, careers education is today still clouded with a constricted mythology which places artificial ceilings on girls' expectations – especially holding back the average and the less able.

Inextricably entangled are the two myths that women do not work after marriage (used as justification for not training them or encouraging their advancement), and that there are some jobs women cannot (or should not) do, simply because they are women. For the benefit of any who need ammunition to use against chauvinistic head teachers, employers (or even careers staff) to dispel the myths, useful material will be found in another book in this series which deals thoroughly with the situation of women and work (Mackie and Pattullo 1977). Brief illustrations may however sharpen the argument meanwhile.

For the non-economic role of women has, in fact, always been a myth. Mrs Gaskell's *Mary Barton*, one of the great and underestimated novels of the nineteenth century, paints a picture of Manchester factory life, where most girls worked. Mary, set like her father against factory work, had but two alternatives – 'going out to service and the dressmaking business'[1]. In fact, the 1841 census records 84,064 women over twenty and 22,174 women under twenty employed as dressmakers – their working hours commonly from 4.0 am to 10.0 pm or the early hours (Neff 1966). By 1919, a government committee reporting on women in industry in the First World War (HM Government 1919) dispelled the remaining clouds of disbelief which persisted, against the brutal evidence of four war-torn years. Women worked. They did 'men's work'. They had stamina. Their productivity was good; their absences few. The War Cabinet, moreover, had said quite decisively that many women worked as the breadwinner or to make up a quite inadequate family income, because their menfolk were in low paid trades susceptible to unemployment. The 1911 census had recorded that 54 per cent of unmarried women worked, 10 per cent of married, 30 per cent of widows. By 1919, 77 per cent of unmarried women were employed. *But only 54 per cent of employed men were married.* The facts were then currently well known.

By 1914, there were already 6,000,000 women in employment, although one and a half million of these were in domestic service. In 1918 it had risen to seven and a quarter million. Ten per cent of workers in metal trades were women, and over half of the cycle and motor force on milling, drilling, handpress, assembling. By 1918 one third of the aircraft industry and 90 per cent of men's jobs in ammunition were covered by women; 60 per cent of shell makers. The myth of women's physical frailness was surely laid to rest in the chemical trades, where

'The greater part of the work is unskilled and consists in the handling of weighty materials. The women were mainly introduced as labourers and in packing, loading and unloading, trucking, wheeling or in general yard work.'

(HM Government 1919:86)

The War Cabinet report dealt a further blow to the 'men's work' syndrome. In acetylene welding 'women did interchangeable jobs with the men ... It was pretty generally accepted that the women's output is equal to the men's', and in the cycle and motor trades: 'There was no clear demarcation between men's work and women's work'. It was, let us be brutally honest, social or political reasons that built the distinction back – not Havelock Ellis's theories on women's inferiority or non-existent evidence of innate incapacities.

The Committee of the Cabinet was, unusually, of three men and two women – Mrs Sidney Webb and Dr Janet Campbell. *They recommended full equal pay for equal work* – fifty years before the 1970 *Equal Pay Act*, still not yet fully honoured by industry in 1978. Evidence to this Committee laid the cause of low pay squarely on 'artificial restrictions on training and employment and is easily remediable'. Attitudes that ring sadly true today emerge.

They rejected the concept of male and female rates of pay and gave no basis whatever for a policy of sacking women to make room for men. On the contrary, it laid the accountability for women's lower position as 'dictated by men's ideas as to what work it is decent and proper for women to do' and declared that 'the long continued exclusion of women from nearly all the better paid occupations has been largely the result of the assumption that these occupations were the sacred preserve of men'   (HM Government 1919:27,265).

Women's right to work

It is, therefore, the more startling and the more serious to see an otherwise admirable careers guide for women published in the same year, encapsulating in its preface all the assumptions that the war had disproved, appearing to endorse the dispensibility of women to second place when jobs are scarce. There is a recurrent danger of this today in both teacher employment and generally. I can see no justice, no equity, no economic or ethical validity in using women conveniently to clean up social and economic problems for a given period, expecting them to work flat out as a supplementary labour force in times of labour crisis (women teachers coping with the post-war birthrate bulge in overcrowded classes) and then telling them that, with thanks, it is no longer convenient to need them, and they are both uneconomic and redundant. What happened to the quality of self-fulfilment? The personal development? The individual right? Is it only valid for what is left over when the boys have grown and taken first choice? But one can sadly understand the attitude that is revealed in the following quotation – what seemed like a realistic recognition of the pressures, public opinion, and conflicts of that time. How insidiously it is echoed today under the guise of 'redeployment' politics which attempt to dismiss married women and part time workers first. It is disturbingly topical, fifty years later.

'The artificial standards necessary during a crisis should be realised as emergency measures, useful as experiences no doubt, but impossible of continuance ... with regard to the employment of educated women, readjustment cannot be very rapid, for two reasons. Firstly because war work has rightly ceased ... Secondly because disabled men must be given the first choice in every occupation while women for the moment stand aside. It is no use insisting that her work has been exceptionally and even surprisingly well done ... but there is an insistent demand for the well prepared and well trained woman; even now in some directions it is difficult to meet this demand. Short training has proved a delusion.'
(Central Bureau for the Employment of Women 1919:2)

It seems to me to strike an especial irony that women should be being advised – and by a woman – to give up their right to economic independence, a social and companiable life outside the home and all that these bring, just when government had finally agreed to enfranchise women by giving them the vote.

Priority for men and the dispensability of women was indeed not universally approved. Mary Allen, writing of the pioneer policewomen during the 1914–18 war, makes it clear that, 'not only was it *not* presumed that their organisation would be terminated with the war, but their every activity was under-taken in order to demonstrate, in the first place, that a force of trained police women was needed, and in the second place, that they were perfectly fitted for their office' (Allen 1925:12).

The War Cabinet report is confirmed in Arthur Marwick's attractive account (1977) but sadder is the regular recession to matriarchal non-working stereotype after each war and in each economic depression. We slip back down Sisyphus' hill struggling with twin boulders of male prejudice and female resignation or apathy. In 1919 a careers guide talks of *forestry* as a successful women's profession, women carrying out hard manual labour and obtaining government acclaim (Central Bureau for the Employment of Women 1919:209). By 1932 the Forestry Commission was refusing to take women at all (Biscoe 1932:20). In 1977, women are almost non-existent in forestry although timber remains a key industry in housing, building, and domestic economy. *Agriculture* is similarly regressive. Van Gogh's peasant women could outlast any modern male labourer. Nor is physical strength at the same premium with increased mechanization. Food is a growth industry. We have, yet, fewer girls in agriculture proportionately than seventy years ago. Women maintained the land in two world wars. In 1932 the demand increased. 'A definite demand exists for stock women on dairy farms' (Biscoe 1932:20). Today, of the 10,884 students on day release in forestry and agriculture, only 895 (8 per cent) are women. Competition from other employment? Prejudice in training and recruitment? Reassertion of priority for men in unemployment? Or the adverse conditioning of rural secondary schools who teach boys about farms and tractors and girls to care for hamsters, hens, and husbands in rural and domestic science?

The most ineradicable piece of sex typing remains the inexor-able path to a clerk's desk, a typist's chair, to a secretary's office, its roots deep in the past also. It has in my view been the princi-pal cause of poverty of aspiration we can identify. When in doubt, type, seems a motto of teachers and girls alike. Of course we need secretaries. But why must we limit them to girls? What traumatic adjustment would a 16 year old boy have to undergo if he learned a supportive role in life – the enabler and not the doer. Why should we pay the dole to unemployed boys who cannot get skilled engineering jobs and whose English and intellect are quite suitable for retraining as shorthand typists, of which we appear to need an inexhaustible supply – the vested interest, of course. The origin of this unbreakable association of typing with girls goes back as usual to the origins of the craft. The 1919 guide sets an all too familiar scene, a cry which has been echoed constantly since then.

> 'But women have unfortunately made their own a special department which has almost universally become a blind alley – typing and shorthand ... the youngest male clerk can become a departmental manager, perhaps a managing director; the girl remains a shorthand typist all her life. While girls have largely "drifted" into this undesirable position, there are other circumstances responsible for their failure to obtain promotion. It is generally assumed by business men that women have neither the taste nor the aptitude for the management of affairs.'
> (Central Bureau for the Employment of Women 1919:175)

The editor was of course writing fifty years ago at a time when girls of university ability were settling for this, *faute de mieux*, not perhaps quite unreasonably, as a better prospect than unemployment or total frustration. Unfortunately they laid the seeds for what follows below; and the costs of their own underachievement. Once behind a typist's desk their chance of later retraining was minimal; it still is.

With what, for example, can one counter the male arrogance, patronage, and complacency of the following – written as recently as 1964?

> 'But it would be a disastrous thing for the economy of this country if there wasn't a steady flow of girls into office work ... general office work of this kind suits many girls. It is true that it doesn't make heavy demands on the intelligence and it is not likely to lead to anything much higher. But then you may not be looking for a more responsible job. It's not a crime not to be ambitious.' (Brown 1964:104)

Unless one is a boy?

It is matched by the less conscious incipient arrogance of the

158

fourteen-year-old boy who writes that 'English is also useful for a secretary in correcting her boss's phraseology' (quoted in Ollerenshaw 1961 : 23), surely the quintessence of my argument that teachers and parents are accountable for allowing both boys and girls to grow up in the expectation that society will provide boys and men with the professional equivalent of a harem of support services in every conceivable range to enable men to do what the rest of us have to do on our own – combine domestic, administrative, professional, and social roles. This is the very worst kind of careers 'advice' – deliberate encouragement not to be adventurous; a sort of reverse womanpower planning to a pre-set role.

I know that many heads and careers teachers have been puzzled by my particular longstanding criticism levelled at the overfacile route from the classroom to the typewriter and secretary's desk which they encourage girls inexorably to follow. Let me spell out why. Secretarial training is skills-based, with no transfer value. There is no ladder with rungs labelled junior management, senior management, executive, above the solid base of shorthand and typing. The qualifications for secretarial work give no exemption for other courses of training and any girl who wants to move across to executive or administrative work would have completely to retrain when competing with graduate and 'A' level entrants or with holders of ONC/D or HNC/D in business studies. Yet many able girls capable of advanced work are persuaded to the 'safety' of 'you can always fall back on typing'. To some extent this would be valid if typing were *additional* to educational qualifications and vocational training, for both sexes, and were used as an added field skill for all. But although secretarial work is relatively highly paid for a college leaver, it reaches a quick ceiling, and stays there. Thus secretaries will remain on, say, Scale 3 on job evaluation while administrative and executive or commercial staff may rise to Scale 10 or more. Women secretaries therefore stay on a low pay ceiling for up to thirty years with no *transferable* training to move sideways as a preliminary to other promotion routes, while boyfriends and husbands move up a long ladder. It is good news, therefore, that the new Business Education Council[2] is proposing to include secretarial modules in its Certificate and Diploma courses whose additional breadth will give students who qualify a base for wider career choice or retraining later. The next step is to persuade more girls to study for further education Business Educational Council courses and fewer for terminal skills alone.

Equal means the same

If, as the provisions of the UK *Sex Discrimination Act, 1975* declare, equal means the same in employment, advertising and careers guidance, and training for employment, it is inconceivable that there should be any doubt that equal must mean the same in all educative processes that prepare for adult life including work. But it is one thing to persuade employers (with difficulty) that 'women's work' is a thing of the past. It is another to persuade the girls. The Northern fifth-form girls were asked about a wide range of issues affecting careers and work and particularly on whether boys' and girls' careers should or could be identical. A central theme running through the questionnaire was their attitudes to 'men's work' and 'women's work', and their own career aspirations. The following quotation is characteristic of over half the responses.

'It has been proved that men are more suited for doing jobs that need physical strength and on the other hand women do jobs in which more emotion and intelligence is needed. However, I think education should be the same in both cases to provide for the extreme of job choice.'

Fifteen-year-old Gillian encapsulates here the main characteristics of her conditioning to accept masculine and feminine stereotypes. Men (by implication all men) are strong but unemotional. Women are weaker, emotional, caring (and interestingly, for Gillian, more intelligent). She implicitly has accepted, also, what I called earlier the rubric of exceptions – the untypicality of opting for the reverse role with a minority choice of career. The implication is that to do so is unmasculine or unfeminine. The girls were asked in the questionnaire whether they would be prepared to take a job in an industry where all, or almost all, the other workers were men; and if so, what difficulties they thought they would meet – if any ? A majority (67·3 per cent) said yes, they would tackle 'men's' work; 32·9 per cent said no. Of the difficulties listed (an open-ended question), discrimination accounted for 53 per cent, distraction or unfair practices 15 per cent, resentment or hostility, 6 per cent, lower pay only 4 per cent. Less than 4 per cent expected to meet any physical difficulties. The most frequent references are 'constant references to my sex'. 'Will say I can't hold the job down,' 'Men think they are superior.' 'Prejudice, especially if the job carries authority.' 'They look down on us.' It does not speak well for the primary and secondary education of past generations of boys exported from our schools that this should be men's image today.

In the context of open-ended training and recruitment to work, a majority of the girls agreed that equality of training was the key to identical careers, and very few supported the industrial view that discrimination in day release is justified because girls get married and are 'lost' to employment (even if the latter were causally true).

	agree %	don't know %	disagree %
Women can do everything that men can do if they are trained the same.	63·3	16·5	20·2
It is not worth educating girls after 16–18 because they get married.	12·0	3·7	84·3

Some, however, took a traditional view. Tracy appeared to be in no doubt that there were vocational subjects as such – her vocation however being a family and part-time work at thirty plus. She was going to use her five 'O' levels and three CSEs (assuming success) by typing at the BBC, and had no greater ambition.

'If girls will have different careers from boys there is no point in girls learning woodwork and engineering, also boys learning domestic science, therefore girls should have different education from boys.'

Diane, by contrast, thought the reverse. Her six 'O' levels and three CSEs were to be applied to nursery nursing and she hoped to be back working full time at thirty plus, after concentrating

on a family at twenty-five. She had grasped the causal relationship between educational options and choice of career – even
if her own choice was traditional.

'Because if a girl is to have the same kind of job as boys she
needs the same education as him, and also homemaking may
prove very useful to boys.'

The girls' assumptions on sex typing in employment were
mostly traditional, and indirectly betrayed the classic assumptions about jobs they saw as needing toughness and strength
(many of which, in fact, do not), and their exclusiveness therefore to men; about women being better at personal services,
counselling, caring; and about the 'suitability' of sex-typed
careers.

'Some jobs suit girls more than boys, e.g. air hostesses and
others, e.g. engineering suits boys more as it is tough.'

I was delighted to be able to show them the Foundry Industry's Training Committee leaflet addressed to 'A'-level school
leavers, showing a photograph of a girl with a degree in production engineering impressively analysing a foundry problem
as a male worker looks on. How many careers teachers actually
look for material showing girls doing non-traditional work (and
the reverse)?

On balance the fifth-form girls still felt that some careers
were more suitable for one sex than another, although the
majority wanted to see completely open opportunity. Carol,
studying for eight 'O' levels but determined to be a typist,
equates men's work with a strong forceful nature. Her idea
of men does not apparently include a male temperament which
could be suitable for 'feminine' jobs.

'I think girls should have feminine jobs if they are that type
of girl. A strong forceful girl can do the same jobs as men.
It all depends on the type of job. Girls should be able to have
the same education as boys as they can do the same job.'

Ailsa, aiming at university and either social work or careers
education, summarizes what the 1975 *Sex Discrimination Act*
(Section 7e) calls a 'genuine occupational qualification' (still
very ill-defined legally).

'Girls and boys should study the same range of subjects and same qualifications, but careers like nursing and working with people's bodies or personal problems should be left to a member of their own sex. Jobs depending on physical stamina should go to the man.'

Here is a need for some in-depth discussion with boys and girls. For we have a good deal of evidence in fact from both wars that, while men are capable of greater feats of strength, women's endurance and *stamina* are on balance greater. Nurses at the moment look after both sexes; and do we seek advice on personal problems only from our own sex? Take pregnant schoolgirls or students. If they want one kind of advice, a nurse or social worker of their own sex may be right. But if they want help to continue their course, sort out Mum and Dad, find a home, keep their student grant, they may rather come to a decisive and competent colleague or teacher. It is indeed in the context of careers education and counselling, a singularly old fashioned and naïve assumption that simply because the young people being advised on future careers happen also to be adolescents going through changes of puberty, and of psychological development into men and women, boys are likely to relate better to a man and girls to a women. I do not believe that many teachers, counsellors, or careers officers could or would wish to limit their role to their own sex. This must be demonstrably unfounded on any realistic evidence, as anyone who has dealt with this age group will know. Young people will identify with anyone who meets their need. A fourteen-year-old girl might need a mother figure who may or may not be the careers teacher or the senior mistress; or she may conversely need a father figure who is as likely to be the bearded art master as the deputy head; and she may need both successively in different weeks. If she is in some kind of trouble she will seek guidance from the most likely person to understand her background, her difficulties, her accent, her shyness, or brashness, and her need for help. She may look for decisive guidance, or for a sensitive listener. I can see no justification for assuming that any of these qualities is immutably locked up exclusively in one sex or another.

The message that comes through strongly from the Survey analyses is that the girls all accepted work as a normal pattern

– but 'feminine work' for the most part. Most chose traditional jobs – a few only, unusual careers. All seemed to stumble through considerable ambivalence between what they wanted – and what they thought Jim and their in-laws and their bosses 'would stand'. One must recognize that tradition dies harder in Jarrow and on Tyneside, in Yorkshire, or rural East Anglia, in Dorset, than in avant-garde London, multi-industrial Birmingham, affluent Surrey or Middlesex. Regional inequalities of opportunity and achievements spring from past conditioned underexpectation influenced by the patterns of local opportunities.

The dual role – for both sexes

Picking up the argument of the earlier masculinity and femininity debate, a central change needed in the careers education of 13–16 year olds *of both sexes* is education for the dual role of work (or unpaid career) and homemaker; either concurrently or intermittently. This may become increasingly commonplace, as careers programmes develop, young people assert new choices, and society's practices and support services adjust to new demands. One hopes, however, that the implicit assumption in this extract for an older but feminist careers guide, that *only* girls will take domestic responsibility, has changed as much as the updated 1978 version of the guide.

'Career planning poses an additional problem for girls. The career has to be satisfying and it will have to fit with domestic responsibilities after marriage ... You will probably be thinking of returning to work when you are in your thirties ... Two stage careers will soon be taken for granted generally. The majority of girls will train and work for a few years before having a family, then temporarily devote all their time to the family before starting the second, *and probably longer*, share of their working lives ... So even if you are getting married soon, it is well worth while to train to the limit of your capability. The higher your qualifications, the wider the choice of training and job opportunities at the second stage of your working life.'   (Miller 1973:16)

Not all girls (or boys) are of course temperamentally equipped to take on a full dual role. The final years at school are a time for appraisal, to think out new approaches to marital partnership, and to early and later needs for qualifications and training. Three routes should be offered to all young people – of both sexes. Either should expect to be able to, or to need to, work full time or part time; and either may be permanently or intermittently the principal wage earner. Either should have the choice of homemaker, domestic and main parent caring for children and home-based family support. And either should have the right to train and study for work or to retrain later for a second or new career.

The relevance of my earlier attack on the 'dependence' syndrome becomes apparent. Education for a career, and the automatic, sole, female responsibility for the full domestic burden (employed or not) are mutually exclusive. I do not just mean the literal domestic burden or the relatively trivial male contribution that carries an aura of progressiveness ('But I do wash up the dishes', say my male colleagues defensively), but the more complex question of the time and freedom of mothers and wives to study, read agendas for serving Committees, keep up with activity and knowledge outside the home without constant implicit guilt at 'neglecting' the family. Take a young male manager heading for early promotion. 'Daddy's working' is acceptable, as he comes in, eats his meal, and settles down with his costing sheets to impress the regional manager arriving tomorrow at the works. He is not available to his three children bubbling with what happened at school, anxious to unburden about some immediate fight with a school friend, needing to argue to go to a party, worried about bullying at school, needing a clean dress or a pressed suit urgently for an unexpected school function. If mother then settles down also with her homework for a shop steward's induction course in the factory, a report about a new deal on the shop floor, with the latest educational research project, with a batch of newsletters from the Women's Institute Advisory Council, with a District or Area Health Authority agenda, and refuses to listen to the children (or to her husband's work problems which he wants to unburden), she is guilty of neglect in their eyes – but he is not. Does not the reverse apply? And should we not bring children up to regard both parents as having rights as well – the right to be listened to, the right to their own support from the other members of the family?

A PEP survey on women and top jobs highlighted some of the problems, and especially the increased tension between home demands and career fulfilment. The more the job satisfaction and the higher the salary, the more the demands on personal time and the more a woman has to lose in giving it up. The authors found a correlation between top jobs and 'particularly conscious and conscientious mothers', but also that the dual career family calls for a higher degree of understanding by both of how the other thinks – and why. Important in this discussion (and against the paternal deprivation on which I touched in Chapter 2) is the better balance women tend to strike than men.

'Characteristic differences between career aims and patterns of men and women from P.E.P. reports, is that women are more likely than men to keep a balance between different aims: to insist on doing a worthwhile job well, but to refuse to let their job commitments take automatic priority over commitments in other directions, especially to their families.'
(Fogarty, Rapoport and Rapoport 1972:42)

The length of the domestic gap is also diminishing steadily. In its evidence to the Expenditure Committee of the House of Commons in 1973, the TUC speaks of the domestic gap as ten years, which, with a five year earlier retirement, reduces women's working life to thirty-five from a man's fifty (if he leaves school at sixteen), although the TUC stress that government and the education service should plan for the thirty-five years notwithstanding. Later experience, however, suggests that if women do return to work, it is now much nearer five years than ten after marriage. Many never give up at all except for very brief spells for childbearing. I am not here concerned with the rightness or otherwise of this, but its reality as a fact. The *Employment Protection Act, 1975*, giving increased maternity rights for re-employment, is likely to accelerate this trend. The number of women *over thirty* who were employed increased from 638,000 in 1960 to 896,000 in 1970, and the Government estimated in 1973 that by 1986 there will be ten million working women and about sixteen and a half million working men (HM Government 1973:20–1).

Training, study, and experience are integrally related to career advancement. In order to be promoted, one needs to acquire either increased technical excellence, or a capacity for policy making, greater breadth and wisdom, understanding how to work with others to achieve synoptic and not over-specialized objectives. Technical excellence comes from increased study, whether formalized or on the job. Women who work and also run a home have much less opportunity than men to carve out 'protected' times in evenings and weekends for private study or for evening classes. The importance of in-service training courses, refresher courses, learning new techniques and fields of knowledge is particularly influential in industrial and managerial work. 'In an era of meritocracy, the channel to the top lies, on the whole, through the obstacle course of functional specialisms' (Rapoport 1974:58). The kind of ethos surrounding girls' education has not traditionally encouraged them to set sights on a series of recurrent training experiences and specialisms, but on a once-for-all skill. Young women who are mentally alert and looking for increased specialism experience are in a relatively smaller minority than their brothers.

I mentioned earlier that at least part of any family problem over children's development or maladjustment, discipline, home environment, was as much due to *paternal* irresponsibility or lack of daily involvement at home, as from maternal absence during the schoolday at paid employment. A number of surveys of men's career development, including Rapoport's, make passing and implicit but regular mention of the double career benefit which ambitious men have, of being able to decrease their time with the family, and increase support from their wives for study or even work leading to promotion – neither of which a woman will be able to have, whether professional or in the middle range of industry or factory work, unless she has trained an unusually progressive husband to help her to bring up unusually adaptable children. Typical perhaps is a thirty-four-year-old quoted by Rapoport who moved from section head to Deputy Director via Henley Staff College – married with one child and a graduate wife working part time. 'The amount of time spent on work has increased, and correspondingly the amount of time spent with his family has decreased.' Is it unfair to ask whether his wife has the same free option? Similarly, a man who moved from assistant to Deputy Director and from £3,000 pa to the £5,000 bracket, via Henley, is described as a 'family man with two children, and his wife is a full time home maker' (Rapoport 1974:180–3). Not for him, my weekly choices of *either* three technical reports on Sunday, *or* mowing two lawns; the July sales on Saturday *or* a dinner party for important colleagues; but no way all four. Had I 'a wife' all would be done by a fresh and relaxed Monday morning. We would do well to educate all girls at school also to anticipate not only the dual married home/work role, but the dual 'single' home/work role – which, if we include all reasons for a single state in 'real terms', is almost a fifth of all women – it will happen to one in five of all schoolgirls in today's classrooms[3]. Not unlinked with this is the desirability of discouraging boys from regarding it as a slur on their masculinity even to suggest that they will have working wives later – and that they are not failures if she ends up earning more than they because of the accident of the job market. Finally, mobility (which means car ownership) and money are vital to success in dual-role survival. The latter means aiming for maximum salary in order to pay for efficient home help and corner-cutting labour-savers. The former is grossly underestimated as a factor for access to scarce opportunities for training or re-education, as well as for domestic survival.

In 1975 I asked a group of rural, adult-education women students, all over thirty, how they managed to get to the GCE 'O'-level foundation course which they were following to top up their inadequate basic secondary education as the first step to a second career. I put their freedom of access both domestic-ally and literally to them. (Rural transport is closing down so fast that to get from village to centre is almost impossible in the evenings.) All seventeen of the women had had to struggle against criticism and guilt because they had left the family to 'fend for themselves' on Thursdays – which really meant mother cooking twice as much the previous day – and had had to negotiate delicately to be brought to, and be collected from, class. Most working-class wives cannot drive the family car even if the husband will release it. They are discouraged by their menfolk who rarely will take time and trouble to teach them, and few will have the now considerable financial sum needed for professional driving lessons. Without a car, a woman is im-mobile compared with men. 'I'm not being driven by a woman, so think on', one Yorkshire farmer told his wife and seventeen-year-old daughter when they moved from the city to an outlying small town – for *his* job. Both had to give up their further education evening classes because he had the car every night and there were no buses after mid-evening. These attitudes begin in school and are tacitly accepted by girls as readily as by boys.

I was not conscious of how great a debt I owed to the enlightened male colleague who made me persevere with learning to drive (in his car) in a maze of inner London traffic, on the grounds that one day my job itself would depend on my being car-mobile, until I left London for the Yorkshire moors. Every girl's careers education ought to include car maintenance and encouragement to learn to drive as young as possible – immeasurably more useful than cooking, which is easily self taught when motivated.

Unpaid careers – educating women for government

The dual role is not only relevant to home and work but to women's current minimal participation in decision-making in government careers, from district councils to Parliament, from trade union to public authorities, from advisory committees to Royal Commissions. The same factors make it difficult for women to take on public office – girls' under expectation on leaving school and their lack of training for leadership; married women's lack of adequate salary, car, and freedom; and in addition, the apparent total unwillingness of the male leadership actively to encourage the greater participation of women by nominating them to office. The extra-mural departments of universities and the adult education service might consider special promotional programmes to attract and train women for community and political work to increase the potential pool – while schools must educate more girls to automatic expectation of future leadership roles.

'These things shall be! A loftier race
Than e'er the world hath known, shall rise
With flame of freedom in their souls
And light of knowledge in their eyes.'

Symonds (1840–93)

It is, I imagine, the dream of every true feminist, and the declared policy of most governments that the 'loftier race' shall be seen to include more women active in its visionary leadership as well as cooking at its hearthstones.

The art of government is not solely locked up in male minds; and is needed at all levels of professional, industrial, political, and community life. To lose half of the wisdom and experience of our country as a silent, unheard voice, is to take into the next century, unchanged, the maxim *An nescis, mi fili, quantilla prudentia regitur orbis*[4]. Nor must the next generation leave their fight to the tiny handful of their sex. The words of Symonds' song, soaring in the clarity of 550 girls' voices, echoed in my mind in 1973 as I sat on the platform of my old school's Hall, as one of England's only three women Deputy Chief Education Officers. But I searched in vain among the distinguished prize-day visitors for another woman – the leadership of education was unquestionably as male as when I left the county for college twenty years earlier. Two years later, in 1975, after local government reorganization, even the few existing top women had almost vanished. The myth that women have made it in the public sector has been bitterly dispelled. As with schools and colleges, reorganization has served to move women from first and second levels to third and fourth tier. It is not enough to deplore; we need to use analysis, research, investigation to find out why. The argument here is however mainly concerned with political, governmental, and voluntary work in the sense of unpaid careers, rather than with women officers in local government. One principle characteristic of British democracy is indeed its reliance on unpaid voluntary but high-powered government through local and regional councils, area boards for health, water, etc., national and regional specialist advisory committees, and voluntary associations and organizations who bridge large crucial gaps in the public service network.

Government is not only equated with Whitehall, Westminster, Edinburgh, or Cardiff. It is everywhere that a community and an organized body of decision makers needs to exist. There has been depressingly slow progress in the nearly seventy years since Brownlow pleaded for more practical women in public service, as long ago as 1911. 'Every woman interested in social improvement can do her share towards convincing the apathetic public that efficiency and economy are secured by electing a fair proportion of women to serve on public bodies' (Brownlow 1911:141). He pleaded for more women on housing committees, asylum committees, hospital and public health boards, for women sanitary inspectors (Southwark's rates *dropped* in the first decade of this century after its efficient women inspectors reorganized both the system and the landlords), more women designers of housing, more women on water authorities. Even the new Midwives Committees (*Midwives Act*, 1902) *were all male*. Brownlow argues indignantly for women committee members. Yet the School Boards had already boasted distinguished women and, by 1895, 900 women were serving as Poor Law Guardians. So why not in local government, on, for example housing committees because 'houses are usually most unsuitably planned and arranged for family requirements' (Brownlow 1911:34).

Today, however, just as we lose ground on regression of opportunity for careers for employment, we lose momentum on women in leadership. There are today still only twenty-seven women MPs (4 per cent), thirty-six life peeresses (18 per cent), four women government ministers. Only 20 per cent of local councillors are women, and only two members of the General Council of the TUC. Scandalously, the Electricity Council and British Gas Corporation and Post Office Governing Council boast no women members (where is woman, the consumer?) (UNESCO 1976).

We have made relatively little progress in the top echelons of public service, where reorganization of local councils has only served to reassert the pattern of male leadership which had been partly eroded over the years. It was for example particularly fitting that International Women's Year should see a woman Lord Mayor (Dame Katherine Ollerenshaw) in Manchester, home of the Pankhursts; but the overall number of women councillors remains only 20 per cent of the total. Even on the education committees – the most likely appointment for women by the men who still govern the political parties – women number considerably fewer than half. Over a full twenty years from 1945–65, two county boroughs averaged 25 per cent and 15 per cent women members only (including co-options); although the rural county threw up 43 per cent (Byrne 1974:64). (Had their Labour party a more positive attitude to using women? Or were there simply more housewives with cars in the county who had time and access?) Today, there are a handful

171

of outstanding women in the leadership of the Association of County Councils and the Association of Metropolitan Authorities (who represent the local education authorities at national level) but they are in a small untypical minority.

The sharpest example is the low participation of women in the major committees that have restructured education in post-war years. The Beloe, Crowther, and Newsom Committees numbered 25 per cent, 20 per cent, and 31 per cent female membership only. The Robbins Committee's female membership was a mere 17 per cent. Plowden (on primary education) broke all records with 50 per cent membership from women[5] but the Bullock Report on Reading and Language had only a third women members, despite the domination of women teachers in the primary sector and in remedial education.

The original Technician Education Council was without a female voice; it now has three, while four of the Business Education Council's twenty-four members are women. But more startlingly, of 103 members of the Universities Central Council on Admissions, in January 1976, UCCA could only produce eight women. I simply do not believe that despite the predominance of professors on UCCA (hence few women), there are only eight women in the entire university sector qualified and willing to tackle this important task. (I am bound in fairness to say that since, of the total candidates who applied, 64·4 per cent were men and 35·6 per cent women, and of those accepted, 63·6 per cent were men and 36·4 per cent women, it has not apparently overtly disadvantaged girls (UCCA Thirteen Report, 1974–5).

Moves like Eleanor McDonald's collated *Who's Who of Women in Management* will become increasingly influential in identifying suitable women for nomination to major Committees and Commissions. The parallel need is for more government ministers to declare a positive policy of appointing women to bodies and committees under their patronage. This is especially vital in the education service.

In those fields in which women have arrived at an active role, there is strong evidence of negative, discriminatory attitudes by government and appointing bodies, not least in the education and training fields. Nor is it wholly true that qualified women are not available to fill the places although government may need to look for deputies and not chiefs, heads of departments and not principals, in seeking women nominations, in the first instance.

While decision-making takes place in an increasingly complex variety of levels and places, Parliament is the obvious key level of influence. Our proportion of women MPs has declined (and by no means all of those who *have* arrived, understand or care about women's deprivation). Interestingly, in Sweden also, although women make up 51 per cent of the electorate, they still account only for 21 per cent of the Riksdag, 19 per cent of County Councillors, and 19 per cent of municipal Councillors. Even in egalitarian Russia the political scene is male-dominated, although there were in 1973, twenty-five women Ministers in the republican Councils. Uzbekistan had a woman president, five autonomous republics a woman head. The 1976 Supreme Soviet elections achieved 31 per cent women; the constituent Soviets, 34 per cent. But these figures are well below the Russian women's contribution to the economic and productive life of the USSR as a whole. George St.Georges asked the secretary of the Moscow Women's Soviet Committee whether this was discrimination? Elena Shibarina thought rather that it was (the familiar tale) that women were still expected to care for household and children as well as employment : hence men had more free time for politics. A large number of women actually invited to stand for the 1970 elections could not do so because of family obligations.

I believe, to my concern, the under-representation of women to be partly also due to an ever increasingly conscious choice on their part to remain at third tier level and to eschew the extra responsibility of the Chief, Head, or Deputy posts. They also, in my experience, fail to take adequate part in the affairs of their professional bodies – in teacher unions, in the Society of Education Officers, and in the local authority associations. It takes both commitment and stamina to add to the already double role of work and homemaking, regular four hour drives across the Midlands to regional meetings, or commuting to London for national meetings. Because however they are absent from the public scene, they are therefore not known or identifiable.

Not all readers, especially outside the UK, will perhaps be familiar with the structure of the careers service, and a brief word of explanation may be helpful.

Following on from the *1944 Education Act*, a further Act of Parliament in 1947 established the power (but not the duty) of Local Education Authorities to run their own Youth Employment Services, which after the raising of the school leaving age in 1947 had increasingly developed their work as not simply finding employment, but advising on the education and training needed for it. Over two succeeding post-war decades the profession of guidance to young people acquired its own ethos and is now substantially represented by members of the Institute of Careers Officers employed by local education authorities and of the Association of Teachers of Careers Education and Guidance who work directly in schools.

In 1973 a new and comprehensive *Employment and Training Act*, established the Manpower Services Commission and the Employment Services and Training Services Agencies. Local Education Authorities not only *must* now provide for a careers service for young school leavers, but *may* help all over school leaving age who need careers guidance, and who are attending educational institutions in Great Britain other than universities, either full time or part time during the day. The powers under Sections 8–10 of the 1973 Act are quite wide. The Careers Officers employed by Education Authorities (but professionally guided by the Department of Employment) are not only expected to advise on the employment that would be suitable and available for school and college leavers of all ages, but to advise and determine what training they need and must be provided with, in order to fit them for their chosen employment.

In the light of the curricular problems touched on in Chapter 4 and the preceding argument here, clearly our main tool of remedial intervention is the careers service. But Careers Officers still tend to be called in only during the last year of a pupil's expected life at the school, clearly too late, since by then the curricular options between the sciences and the arts, the kind of pre-emptive subject choices which HMI Inspectorate have criticized, and the expectations and attitudes of the girls themselves, have already been conditioned, moulded, and set to 'feminine' models. It becomes increasingly apparent, therefore, that the actual vocational guidance offered by the careers officer both has to start lower down the school – preferably at thirteen plus before girls started dropping maths and science, and boys, languages and creative arts, and must be complemented by informed and sensitive advice and guidance from teaching staff within the school who know their youngsters well and can advise in the context of the whole of their school work and of their personal and temperamental strengths and weaknesses.

In the same way in which I have criticized school textbooks and readers, no shrewd look at careers work can overlook the growing problem of stereotyping in careers literature, films, media materials. Under the *Sex Discrimination Act, 1975*, discrimination in advertising is now unlawful, and some of the more blatant job and recruitment posters, booklets and advertisements are being altered. Much can be done by enlightened employers and industries in the way in which they select photographs to illustrate jobs showing both sexes in untypical work, selecting successful examples to quote, referring to *young people* and not to 'he' and 'him' throughout. Girls of fifteen are particularly impressionable to what is expected of them; and they identify with what they see other girls doing – and doing happily – preferably with a boy around too.

A review of the current traditional glossy guides and even government-sponsored careers booklets has so far shown an almost complete reflection of the stereotyping of employment, documented elsewhere. One positive, non-legal result from the *Sex Discrimination Act, 1975* is that its powers over controlling discrimination in advertising have produced a reflected climate in which publishers are beginning voluntarily to look at their careers literature in the context of the Act, and much of this is being monitored effectively to reduce stereotyping and to encourage positive discrimination in presentation. This is a key area of influence and there is still need for the imposition of national guidelines on non-sexist presentation.

Some innovatory material is now being produced. The Careers Research and Advisory Centre have published a lively new cartoon-illustrated careers workbook to help students to question their own sex stereotypes and to consider new and alternating roles (Jones, Marsh, and Watts 1976). On a different but equally refreshing wavelength is *The Gender Trap* series (Adams and Laurikietis 1976) of which the second book, *Sex and Marriage* is ideal material for use with fourth- and fifth-year girls. It uses lively but simply written material to make girls question many of the double standards applied to young men and young women in sex and marriage, and is an unusual combination of relevant facts, straight ideas, and well-presented questions to students based on the 'at times' trenchant material.

Careers counsellors are not necessarily free of prejudice. One study shows that although counsellors accepted equally clients whose aims either deviated or conformed to sex-role types, they did not approve as highly of deviant goals as of conforming choice. Clients deviating strongly were ranked as needing further counselling in 'self-understanding' (Thomas and Steward 1975:352–7)!

Careers officers have often, however, led the way in breaking new ground against cycles of discrimination and inequality in employment – for girls, for immigrants, for the less able, for all disadvantaged groups. But their service is grossly under-staffed and often underestimated. The 1971 HMI Survey of careers education spells out also a depressing tale of non-provision of careers education in over half of the schools. The full report (DES 1973) should be read by anyone concerned with the field – for the public expenditure cuts have now reduced still further since then, the number of careers officers and careers teachers – apparently regarded by LEAs and schools still as 'dispensable' in times of crisis.

Concern about the quality and adequacy of careers education was a theme running through Fogelman's survey of school leavers – 'I do feel that careers guidance was limited by the confines of straight society and that it was an attempt to put someone in a job rather than find a job to suit them' (and in particular, the sixth form leavers strongly criticized school-teachers' apparent total lack of knowledge of polytechnics, FE colleges, industry, and commerce – of anything other than academic higher education) (Fogelman 1972:14). This is partly an attitudinal problem and partly a resource one. We cannot afford to waste young brains and ability – female or male – needed in productive industry and commerce and in skilled trades, by wrong training and poor career-orientation. We allege we are paying for equal opportunity. Government must monitor the public expenditure cuts and reinstate the proper establishment of careers staff which HM Inspectorate and the Department of Employment themselves recommend if pupils are to find their way to the opportunities, some of which the next chapter unfolds.

SIX

Tertiary education – the alternative routes

'I aim at securing for all human beings training in all that which is proper for their common humanity.'

COMENIUS (17th Century)

'There is a method by which we may test the quality of the schools: we can look at the quality of the thing produced . . . I ask then, what are girls worth when their education is finished? What are they good for?'

EMILY DAVIES, 1861.

With all the ephemeral protection that an 'academic' education gave to us, I have to admit that the implication of Comenius' universal training for completeness, and the extension of opportunity to every girl, so dear to Emily Davies' heart, was not on my conscious horizon on that graduation afternoon in July,

1957, when the last hurdle in my particular educational obstacle-race fell to the ground. In the warm glow of ivy-clad redbrick cloisters, the lawns speckled with gowns and mortar-boards and clinking with tea-cups, we clutched our vital parchment; and did not know that we were only 1·6 per cent of our age group; nor I, that I then represented the minute 0·65 per cent of girls from my rural county to reach university at all and escape from the drudgery of an office stool; or the tramline to 'girls' courses' at the Technical College – carefully limited in scope, span, and length by the conditioned thinking of the male-dominated technical, scientific, and commercial 'tertiary sector', then the most powerful influence in the further education colleges, which were then the only alternative to universities and the prestigious higher education sector.

This chapter is in fact mainly about the alternatives offered (or not offered) to the then remaining 98 per cent of girls – as time has rolled on, to women at the peak of career, job, or family life; and to the 90 per cent of girls today who still do not reach the green lawns of Academe. It is about double standards; and about compounded inequality, since the answer to Emily Davies, of course, will depend quite distinctively on which girls we look at, in which regions and from which ability range or social class. It is above all at the tertiary stage that the warp and woof of inequality and discrimination are interwoven to the greatest disadvantage of women – and of particular groups of women. Priority for the gifted, the urban, the South, compounds the inequality of inadequate resources and opportunity for the rest – rural, average, Northern, and the non-academic. Who has, over the years, monitored for these? In brief space we can only touch the surface of this complex area, and I am selecting some strands only across the sectors to illustrate past trends and present needs in the further education and training of girls and women.

Firstly, however, a brief look back at the opportunities of my less fortunate peer group. In 1953, when I left school in that small cathedral city, there was little difference between girls' and boys' performance overall at sixteen plus (11·13 per cent of boys and 10·27 per cent of girls achieved five 'O' level passes). But the achievement gap widened disturbingly at seventeen and eighteen years. Of those achieving GCE 'A' Level, 5·4 per cent of boys achieved two 'A' levels, and 3·77 per cent three 'A' levels;

179

but the figures for girls were only 2·79 per cent and 1·62 per cent respectively. Ninety-eight per cent of girls were therefore unqualified for university entrance; and ninety-seven per cent unqualified for *advanced* further education. It is chastening to see how few of the men and women now aged 40–45 achieved full-time, post-school education at all:

Destination of school leavers, 1953

	boys %	girls %
university	2·33	1·06
teacher training	0·25	1·96
further education	7·01	10·06

(Source: DES *Statistics of Education 1953*)

It follows that the chance for the remainder of this generation of leavers (and for many of those in further education) to advance themselves, would depend on later day-release from employment, on grants and awards for later full-time study, on a second chance through adult education. This has proved impossible for most women because of the prejudice against investing in training and vocational education for women. Because, however, of the crucial relationship between the achievement of vocational qualifications and latter access to skilled employment, economic independence, equal pay, and promotion, the contrasting trends of women's achievements in further education with those in higher education over the last two decades are an important background to the wider but still limited opportunities offered to the female 51 per cent of the population today.

It is disheartening to see that after twenty-five years the gap of achievement is as great as ever in higher and in advanced technical education.

It is widely alleged that the under-recruitment of women to higher education is offset by their greater participation in further education. In 1975 men outnumbered women overall by two to one on *non-advanced* courses (323,570 women to 641,323 men) but by three to one at *advanced* level (61,310 women to

Percentage of school leavers 1975

	boys %	girls %
degree courses	8·2	4·9
teacher training	0·8	3·5
HND/HNC	0·4	0·2

(Source: DES *Statistics 1975* 2:Table 13)

188,379 men). And this is the only legitimate equivalent to higher education for those qualified for the latter. Moreover in the past, to a greater extent than now, those girl leavers who did qualify for higher education used their qualifications proportionately more for teacher training than university entrance, as *Table 6(1)* shows. This still significant practice today has important implications for the restructuring of higher education. The more able girls who would have trained as teachers, and cannot because of the cutback in teacher training, will be competing even more with boys for diminishing university and polytechnic places – with fewer relevant qualifications for the non-arts based courses.

The position of women staff in teacher education is touched on in the following chapter. The educational rationale behind the integration of teacher training into the mainstream of further education and higher education is, in my view, sound (in addition to obvious economic benefits), discouraging, as it will, the isolation from external industrial, commercial, and technical influences that the typical, single-sex rural college, or even co-educational urban college set apart from its neighbours, inevitably has reinforced in the past. The school:college:school syndrome which leaves so many teachers ignorant of (and uninterested in) the outside world of work, has been an unhelpful counter to developing new attitudes in school teachers. The dangers of overswift reorganization lie rather in the underqualification of girl school leavers for alternative courses of study and the need – not to develop 'special' courses for them – to pay for bridging courses to enable them to move into new areas of study, for which their school qualifications are not suitable.

Table 6(1) Destination of School Leavers entering higher education (England and Wales) 1967

Percentage of those holding qualifications as follows	universities		colleges of education		advanced further education	
	B %	G %	B %	G %	B %	G %
3 or more 'A' levels	68·3	57·7	2·7	15·4	10·7	6·7
2 'A' levels	26·1	12·5	11·0	41·4	22·0	9·5
1 'A' level	1·1	0·2	15·5	51·2	21·4	6·5
5 or more 'O' levels but no 'A' levels	0·2	0·4	4·7	12·2	4·0	0·3

Note: Percentages are of leavers with the appropriate level of qualification – not of the age group. Thus of those leaving with 2 'A' levels, 26% of boys but only 12% of girls went to university; but only 11% of boys with 2 'A' levels used them to enter teacher training as against 41% of girls. The remaining leavers will have entered non-advanced FE, professional training, or employment.

It is above all the tertiary sector that provides technical education for industry and commerce, from technicians to technologists, from agriculture to engineering, social work to business management. Equally important is the *adult education* sector within further education, which provides non-vocational education for leisure, recreation, government, literacy to those who have failed earlier in a fallible school system; general education to those who want to develop their minds (and characters) without a specific employment outlet in mind.

Further education is a knotted skein of interwoven strands of planning and provision, organization and reorganization, expansion and recession. While schooling is compulsory, post-schooling is not. Local authorities must provide a school place for every child; but the *level* of provision of further and higher education has never been fixed by national standards. The *Education Act, 1944*, makes it possible for local government to provide as much or as little further (as distinct from higher) education as we choose – or so it has been held for the last thirty years. I disagree. In my view, the wording of the Act could be held to make it *mandatory* for provision to meet the level of *real demand*, for all kinds of tertiary education.

'Section 41 : Subject as hereinafter provided, it shall be the duty of every local education authority to secure the provision for their area of adequate facilities for further education, that is to say :

(a) full-time and part-time education for persons over compulsory school age; and
(b) leisure-time occupation, in such organized cultural training and recreative activities as are suited to their requirements, for any persons over compulsory school age who are able and willing to profit by the facilities provided for that purpose.'

There is nothing in this wording to justify the dichotomy of the Robbins' principle of the 'right' of every eighteen year old with appropriate academic 'A' levels to a university place *mandatorily*; and the specious and questionable principle of making further (as distinct from higher) education students fight for a declining pool of *discretionary* grants which are the first target of cuts in recession by hard-pressed, near-bankrupt, local education authorities. I am here asserting that whatever the law says, it is indirect discrimination against women to deny FE students the same right to grants and awards and to the protection of their courses, that higher education students enjoy. Because FE is the only sector in which women predominate and to which women beyond school leaving age can look for re-education and retraining to mop up their broken or inadequate past education, when they return to work after bearing an unfair share of the domestic burden.

In my view, the words of Section 41 (a) of the *1944 Education Act* above imply *no* limit on the demand or provision for further education, and the inclusion of 'any persons ... able and willing to profit by the facilities' in S.41 (b) reinforces this interpretation. But while central government attempts to control the number of higher education places in universities and colleges recruiting nationally, by Planning Papers and controls of centrally determined expenditure, local government adopts an entrepreneurial approach and develops courses on a *demand* factor from both students and the employment sector.

We have tended indeed quite consciously to plan for continued inequality at governmental level in a way that matches

very ill the logic and parity of the French quinquennial development plans. When the Robbins Committee reported in 1963, it
drew attention to the increased demand for higher education
from the generation of young people who represented the post-
war 'bulge' of the 1940s and gave an expensive, but generally
sound, clarion call that higher education should be equally
accessible to all qualified to profit from further study – a principle much vaunted in prestigious speeches since 1963, but which
we have failed to achieve against perpetuated inequalities between sexes, regions, and social classes, simply because young
people from the North, girls, and working-class school leavers
are still seriously under-represented at universities and in advanced further and higher education.

The Robbins Committee stated unequivocally that:

> 'Throughout our Report *we have assumed as an axiom that*
> *courses of higher education should be available for all those*
> *who are qualified by ability and attainment to pursue them*
> *and who wish to do so* ... If challenged, however, we would
> vindicate (this principle) on two grounds. First, conceiving
> education as a means, we do not believe that modern societies
> can achieve their aims of economic growth and higher cul-
> tural standards *without making the most of the talents of*
> *their citizens.* This is obviously necessary if we are to com-
> pete with other highly developed countries in an era of
> rapid technological and social advance ... to realize the
> aspirations of a modern community as regards both wealth
> and culture, a fully educated population is necessary.'
>
> (Robbins Committee 1963, Vol 1. 8–10)

The Committee went on to say that 'the good society desires
equality of opportunity for its citizens to become not merely
good producers but good men and women'. It is unbelievable
that any government could endorse this for potential graduates
and not for the much needed technologists and technicians
produced by the FE sector.

But the tenor of the Committee's report – and many of its
tables – also assumes that the major expansion will go to young
men rather than to young women. This assumption has – rather
incredibly, considering the concurrent widespread European
and Transatlantic debates on improving equal opportunity for

women – been translated meekly, firmly, and unquestioningly into English governmental planning. The Planning Paper published by the Department of Education and Science in 1970, on to which later plans have been built, assumed a constant gap of feminine under-achievement, with no proposals for narrowing the gulf:

'The respective proportions of boy and girl school leavers with 3 or more "A" level passes, and with 2 "A" levels, who proceed to university have been assumed to regain by 1971 the corresponding proportions achieved in the early 1960s, *and to remain constant* from 1971 onwards.' (DES 1970:38)

The Paper went on to say that:

'The proportions of school leavers with 1 "A" level who enter fulltime and sandwich advanced courses in further education would rise by 1981 to 28·5% for boys and 16% for girls. In absolute numbers, these assumptions for colleges of education and advanced further education imply *a doubling of the numbers of boy school leavers* with 1 "A" level proceeding to higher education (from 3,500 in 1967 to 7,000 in 1981), *but a fairly constant number* of girl school leavers (about 5,500).'
(DES 1970:38)

In my view, this has a quite reprehensible ring of male complacency. It may be argued that the government was merely planning on the basis of known trends, and that it could not legislate for equality against factors of social conditioning and failure by girls to exercise their 'choice' of access to higher education. I believe this to be thoroughly and deplorably specious. The Robbins Committee principle of a right to a place has been theoretically accepted in government's planning up to 1980; but then ignored in its actual planning, for 50 per cent of its clientele.[1]

Higher education

Although the growth rate of women holding new university awards at universities between 1960 and 1972 rose by 211 per cent compared with male growth rates of 154 per cent, men still outnumbered women by two to one (32,000 men and 16,000 women). This is a pattern replicated in other European countries. In 1974 the *total* university award holders remained in this ratio – 100,107 men and 51,455 women. In 1975 women represented only 35·3 per cent of all full-time university undergraduates – and equally, only a third of full-time polytechnic students on degree courses (11,785 women to 20,520 men) (DES *Statistics of Education 1975*, Vol. 3).

It is superfluous to repeat in detail the sextyping of subjects studied by women in HE and in advanced FE – the pattern basically (and for obvious causal reasons) almost completely replicates the schools' patterns. Students and interested readers should analyse for themselves the now comprehensive published statistics of the DES (vols. 3 and 6 of the 1975 statistics cover this field) which show some interesting trends. Women's proportion of business studies and social administration courses at degree level is for example growing steadily and encouragingly, and noticeably is again faster in polytechnics than in universities. Careers staff should look seriously at business and management degrees as alternatives for their girls to the doubtfully marketable 'arts degrees for all'; and at the vocationally slanted Higher National BEC award in preference to the – in my view – doubtful Diploma in Higher Education. The latter will carry less weight as a two-year qualification than an arts degree, and will be considerably less relevant to administration, business, and commerce than the BEC awards with their balance of common core and vocational option modules. This is an important growth area for women, particularly in the context of training them for decision-making and more senior office. A second reverse trend is that women's proportion of nontraditional degree work is narrowing more significantly in universities than in polytechnics and in advanced FE – confirming the school pattern where the sextyping gap is sharper in CSE than in GCE. The academic girl seems consistently readier to break the net.

Alternatives to academic education

The base on which we are building is surely the most uneven, listing foundation imaginable for the achievement of an equality which should be as impeccably even as that of a spirit level. The alternatives to a liberal university education have changed and widened more over the last two postwar decades than at any time in our history. Fifty years ago there was little between the professions (and teaching was still limping into last place as a profession as such) and the craft and technical classes mostly offered at 'night school' in technical institutes whose origins lay in the nineteenth century science and art classes grant aided by the special Government Board which preceded the establishment of a Ministry.

The key influence of technical training as well as secondary education was not overlooked even then. By 1903, the London County Council was, for example, offering substantial technical scholarships and exhibitions. Girls in London at that time accounted for nearly half of all junior technical scholarships; but predictably, of 293 evening exhibitioners in science and technology, only five were young women (London Statistics 1903, XIV). Discrimination against the training of women for employment has deep roots in the past. For the later extension of the opening of central technical classes for women in London brought a now only too familiar reaction from men trade unionists of the Metropolitan Trades Councils who condemned the move because they alleged the LCC was using working men's money 'to equip their unscrupulous competitors'. Mary MacArthur, the only woman member in the Trades Council, successfully fought them on the grounds that they were only holding back their own deprived sisters and daughters and leaving the way open for middle-class women who could pay for instruction. The men gave in (MacArthur 1908). We can only regret the subsequent passing of the National Federation of Women Workers who then had 3,000 members, twenty-seven branches, and two paid officials, crossing twelve industries, in 1908. One wonders how far the natural isolation and individualism of adolescent girls leads to their later disinclination to organize themselves in associations and protective or support groups. This is one respect in which the group approach of the Women's Liberation collectives is such an excellent development.

Half a century later, in 1957, there were 1,926,000 students in further (non-university) education in England and Wales. Today there are 3,688,000. While twenty-five years ago the alternatives for my fellow school leavers were mainly limited to *non-advanced* further education (polytechnics were in their infancy, sandwich courses unborn, and Higher National Diplomas were available in only a very limited range of subjects), today students have an almost bewildering option of vocational courses in establishments from rural local colleges through large urban colleges of technology to polytechnics which include teachers' education, art and design, and growing departments of business and management education and social administration. New industries spawn new courses from computer technology to food refrigeration. But girls have not increased their relative take-up of technical courses – because they still lack the base qualifications in the same measure as they did twenty or fifty years ago, by comparison with their brothers. With the sole exception of non-vocational adult education classes where women outnumber men, the growth rate has, however, been heavily weighted in favour of men – both in types of course and methods of study which are traditionally male-oriented.

For reasons of space, the statistical position of women in FE is not recapitulated – basically that they predominate on lower level, non-advanced courses in arts subjects or in skills-based rather than career-based training – in order to illustrate two deeper problems. (Those seeking details will find them in the DES statistics.) The first problem is the male ethos of further education as compared with higher education. The second is the 'compound interest of inequality', in this case regional and rural/urban.

We found in the secondary school sector that girls study nearly as long as boys; that their pass rates are often higher; their general education better, but that the moment they were given apparent freedom of curricular choice, they appeared more strongly to reinforce stereotyped views of their future roles. I suggested that the pattern of staffing and of teachers' different roles in the schools, as seen through girls' eyes, was strongly influential. The tertiary sector is of course immeasurably more complex. To look at it through the eyes of our girl leavers would be a sharp contrast to the schools they are leaving. The male ethos of an FE college is probably the biggest single deterrent to the development of new attitudes in young women in the post-school sector. Yet it is difficult to know how to alter it in the short term.

Let us hypothesise the situation of four girls. *Jean*, from a Northern mill town will probably attend the local middle-sized technical college. It will, typically, have a male principal almost certainly an ex-engineer). Ninety per cent of the staff will be male, including the registrar. The only women she will see will be the lecturers in charge of secretarial studies, the head of catering and welfare studies and possibly one or two women lecturers in English and foreign languages, the secretary, and the cleaners. If Jean is studying business studies, her class will be fairly mixed; if secretarial skills, almost all female. If she has overcome her careers teacher's opposition and the repressive atmosphere and has carved her way into a technical drawing class ('You'll find it difficult to get a job anywhere afterwards') she will be one of only 5 per cent. If she is on day release for anything but typing or clerical work, she will be outnumbered by young men by ten to one. The sports facilities will almost certainly be limited to rugger or soccer, and the college will be dominated by workshops and boilersuits, except in the new block built to house expanding BEC and TEC middle range courses in non-craft subject areas. The college may not lack in good will. It nevertheless is organized for a male world.

Alison's college in a larger rural county is more like a community college, with a well developed adult education department to which her mother also comes on the village bus twice a week during the day to study for GCE at the age of thirty-five to help her to prepare for a return to work. Like Jean, Alison has had to fight (unsuccessfully) for her grant for a two-year course – in her case – an ONC in hotel catering. Her authority, like Jean's, is poor in rate yield and has had to cut discretionary grants. Alison will not qualify until she takes HND (which carries a mandatory grant) in two years' time. Alison is also fighting the county because they pay her brother a motor-bike allowance under the county's transport aid scheme to enable him to get to the polytechnic over the county boundary; but they will not pay for her, although there are no evening buses back to the village from her college. She is considering taking a case under Section 23 of the *Sex Discrimination Act, 1975* on the grounds that if it were her brother they would award the allowance. Her mother does not qualify for a grant either – her basic re-education, which is what most mature women need, is not regarded as 'economically necessary'. They are lucky: Alison's father is a secure farmer who can fund them. How different from the Robbins principle. (No one asked me at eighteen whether my Medieval French, Latin, and modern French was likely to be useful to the community or not; academic students are still just as unfairly favoured.) Alison's rural college is more likely to have one of the nineteen women principals or twenty-two vice-principals (out of 537) in the country; a woman head of adult education and women in the liberal studies department. But it still will not have more than 10 per cent women staff overall and, despite heavy unemployment of males in the county, the cleaners and secretaries will still be women.

Julia decided on a polytechnic at eighteen plus to take HND in science subjects. There were no hostel places so she shares a flat with a girl friend. The leadership of her polytechnic will inevitably be male – there are no women directors or deputy directors of polytechnics; only 3 per cent women heads of departments; no women readers (out of thirty-four); and only 12 per cent women staff overall. Of those, Julia will have gradually noticed that almost all are ordinary lecturers. In fact in polytechnics 93 per cent of women staff are of lecturer grade II and below, and only 7 per cent of senior lecturer and above. Equal pay becomes a myth when women cluster round the bottom of the grading graph.

Maria is most typical of the students of the next few years. As teacher education is cut and more colleges and polytechnics diversify, offering technology, arts, and education, more students may want to keep their options open and seek a college where they can switch courses in mid-stream. Living in Greater London she had the choice of over twenty large colleges and polytechnics and a very advanced careers service. Having decided against teaching she is discussing with staff in two colleges, whether to study for the Diploma in Higher Education or whether to opt for a vocational course under the Business or Technician Education Councils (she has two 'A' levels and five 'O' Levels and has a very open mind). It is hoped that the increased flexibility of the new modular courses, and the multidisciplinary organization of amalgamated colleges, may persuade more of the able girls to look more widely than traditional arts subjects or the (diminishing) teacher-training field. Maria will probably notice in her reorganized college of higher education (an amalgamation of three colleges including teacher training) that more of the women lecturers are teaching educational studies; but that the director, deputy director, and head of academic studies will be male.

Aggregated inequality of region, provision, ability

National statistics hide both regional and rural under-achievement. Despite six volumes of annual published DES statistics (now fully sex-divided as a result of discreet but firm feminism in the corridors of power) there are still some questions of correlation which they cannot answer. *Table 6(2)* illustrates disturbing scales of regional differences in recruitment to FE –

Table 6(2) (a) All students at grant-aided further education establishments. Regional variations in take-up, 1974

| | percentage of age group | | | |
| | 16–17 | | 18–20 | |
region	men %	women %	men %	women %
National average	41·1	31·2	32·2	18·4
North	41·6	29·7	31·1	13·5
East Anglia	34·6	27·9	24·2	13·6
South West	35·4	31·0	28·3	14·9
Greater London	45·4	30·1	46·5	28·5

(Source: DES *Statistics of Education 1974*, Vol. 3, Table 10)

(b) School leavers going on to further education (England and Wales) 1974. Regional variations

	boys %	girls %
All leavers going on to full-time further education:		
National average	16·9	23·04
South East (excluding Greater London)	20·4	27·2
South West	21·7	27.6
North	12·1	18·6
Yorkshire and Humberside	13·9	19·6

Source: DES *Statistics of Education 1974*, Vol. 2, Table 17)

for both sexes – which raise serious problems in policy and planning. Twice as many men as women enrol nationally – but nearly four times as many men in Greater London as women in the north. And only 18 per cent of northern girl leavers went on to further education, as compared with 27 per cent in the south west.

I attempted in 1973 to break down the national DES Statistics regionally, to illustrate my suspicions that the often quoted higher proportion of girls going on to FE (see *Table 6(2)* – 23 per cent nationally for 17 per cent of boys) concealed nevertheless continuing under-achievement. I suspected girls were syphoned on to lower-level courses, skills-based and not careerbased, sextyped as 'women's courses', and leading inexorably to lower paid employment. I expected to find rural/urban differences, and correlations between high levels of local provision and higher take-up by local students.

The accumulated available government statistics returned by colleges could however not answer basic questions, like what relative proportions of women and men were on full-time advanced courses in study area A, from rural and urban LEAs B and C. It is greatly to the credit of the Regional Advisory Council for Further Education in the East Midlands (RACOFEEM) that it sponsored a special survey of fifty colleges and polytechnics in its area to find out precisely where women students were – and were not – and subsequently launched a seminar 'Wasted Womanpower' on June 6, 1973 to persuade an audience of industrialists, teachers, careers officers, and LEA senior staff, to consider positive assertive programmes to remedy the inequalities we had then uncovered. The sample survey illustrates many points that have since emerged as more widely valid.

First, relative regional under-achievement acted to the further disadvantage of women. There were 86,071 male students and 68,535 female students overall, thus illustrating that proportionately fewer women than the national average go on to further education in the East Midlands – since nationally, in reverse, women outnumber men in further education *overall* (including adult education and evening classes). Second, proportionately more men were on advanced courses, on semi-advanced courses (vocational diplomas), and more on intermediate courses. Only on lowest-level courses did women outnumber men. No way were the FE opportunities equivalent to the missing HE female take-up.

The divisions are important diagnostically and cannot be obtained, nor cross-related to areas, from published national statistics.

Table 6(3) East Midlands 1973

	Students by level of course			
level	men		women	
A1 (degree equivalent)	5,741	(6·7)	1,129	(1·7)
A2 (advanced)	11,608	(13·5)	1,175	(2·5)
B (intermediate, technician)	22,740	(26·4)	6,733	(9·8)
C (craft Level)	29,731	(34·5)	35,006	(51.1)
Unclassified (adult education, evening classes, etc.)	16,251	(18·8)	23,917	(34·9)
	86,071	(100)	68,535	(100)

Note: % of all students of same sex in sample in brackets

In fact three quarters of women were on the lowest level of courses as against only half of men. A fifth of all men were on advanced courses; fewer than one twentieth of women. (This situation is mirrored in the North East, where women's under-achievement is even more marked.)

The distribution across the region was moreover uneven in a highly significant way. Three of the five partly urban counties had their further educational provision concentrated in a large regional centre (the three county boroughs) with a university, a polytechnic, and a number of larger colleges of further education designated for advanced courses. These had consistently and proportionately more women enrolled on advanced courses. The two rural counties with no such large centre, no higher education provision, and fewer and smaller colleges, had few or no girls at all enrolled at *advanced* level. The results were so consistent across all levels of courses and all areas of study, as to suggest a prima facie correlation between *local* availability

of provision and higher take-up at all levels. This has majo
policy implications for the present reorganization of highe
education in which it is mainly rural and smaller colleges tha
are closing, and mainly urban and larger regionally centree
colleges that are remaining or being absorbed. There is a stron
argument here that the presence itself of local *advanced* pro
vision as well as of lower-level courses stimulates take-up; and
that the lack of it depresses the level of demand. This is exacer
bated by the almost total lack of residential hostels for *furthe*
education students, the lack of public transport in the rura
areas making access to other countries almost impossible, and
LEA policy that students must study in the home county if the
relevant course is available. The domestic ties of women will
however, make it almost certain that they will need to limi
their horizons to colleges within easy travelling distance.

When the cross relationship of take-up by each of the five
counties is analysed, the variations of inequality are disturbingl
aggregated further. Lower levels of FE provision, fewer womer
in FE, fewer or no women at advanced level, lower than average
proportion of women on day release, all correlate highly in two
mainly rural counties by marked contrast to their semi-urbar
neighbours showing proportionately higher female achieve
ment, linked with proportionately higher provision.

Analyses cross-relating subject area to level of course showed
other significant trends. Only 0·6 per cent of students on *techni*
cal courses were women; and only 26 per cent of those study
ing science. And while women did account for 58 per cent of
business studies students, they outnumbered men by three to
one at C (low) level (mainly secretarial). But 37 per cent of male
business studies students were on advanced courses, whereas
only 12 per cent of women reached this level. Even in social
studies, traditionally a women's sphere, *nine tenths* of the men
students were on advanced courses, but only a quarter of the
women students (42 per cent of women students of social
studies were on C level courses, but only 5 per cent of the men)

Suspecting some of these findings in advance, we had asked
colleges for subjective informed opinions as to probable causes
of women's under-recruitment, under-achievement, and their
restriction to traditional study areas. A majority of colleges
commented trenchantly and adversely on women's lack of basic
grounding in maths and physical sciences, and laid the blame

194

squarely at the doors of the schools. Practical obstacles quoted as preventing women and girls from attending *advanced* courses included discrimination against married women by LEA grants and award officers, social immobility because of marriage on part-time advanced courses, and discriminatory attitudes of employers against the release of women for study – industry's 'tendency to regard women as a temporary work force'. One polytechnic was certain that more women would apply for advanced courses in technology and construction 'if they had confidence that their chances would not be prejudiced when applying for employment'. Discrimination by employers against day release and industrial training for women was also a widely-quoted cause. Traditional attitudes by girls and poor careers advice was the third major disadvantage quoted. Girls' own feeling that 'they are less acceptable to industry and commerce than equally qualified males' combined with self-imposed dom-estic responsibilities came through clearly as pervading the survey. Lack of knowledge of non-academic FE courses by girls from grammar schools led, several colleges suggested, to under-achievement even in traditional areas of study. The survey also highlighted substantial differences in patterns of day release enrolment as between both different geographical areas and different occupational study areas – all cumulatively dis-advantageous to girls.

The part-time route

Of all of the factors for disadvantage, which could be reversed into a positive policy for improving the further education and training of women, the part-time route stands out as tradition-ally the most discriminatory and potentially the most visionary. There are two angles to this – day release from employment; and courses and grant aid for those (mainly women) wishing to retrain or re-educate for a return to work (or, as postulated in Chapter 5, for an unpaid career in government or community work).

In terms of school leavers, day release for study remains one of the major and continuing inequalities. It is well documented elsewhere,[2] but it is worth a brief reminder of the scale of disadvantage.

The Henniker–Heaton report of 1964, set a brave target of an additional 250,000 boys and girls by 1970. The Committee recommended strongly that girls be given parity of day release, rejecting as unacceptable the argument that 'girls are not likely to make a career in industry or commerce and therefore have little need of training and education'. Henniker–Heaton endorsed the Carr report's 1956 recommendation for more girl technicians, more training for women in sales planning, market research, and work study, and more day release training in sectors 'traditionally regarded as women's occupations'. For three-quarters of girls and women, study will remain a part-time route to achievement to be fitted in with employment or marriage (or both). If we are to use and effectively direct half of the female brains in the country towards economic productivity, it will be through part-time further education that the major expansion must come.

But it seems characteristic of the intermittent hypocrisy of government that educationalists since the *Fisher Act* of 1918 have pleaded for compulsory national day release or continuing education – for the future economic producers of our wealth – without any success in narrowing the inequality gap in achieving day release (or an equivalent educational alternative) for all, across all barriers of sex, ability, or region. It cannot be accidental that West Germany, for many years economically in our advance, has a system of compulsory part-time continuing education and training for young people who leave at or after fifteen, until the age of eighteen years. Investment in the young has always brought benefits to the older.

The trend makes depressing reading. Provisional figures for 1977 are no more encouraging.

Table 6(4) Part-time day students under 18 as percentage of population not receiving full-time education

	male	*female*
1956	17·7	4·43
1963	30·2	7·1
1971	41·0	11·7
1974	37·6	12·4

Source: DES *Stastics of Education 1977.*

Regional inequalities persist. The North and the East Midlands are, for example, consistently below the national average. There is a further subdivision of disadvantage – by different industries. Further broken down by occupation, average figures for day release in textiles, distribution, clothing, and footwear are, for example, less than 3 per cent for girls; and these are office workers, not operatives, a hidden form of discrimination within the sex (priority for the able and the 'respectable' traditions, again). Insurance and banking release less than 1 per cent of young women.

There is in fact a general misconception about *day and block release* for further education that it mostly represents a day at the local technical college for school leavers; typing for girls and welding for boys. The dimension of employment-sponsored release for further education for young adults rather than school leavers is however the major area where discrimination rather than inequality holds back older women from economic independence, from acquiring advanced qualifications, promotion, and real work mobility. Some countries describe this training for career advancement after about eighteen plus as 'paid educational leave', but the principle is the same – payment of salary by employers for employees to study during working hours. My arguments in the earlier chapters about *why* we educate recur. Careers (not domesticity) for women, even if interrupted mean employer investment in women. We will not accept less. The age difference is sharpened by the breakdown of the total further education day release figures. When figures are analysed again *by age*, the craft apprenticeship pattern of the under eighteens is replaced by a route to a career, through professional qualifications. Courses for intermediate and advanced diplomas and certificates in insurance, banking, accountancy, business administration, technical, and technological skills, depend on day release *over eighteen*; and here men outnumber women by up to 100 to one, not by the four to one so often quoted for the school leaver. The figures below show, for example, that men receive proportionately more release by employers from 18–21 for *career-based* vocational courses[3] while investment in young women over eighteen drops dramatically and proportionately more, for the key years of 19–20 – and thereafter.

Table 6(5) Students on day release at further education establishments 1974

age	male	female
16	61,203	17,836
17	93,229	23,943
18	81,285	14,127
19	60,863	8,033
20	38,365	4,993
21 and over	117,117	31,843
total	452,062	100,775

The provisional overall figures for 1975 and 1976 show a further decline (not advance) for both sexes, but a constant sex gap, of an overall four to one ratio in favour of men. Day release for the men aged 19–21 is the key that enables them to represent future budding young managers, sales distributors, technicians, accountants, surveyors, computer technologists, skilled supervisors and foremen, leading craftsmen, high on job evaluation charts. How can women achieve equal pay, if they cannot achieve equal release from employment for training for *career-based* technical and professional qualifications?

I have perhaps laboured the point because I am so often (wrongly) told that the lower proportion of young women on career-linked courses is only because they choose to opt out. I do not believe the trends illustrated support this. At each stage it is the courses that depend on *employer* sponsorship that show the most startling weighting in favour of men, and in my view clearly reflect persistently adverse employer (and often college) attitudes which amount to discrimination. Of sandwich course students in 1974 in England and Wales for example (that is, those which depend on either employer-sponsorship or placement in employment for part of the course), 36,000 were men but only 7,300 women. Again, the key difference is for the *over twenty-one* and not the under eighteen age group.

Table 6(6) Sandwich course students at grant-aided FE establishments, 1974

age	male	female
16	600	400
18	3,695	1,227
21	18,181	2,306

The differential may be partly because more sandwich courses are science or technology-based, for which fewer women are qualified; partly because there are more men over twenty-one overall in higher education; but is also partly because employers are less willing to sponsor young women through fear of 'wastage' – despite all the evidence from Sullerot onwards that qualified women drop out less after marriage or return more quickly. Women's proportion of HND (full-time) and HNC (part-time with day release) is similarly only about half the rate of their participation in university studies, relative to men. They accounted for 34 per cent of university students in 1974; but only 19 per cent of HND students and 13 per cent of HNC students, in 1974.

I am conscious that my argument has tended to centre on the quantitive rather than the diagnostic; but not wholly without reason. Growth rates and the numbers game have been used for too many years by the government of education to soothe our stringent questioning of their failure to attack inequality. The sex gap in FE is still a Grand Canyon, not a small fissure. My own arithmetic, estimating the outcome of the placebo of 'natural trends are closing the gap without intervention' is that it will be the year 2084 before 'natural trends' arrive even at an overall 2 : 1 male to female ratio in advanced and technological FE and training, leave aside parity. A recent report places it more modestly at thirty years hence (London and Home Counties 1976). Neither I, nor the generations ahead for whom we are fighting, are prepared to wait for an illusory long-term millennium. We have to invent break-in strategies along the way, using positive discrimination in favour of the disadvantaged if we are to exploit the skills, gifts, and full potential of women.

The economic argument is too often forgotten. Nearly twenty

years ago the McMeeking Report said astringently that, 'It is little short of folly when national resources are already taxed by the demands of science, technology, business and the professions, for firms to regard the potential contribution to be made by women as something they can afford to ignore' (McMeeking Committee 1959). It fell – of course – on deaf ears. This country is falling behind our competitors in both productivity and inventiveness not so much because of lack of top technologists – although they are a constant need – as because of under-provision of skilled technicians, industrial workers, and trained craftsmen to back up the minority of specialists. And it is to the unexploited pool of girls and young women to whom we should be looking. Curricular stereotyping in FE, which results in only 6,476 women studying engineering and technology at non-advanced level as against 373,119 men, but a derisory 953 women out of 57,156 at 'A' level, is uneconomic in terms of the country's potential skills. That employment patterns are in fact linked to education and training is indeed sharpened by the Russian experience, which although I do not commend it necessarily in other respects, should give us cause to look at our own post-school influences. Russian women account for 70 per cent of doctors, 30 per cent of engineers, 58 per cent of agricultural scientists, and 48 per cent of industrial workers. Half of the trade-union membership is female – and they participate (St.Georges 1975).

The symptoms and cures needed to tackle the 'rubric of exceptions', which I discussed earlier, causing girls and women to shy away from breaking traditional patterns of choice and behaviour, differ in depth and in character for school leavers on the one hand, and for the 'lost generations' of older women over twenty-five or over thirty whose second chance depends on programmes of deliberate, positive discrimination. In distinguishing the warp and woof of inequality against discrimination, I have made clear my view that the complete breakdown of all the mechanistic barriers of primary and secondary school sex differentiation will need a fundamental review of aims and objectives for equality and the retraining of teachers to recognize, and correct, their unconscious reinforcement of sex differentiation. But I have attacked, also, the directly *discriminatory* practices of withholding the full curriculum or the full range of activities and patterns of behaviour from either sex –

girl or boy. By changing the previous base, we will begin to change the post-school pattern.

Some immediate action is, however, essential meanwhile in the tertiary sector. First, FE has the unique chance to remedy past deficiencies both in basic education and in male and female attitudes. Over half of all secondary schools provide no real careers education, even in the fifth year, which includes the cafeteria choice of options and the post-school world of work. FE colleges should take major responsibility in influencing the structure of school curricula and timetables and in injecting into school's fourth- and fifth-year programmes, substantial material about the real world of work to *encourage* girls to learn to survive in an 'unfeminine' environment with determination, poise, and relaxation. Lecturers who deliberately reflect the job market in persuading girls to 'safe' courses hitherto linked to so-called women's work are discriminating; and may be liable under the new anti-discrimination legislation. They are certainly not educating for life or for personal fulfilment. *Linked course* schemes with schools should deliberately place girls not only in traditionally male study areas, but into a wider range of courses readily attractive to girls who – whatever we may feel – have in fact just left five or eight years of female conditioning. Those unsympathetic to encouraging girls to train and work in competition with boys (and these exist in very substantial numbers in FE) raise chauvinistic spectres of girl miners and bricklayers and 'butch' transport drivers as a classic negative reaction calculated to destroy the concept of interchangeability as socially and publicly unrealistic. But why not centre on at least electrical engineering; draughtsmanship; administration rather than typing; catering and not cooking; supervision and not assembly line work, as preliminary expansion areas for young women?

Every college should also have not only *crèche* facilities, but also holiday playgroups for older children. The economics? I would cut back drastically on sports facilities, both in the youth service in FE, and more generally (we cater predominantly for men) and redirect building improvement programmes and the budget for part-time tutors to child-care. We are still a healthy nation – the 1902 crisis is long past. There is now a solid existing investment of recreational facilities in most if not all areas (often under-used in out-of-school or college hours because of divisive 'sector' organization). No more money for sport until young women's need for child-care resources to release them from home ties offers them the full outward freedom o their brothers. Second, I would levy industry with a smal child-care tax unless they were already providing facilities Much wealth has been built on exploiting female labour, especi ally part-time labour, in the past, and will continue to be made Women are a steady reliable labour force. They will be the more reliable for having the secure care of their children assured. We are merely claiming our 'back pay' of investment from the last hundred years of under-provision.

Grants and awards

The refusal of successive governments to restructure the system of grants and awards, to remove the implicit discrimination against those unfortunate enough to be non-academic, voca tionally-oriented (and mostly female), by making the grants discretionary for the non-advanced courses which we offer them, is a major hurdle over which fewer women can ride.

Local authorities and central government should be pressed to alter the *grants and awards* regulations to allow grants for two categories of student as a right, and not a discretionary privilege to be fought for. First, because by the trends identified in the secondary sector, it will be seen that we face decades before 'natural trends' eliminate the curricular gap – unless we establish compulsory basic core education, of which more later School leavers, but especially girls, will still need bridging courses to make up deficient *basic* subjects in order to go on to further study. It is economic nonsense, and clear discrimina tion against any youngster whose secondary education has left her or him without the basic tools for further crucial study and training, to deny a grant for key-subject study when academic and well-educated eighteen-year olds have an automatic right to a grant to read old Norse. We cannot afford an uneconomic ally under-educated labour force – of either sex. And the only way that young women over sixteen will now acquire maths and science is by further, post-school, study. Their need for bridging courses in technical drawing and the handicrafts is also keen, to open the door to technical and skilled craft train ing. I remain to be convinced that we cannot afford relatively

mall sums to bring all school leavers up to a survival kit level
of scientific and numerate study.

Second, even if we swept all teachers on a tide of enthusiasm
to the shores of a common curriculum by next September – an
interesting but unlikely phenomenon – we still face generations
of older women needing not only retraining but basic education.
Curricular statistics of the last two decades show far greater
polarity of girl:boy achievement even than today. My generation and the intervening ones had poor fare in our time, in a
period up to 1959 of stark educational rationing (except for the
tiny minority of us who crept through holes in the network).
Married women now wishing to return to work – *and* single
women under-achieving because of past discriminatory educational and training practices – should have the *right* to grants
for GCE 'O' and 'A' level courses where these can be seen to
be needed as entry requirements for further courses. It is a matter
for regret that Section 47 of the *Sex Discrimination Act, 1975,*
which enables exempted training programmes to cater for
women only (or men only) wishing to enter areas of work
hitherto wholly or mainly reserved for the opposite sex, ex-
cludes special educational programmes. Most women cannot
retrain until they have *first* topped up their basic education in
missing sciences, maths, and technical studies; and therefore
end up on the inexorable tramline to training over a hot stove
or a cold typewriter.

This is not the place to debate the cutbacks in higher education which have escalated since the oddly named White paper
of 1972, 'Education: A Framework for Expansion' (since when
we have seen the worst planned, and unplanned, recession and
cuts since the 1922 Geddes axe). The latest discussion document
(DES 1978) postulates a possible ultimate halving of higher
education provision. Since our GNP will not be halved, I suggest we have a pool of resources for potential redeployment
elsewhere – money, staff, and buildings.

The resources for extra further education grants needed by
redesignating more as mandatory, should – unless government is
seriously contending that it cannot afford the level of re-
education and re-training that its European competitors have
accepted – be found from redeployment by borrowing from
the higher education sector. I am constantly told that it would
be politically and educationally unacceptable to ration awards

for university and polytechnic courses in order to pay for lowe[r] level courses. It is a policy and a logic that defeats me. We do i[n] fact ruthlessly ration non-advanced awards even in key tech[-] nical areas. Why not advanced courses? Is it coincidence tha[t] the student body in the protected mandatory HE sector (in[-] cluding vocational advanced FE, as we have seen) is predom[i-] nantly male; and the vulnerable non-advanced students pre[-] dominantly female? Either all students may need to justify th[e] worth of their studies; or, if we preserve the concept of equa[l] and open educational opportunity, on the Robbins principle[,] then all have in fact the right (not the negotiable charitabl[e] privilege) to state aid for *basic* and necessary education. Afte[r] years of adminstering the education service – including award[s] – I do not accept that we cannot invent acceptable criteria t[o] prevent abuse and waste. We already have, for most di[s] cretionary schemes. This *right* to a re-education (recurren[t] education, perhaps) grant, would be the second major life chance for improving the condition of women.

Adult education is in fact the only sector in which wome[n] predominate – 58 per cent of all registered students in extra[-] mural university classes and WEA, and 73 per cent of student[s] on non-vocational adult education courses in the FE sector i[n] 1975 (DES *Statistics of Education, 1975*, Vol. 3, Tables 70, 74[).] The full DES statistics are worth further study. Unlike schoo[l] and vocational FE, adult education has narrowed the curricula[r] gap of sextyping and is a vital bridge link for women to to[p] up their deficiencies, either for general educational reasons o[r] as recruitment qualifications for the next stage. In 1975, 5,27[3] women (7,274 men) were for example studying physical science[s] in adult education outside the LEA sector – almost certainly i[n] fact as a basis for recruitment to further vocational courses.

The adult education sector is well documented elsewhere[,] including the dedicated and imaginative provision of the adul[t] education centres, maintained by LEAs, WEA, and extra-mura[l] departments in universities, in which women are the main bene[-] ficiaries.[4] Not only do they study the widest range of subjects[,] crafts and skills that any European country can offer, it ha[s] been the adult education centres which have most experimente[d] with confidence-raising courses for older women, the better t[o] equip them for both work and community development. Adul[t] education has pioneered training of pre-school playgrou[p] eaders; and this is the only sector to take education to where people are, instead of expecting them to come to us. Classes in village halls, factories, clinics, and Women's Institutes and Townswomen's Guilds supplement school and college-based classes needing more sophisticated resources. But it has to be said that, although of both students and tutors, most are women, we do not sufficiently reach working-class woman, the inarticulate, the cut-off housewife without transport (whether on an ll-served housing estate or in a rural village), the single women ied at home to elderly dependents, the one-parent mum with chool-age children. Evidence of the Russell Committee from 1969–73, while it included interesting experimental work, admitted that the majority of students were middle class or what might be called 'skilled artisan'. The work is not less worthwhile because it is helping a limited range of women whose need is great and whose life is much enriched. It is simply yet another to her who hath shall be given'. We have yet to find the breakthrough threshold for the many others unreached.

I quote below, a housewife speaking in the 1930s to Margery Spring Rice in a survey on the health of 1,250 married women of the poorer families. Lest readers question its topical relevance, almost identical outbursts were poured out to me by women rehoused from the security of inner-city terraces onto a depressed council estate in the North in 1975 ('I daren't not be in when Jim comes in from the works for his tea').

> 'I believe myself that one of the biggest difficulties we mothers have is our husbands do not realise we ever need any leisure time. My life for many years consisted of being penned in a kitchen 9 feet square, every fourteen months a baby ... So many of our men think we should not go out until the children are grown up. We do not want to be neglecting the home but we do feel we like to have a little look round the shops, or if we go to the clinic we can just have a few minutes ... It isn't the men are unkind. It is the old idea we should always be at home.' (Spring Rice 1939:94)

Two factors have changed: two have not. With modern knowledge of contraception, few if any women now need to bear the killing burden of 'every fourteen months a baby'; and while most of the 1,250 women in 1935 shared then the restrictiveness of being penned in a tiny kitchen, few modern housewives are so constrained. But the implicit guilt of 'going out before the children grow up', and the expectation that the wife will always be at home – when Joe wants her – are still very recognizable and still die harder in some groups of women in the poorer families, in the North especially, than the emancipated, well educated women predominantly from the South who are the major feminist voices, often realize. Rather like the principle of Weight Watchers or Alcoholics Anonymous, the great contribution of unstructured women's groups and collectives, is the sharing of experience and of what seems like guilt, of inadequacy, of insufficiency. The mere realization that twenty other women feel, experience, and act the same as we do gives us immediate relief and scales down the problems to more manageable and less daunting size.

The need to help housebound women to their first step in re education – and access to the external world – is as real today as in Margery Spring Rice's 1939 survey. Ann Oakley, writing in 1974, even quotes one of her working housewives as regarding home as a prison, and life as chained:

'I think I regard my home as a prison; I did say that to Dr Robinson once. He said I was a very insecure person. But to me it *is* a prison because I'm not allowed freedom on my own bat. My husband can come and go as he pleases. Like Saturday for example, he's going to watch Fulham play football, but if I came home and said I was going on an outing – like a work outing – I wouldn't be allowed to go. I say to him: "You've got your freedom – it's only fair that I should go out", and he says, "It's all right for a man, but it's not all right for a woman".'
(Oakley 1977:150)

The lost generations

If under-achievement is still with today's girls, how much more with yesterdays' – who are still today's women. In over a third of our LEAs as late as 1958, the selection rate for grammar school education was as low as 15 per cent. As late as 1959 at least eight rural counties and three large urban authorities still had children in unreorganized, all-age schools. Secondary modern schools rarely had sixth forms before about 1965. Three quarters of yesterday's girls left school at fifteen or before

After all, only 12 per cent of girls remained at school beyond the school-leaving age in 1952; only 16 per cent in 1956; only 25 per cent in 1967. The remainder left at fifteen plus, without any examination successes as a key to future retraining – unless they have been able to study again since. One policy attitude, which hinders the concept of recurrent education, is the traditional prestige of the full-time route, equated with, as a rule, advanced study, and to which our rationale of resource-allocation is weighted. Despite however the Cinderella-status of the non-vocational sector, it is here that some of the newer approaches have mushroomed, meeting new demands with (as usual) minimal resources.

The needs of older women not yet ready to consider examination or vocational courses are beginning to be met by a variety of new programmes, of which only one or two characteristic examples can be given. Hatfield Polytechnic's *New Opportunities for Women* ten-week introductory bridging course for women returners has now led on to the establishment of a part-time degree course at Hatfield. The experimental project has led to widely differing 'Now' courses of which Newcastle University's Department of Adult Education course is particularly interesting, being arranged in co-operation with the Open University (the original provision has expanded to four courses). Similarly the *Fresh Horizons* part-time course at the London City Literary Institute for housewives, which was also a bridging course, has now been extended to include a full-time course. Both aim to encourage progress to an institution of higher education. Perhaps the most far reaching is the *Open College* concept of Nelson and Colne CFE in the North West, offering mature women and men up to thirty different study units using the resources of three other CFEs and a polytechnic and the validation of the University of Lancaster.

There are, however, severe problems of finance and resources. Because of the vulnerable status of adult and part-time further education as allegedly 'non-mandatory' the severe cuts in public expenditure since 1970 have fallen disproportionately on part-time and non-vocational education, cutting back opportunities for women in the one sector which they can reach and for which no formal qualifications are needed. It is, in my view, the duty of the Secretary of State to monitor the cuts that local authorities and University Extra Mural Departments and the

Worker's Educational Association (WEA) have had to levy on the adult education sector, because of the recession and because it is (wrongly) regarded as discretionary, and to plan a positive programme, in co-operation with the new Committee for Adult and Continuing Education, to extend opportunities for adults – men as well as women – who need their second chance. Most, after all, never had their first chance at all in the educational poverty of the 1950s.

I unshakeably believe that Section 41 of the 1944 Act, quoted earlier, lays a *duty* on government to provide adult education at the level of demand; and is not a permissive power. If government in general is serious about investing in equality for women, and if any Labour government in particular believes in Tawney's doctrine that:

> 'Capricious educational inequalities which make it impossible for the nation to develop the full power of its children, are not merely, as they always were, offensive to humanity and good sense; they are an economic burden which we cannot afford to carry.'
>
> (WEA 1934)

then government must protect such few rungs in the ladder as will safeguard the adults who were not able as children to overcome capricious inequalities. Adult education, albeit partly culture-centred, has made great strides in the last five years in diagnosing and developing schemes to reach the educationally and socially disadvantaged – where they are. For the first time we are in sight of real contact with, and help for, those rejected by the rest of the education system. And gradually the move from culture classes to unstructured community confidence building is breaking through to women in need. Any special concentration on needs of adult women cannot allow with detached complacency the half destruction of the adult education service that many have taken twenty years to develop into outgoing community development. Alas for the days of specific percentage grants. A 50 per cent government grant for every £1,000 spent on adult education programmes aimed at drawing women back into outward, non-domestic life, would transform most adult education services.

Recurrent education

There is not only a growing consciousness that the needs of special groups as we constantly identify them, for second-chance education or for retraining, would be met by a planned system of recurrent education, involving periods of paid educational leave and the principles of client-credits to be used at intervals and academic credits to be given for modular and intermittent study. There is also a recognition that structural changes in society – reshaping of industry, changes in employment patterns, more dual career families – will create demands for new patterns of education.

In the forefront of these is the Open University, with four characteristics that make its courses both suitable for and accessible to mature students in general, to women in particular; and to women at home. It uses distance tuition, highly structured teaching units, and television and radio. It does not necessarily require formal entry qualifications. Its degrees can be taken over a period of years; and its cost is proportionately less than other forms of higher education. Naomi McIntosh, Pro-Vice-Chancellor, writing in 1973, said:

'Many people, as the Open University started its courses in 1971, feared that it might become "a haven for housebound *Guardian* housewives". Others viewed the expansion of educational opportunities for women as a priority somewhat akin to the problem of expanding the opportunities for that other notable majority group – the working class.'

(McIntosh 1973:10)

In the event, 27 per cent of the first-year students were women. Interestingly, the proportion of applications from women rose from 30 per cent in 1970 to 42·6 per cent in 1973. It was 41·9 per cent in 1976. The OU has tried to develop a policy of positive discrimination towards women, particularly to encourage recruitment to science-based courses, because it recognized that its early pattern of application and recruitment seemed to produce a higher wastage. In the early years, at least, women finally both registered at a higher rate and persisted better in their studies. Since the 1973 study the OU has developed a very creative policy towards not only degree but foundation and post-experience courses; and on discovering that fewer women than men had heard of the OU, developed advertisement campaigns directed at female readers and viewers.

The work of the OU is by now well known and its 'lifeline' relevance obvious – what is less obvious is the recurrent indirect discrimination that entitles full-time university students to complete grant aid, but OU students only to the cost of annual summer schools and minimal book and travel grants (if the LEA so chooses – the latter are again discretionary). The whole ethos of disadvantage and 'non respectability' which surrounds part-time study is a root cause of much indirect discrimination in our resource allocation, and should be attacked at policy level. Possible further policy developments are included in the concluding chapter. Before then the situation and roles of teaching staff are discussed.

SEVEN

Women and teaching

'Dux femina facti'
(A woman the head of their enterprise.)

VIRGIL (Aeneid IV)

'and gladly wolde he lerne, and gladly teche.'

CHAUCER, Prologue (Clerk of Oxenforde)

The most important single educational life-chance a child has, as she clambers up her educational ladder, is probably the quality and vision – or the limitations – of her teachers. No single influence for conservation or change, for creating insurmountable hurdles or new opportunities, will ever be as seminal as that of the teachers in our schools – of both sexes.

Back to June 1945 and the crucial 'scholarship' interview

which would unlock me from four years of further boredom at the all-age unreorganized village school.[1] I concentrated hard. 'And what', enquired the grammar-school headmistress, 'do you want to be when you grow up?'. My reply was as unhesitating as it was decisive. 'I want to be a teacher.' 'Do you? Why?' The question left me (unusually) speechless. I had no idea, only a long, unexamined certainty assuredly not born of the unhappy example of the cliff-top school. My family had staffed a fair number of hospitals over the years; but not an identifiable pedagogue among them. Yet already, at eleven, the adult road to happiness seemed to lead me back to a classroom.

Teaching has in fact traditionally attracted girls of proportionately higher academic ability than the equivalent male entrants to colleges of education. As *Table 6(1)* showed, a very high proportion of girls with three 'A' levels (15–17 per cent) and with two 'A' levels (41–7 per cent) entered teacher training in 1967, eleven years ago, instead of going to university like the 68 per cent of boys with 3 'A' levels and 26 per cent of boys with two 'A' levels, who aimed at graduate rather than certificate qualifications. It is reasonable to hypothesize from the figures that the average woman teacher student was more able than the average male teacher student, and that proportionately more women teachers qualifying were in the top ability band than men students (because more men and fewer women opted for universities and advanced FE). It follows that more women should have been capable of reaching the top of the teaching profession; and they have not. A later section on the staffing of our schools and colleges shows indeed a disturbing decline, in fact, of top women in the education service.

It is perhaps important to stress that the presence of women in the leadership of schools and colleges is not only necessary in order to offer women themselves promotion to challenging personal development and economic equality. It is crucial that both girls and boys actually *see* women in leadership, management, government, making decisions in their daily lives, if we are to break the cycle of under-achievement. As long as children see men taking the top posts, decisions, and higher pay, and women tacitly accepting this from a constant middle role of an Aristotelian 'golden mean', children will believe what they see and not what we say. They will credit the evidence of their eyes and not our exhortations that women are equal to men, have equal talent, and equal responsibility and rights.

I believe it is important for us to understand the undercurrents beneath present trends if we are to disentangle the different reasons for needing a major restructuring of the teaching profession, with both men and women evenly represented at all stages from pre-school to professors, primaries to polytechnics – and probationers to principals.

I see these as having roots in the past, as do so many of the issues and problems that influence equality or discrimination. A brief historical flashback provides a framework for understanding the present.

There is a growing and extremely well documented literature on the history of the main development of the teaching profession and, latterly, on the specific question of women teachers, and there is little point in summarizing it here at any length. It is indeed a matter of some regret that academics in education have not studied in equal depth the problem of the employment and promotion prospects of the non-professional, non-academic woman whom we have turned out from our schools so ill-equipped to achieve the equal pay, the free recruitment, and the relative mobility which teaching has offered so many. Asher Tropp's historical account of the teaching profession (1957) has now been overtaken by an admirably thorough and revealing analysis of women teachers since the turn of the century by Geoffrey Partington (1976), while Hilsum and Start's research (1974) analyses in considerable detail some of the reasons why women and men teachers are (or are not) promoted.

Women's commitment to teaching is a tradition second only to her domestic role, throughout recorded history and in both East and West, and has acquired an aura of 'inborn gifts' and extended maternality that seems ineradicable. It is curiously noticeable that from the earliest days of state education, women have gravitated to and concentrated on younger children, on the infant and junior schools, the elementary and non-advanced sectors within the profession. In Victorian times this was of course for practical as well as attitudinal reasons; women themselves had such a poor basic education that they were not yet competent to teach advanced work – hence the pioneering of Frances Buss, Dorothea Beale, Emily Davies. Understandable though it was that women should settle then for less exacting, less advanced work (which was still an improvement on the largely unpaid drudgery of governess employment), it is sad that women teachers should so quickly have set a pattern, which we now seem unable to break, of more limited career horizons, concentration on the lower rungs of responsibility, and over-docile acceptance of less well-paid teaching posts.

There is nothing new about the unthinking path which women tread to the classroom. We were slow to see alternatives from the start.

'In June 1900, a hundred students went down from a famous women's college. 75 of them were going to teach and all the rest were going home to arrange the flowers. Six years later, another 100 were going down; but this time only 50 were going to be teachers; two were to be journalists, one a doctor in India, one an expert on foods, one a hospital almoner, one a missionary, one an author – and the rest were going home. By 1913 the teachers had dwindled to 13%. By 1932, only 22% were teachers, and none were going back home to idleness, and 10 were to be barristers and 10 journalists.

(Biscoe 1932:7)

At the turn of the century in 1904, women were in the majority in the elementary schools – 69·5 per cent of all certificated teachers and a reassuring 56 per cent of all elementary headships. By 1914 the elementary sector had not altered; but already the different pattern in the secondary grammar schools was becoming evident (later to become all too familiar). The total teaching force was fairly evenly divided between the sexes – about 52 per cent to 48 per cent in favour of men; but men accounted for 65·7 per cent of headships, women only 34·3 per cent (HM Government 1919:20). This again was a causal relationship, since women had not been educated to an advanced level of personal education in sufficient numbers, themselves to be competent to teach advanced secondary education.

Before the Second World War, 66 per cent of the teaching profession were women (and it is important to remember that they were then *all* unmarried). By 1951, the teaching force (with the help of the 1947 Emergency Training Scheme which planned places for 9,000 men and 4,000 women being demobilized or otherwise specially recruited) had reached 225,000, split again between two thirds women (140,250) and one third men (DES 1963). One extraordinary symptom however of governmental double-think was that the Ministry planned teacher supply and expansion on twin dimensions of 'women teachers' and 'men teachers' long after two World Wars had illustrated women's interchangeability with men in the labour market when need arose.

The characteristics and distribution of women teachers

The normative approach, which I questioned in the context of children in schools, is in my view equally inappropriate when discussing teachers. Their influence on children and on their personal opportunities, will be more affected by Dahrendorf's inequalities of 'social differentiations of rank' and 'social stratification of status' than by their sex alone. Characteristics of status such as full-time:part-time; married:single; graduate:non-graduate, are more divisive than sex alone. Women teachers trained in rural, single-sex colleges before 1955 may have more in common with older men teachers, from the same background, than with younger women leaving a multidisciplinary department of a modern urban polytechnic. Although we tend to discuss teachers by sector and by sex, women teachers are more idiosyncratic in relation to their various status factors. Whether or not they have dependents is more relevant than whether they are married or single. Anyone who doubts this should read *Please Ms* with its thoughtful, if sad, commentary on the difficulties of unmarried teacher mothers (One Parent Families 1975). It has taken the implications of the *Sex Discrimination Act, 1975*, to lend power to the arms of those of us who have had to fight for years against the unthinking sacking of unmarried women teachers with children, regardless of their individual personal circumstances. (I have yet to see the putative father, often also in teaching, sacked, even when known.)

Similarly, the distinction between *full-time* and *part-time* is a more influential factor than sex alone, although we know that most part-timers are in fact women. *Age* is also highly relevant because the educational environment from which the teachers were produced will have heavily conditioned their attitudes as well as their skills.

The inexorable path to teaching is still hammered out. Fogelman's selection of sixth-form opinion includes some stringent criticisms by students of sex-typed career assumptions by their former schools.

'Emphasis was put on the teaching profession for anyone who chose to go to college. As teaching did not interest me, I found that it was rather difficult to find any information regarding other courses.'

'Little help was given by my school to the pupil who did not want to take up teaching. I found myself "one alone" among 50 to 60 girls all going on to college/university. I know that many had no particular leaning towards teaching, but just drifted into it because of no knowledge of an alternative.'

'I have found that many of the students at colleges of education are not there because they want to teach, but because their schools and home persuaded them to go to college, and because they themselves had no other ideas of what to do.'

(Fogelman 1972:10–11)

McNamara (1972) quotes extensively to support the 'compatible with marriage' syndrome, while his own research into a sample of student teachers confirms that a majority of women students make the decision to teach at a relatively early school age. What we do not know however is how many would have still done so if persuaded by careers teachers that business management, administration, medicine, dentistry, consultancy roles as architects, planners, designers, journalism, are all equally compatible with marriage and children. Given, of course, some of the sex-role restructuring we discussed in earlier chapters.

The distribution of women teachers in schools

All figures that follow are for England and Wales unless otherwise shown. In the primary sector women dominate overall by more than three to one, but when the teaching force is analysed by type of school, decidedly different patterns emerge. *Table 7(1)* gives the total distribution of teachers for 1975 which shows clearly the concentration of men in the junior sector, although we now have about 2,400 male teachers in the infant sector – a welcome breakthrough on the lines discussed earlier.

Table 7(1) Distribution of teachers – primary schools 1975
(a) *Numbers*

	men	women	total
infant	324	37,507	37,381
first	2,062	15,305	17,367
junior with infant	21,112	60,442	81,554
first and middle	1,086	3,109	4,195
junior	18,506	33,435	51,941
	43,090	149,798	192,888
Middle deemed primary	2,978	5,262	8,240

(b) *Sex balance in each sector*

	men %	women %
infant	0·9	99·1
first	11·9	88·1
junior	25·9	74·1
first and middle	25·9	74·1
junior	35·6	64·37
middle	36·1	63·9

(c) *Overall sex balance*

men %	women %
22·3	77·7

Source: DES *Statistics of Education 1975, Schools,* Table 14, (excluding independent schools)

When however the figures are compared with those in *Tables 7(2)* and(3) following, it will be seen that although men represented only 22 per cent of primary teachers overall in 1974 they carried 57 per cent of headships and 40 per cent of deputy headships – the leadership role. (They also represented 63 per cent of scale 5 and 41·0 per cent of scale 4 posts.)

Table 7(2) Primary school teachers 1974

	men	women	total
all teachers	45,667	148,414	194,081
headships	13,565	10,215	23,780
deputy headships	7,092	10,788	17,880
senior master/mistress	22	47	69
Scale 5	48	28	76
Scale 4	774	1,096	1,870

Percentages of relevant group by sex

	men	women
all teachers	23·5	76·5
headships	57·0	43·0
deputy headships	40·0	60·0
sentior master/mistress	32·0	68·0
Scale 5	63·0	37·0
Scale 4	41·0	59·0

Source: DES *Statistics of Education 1974*, Vol. 4, *Teachers*

Table 7(3) Decline in proportion of women in senior posts, schools 1965–74

	Sex balance – Percentages			
	1965		1974	
Teachers	male %	female %	male %	female %
Primary				
all teachers	26·0	74·0	22·3	77·7
headships	49·2	50·8	57·0	43·0
deputy headships	37·4	62·6	40·0	60·0
Secondary				
all teachers	58·8	41·2	56·5	43·5
headships	76·3	23·7	81·2	18·8
deputy headships	60·0	40·0	65·0	35·0
second master/mistress	33·2	66·8	34·0	66·0

Source: DES *Statistics of Education 1965–74: Teaching staff.*

Table 7(4) Distribution of teachers – secondary schools, 1975
a) Numbers

Schools	men	women	total
modern	20,191	16,665	36,856
grammar	11,547	8,384	19,931
technical	580	438	1,018
comprehensive	80,428	58,190	138,618
other	3,025	2,504	5,529
	115,771	86,181	201,952
middle deemed secondary	3,637	4,001	7,638
direct grant grammar	3,533	2,767	6,300

b) Sex balance in each sector

	men %	women %
modern	54·8	45·2
grammar	57·9	42·1
technical	57·0	43·0
comprehensive	58·0	42·0
other	54·7	45·3
middle deemed secondary	47·6	52·4
direct grant grammar	56·1	43·9

c) Overall sex balance

men %	women %
56·9	43·1

Source : DES Statistics of Education 1975, Schools and Teachers.

More disturbing to both the prospects of women teachers and the implication for children's attitudes, the proportion of women in leadership roles has actually declined from 1965 to 1974 and provisional statistics since then suggest a continuing trend of decline. The adverse implications of this are obvious.

The decline in women holding headships and senior position (despite an increase overall in women staff) is, however, much more serious (see *Table 7(3)*), partly because it is more acute than in the primary sector and partly because it is, as we have seen, even more important for adolescent girls to identify with leadership models. (The second master/mistress question is discussed separately below.)

The secondary pattern is both very different and more complex. *Table 7(4)* gives the distribution of teachers by type of school. Women are in an overall minority, although the sex balance is generally more even.

How pupils see staff

We have already noted the feminization of the pre-school and primary sector – and the importance to girls of having both male and female models with whom they can identify in their formative years. But the polarization of roles between women staff as supportive, subordinate, maternal, and caring, and men as the leaders, heads, active members of staff (football, outdoor pursuits, school journeys), and dealing with boys and older children, is not only constant, but increasing. (In 1975 there were in any event no male nursery teachers and only a small minority of men teachers in infant and first schools.) In those schools with a woman head (43 per cent in 1974) pupils will have seen women in authority and in control; but those coming from schools with a headmaster, and probably also men teaching primary science and football (the existing 'male' preserves) may have already begun to conceptualize women as the supporters, not the leaders. It is true that, of the graduate scientists in primary schools in 1974, 653 were men and 1,000 were women – although this is still a disproportionate male bias given the overall proportion of women to men in primary education. But in fact, 311 out of the 653 men were physicists or chemists, while only 235 out of the 1,000 women were either, while on the other hand, 501 women science teachers were biologists; but only 118 men. The association of women with natural and men with physical sciences is unlikely to be significantly shaken as long as this pattern persists so early in children's education, which partly explains also the masculine-oriented primary cience projects we more frequently see. Similarly, of the 1,416 rimary French teachers, 1,024 were women (DES *Statistics of ducation*, Vol. 4, *Teachers*: Table 17), implicitly registering with both boys and girls that this is a field in which women xcel. While it is comforting to be able to establish that girls nay expect to achieve high standards like their teachers, it waters the seeds sown in earlier years and starts the germination of assumptions which are taken on to the contrasting secondary chools.

How Alice or Jane will see men and women teachers when hey put on their new secondary school uniform in September will depend on their school – single sex, mixed, grammar, modrn, comprehensive. They would of course expect to see a irls' school led and mainly staffed by women (although eleven of the seven hundred or so girls' schools, leaving out indeendent schools, do have a headmaster!). What they may not xpect is that the 15 per cent male teachers out of twenty-five housand in girls' schools should predominantly be heads of epartments, and/or teaching maths and science, mirroring more harply the growing primary pattern. The message is implicitly earned again – they are male fields. (Yet the girls' schools do ucceed in encouraging more girls to read science than mixed chools. Do women science teachers push girls more? Do nen teachers in girls' schools take those posts in the irst place precisely because they want to encourage girls to levelop?)

The pattern varies considerably moreover between different ypes of co-educational schools. In mixed grammar schools, men utnumber women by nearly two to one. In secondary modern chools the balance is nearly even (fifteen to twelve thousand). 3ut in comprehensive schools the proportion of men is steadily rowing, currently nearly 60 per cent to women's 40 per cent verall. Suddenly, girls are seeing a world, as they adjust to the ew environment, in which women not only are not the main nfluence, but they are generally in a minority. At least, nearly alf of all primary schools still have women heads and deputy eads; but fewer than one fifth of secondary schools have headnistresses and only a third have women deputies. This is not only important because it sets a pattern for girls (and boys), but ecause it leads to a quite different ethos in mixed schools in articular, which are male dominated, from those where both men and women share the leadership. There is a typical pattern of organization which has important implications in the context of both sex typing and the hidden curriculum. I am quoting in full because Bennett's analysis is absolutely typical of so many schools in all four LEA areas where I have administered education, and in the areas surveyed in 1968 and more recently. Bennett appears to be writing for an audience of teachers, educational planners, advisers. He postulates the following as a structure which he sees as not open to question. I believe both teachers and parents will recognize this pattern. Both of the schools quoted below are co-educational.

'It may be helpful to look at the formal staff structure of two hypothetical schools. Each school of course has a headmaster. In the first, and English school, there is a deputy headmaster who deputises for the head as necessary and who is in charge of the general day to day running of the school. He is responsible for the discipline of boys in the school and for the supervision of male student-teachers in conjunction with heads of departments. A senior mistress is responsible for the discipline of girls and supervises female student-teachers. She also co-ordinates house matters and has a particular responsibility for social functions in the school. She has a scheme of general administrative jobs.' (Bennett 1972:46)

Bennett's book is aimed, one might add, at the in-service training market.

The phraseology is revealing. The head is male 'of course'. The assumption of complete sex typing of men dealing with boys and women dealing with girls is not questioned – either in the context of discipline or in relation to supervision. Typically the senior mistress is landed with the social side – an extension of the domestic syndrome since it usually means organizing food, drink, transport, and support services.

'In the second school, a Scottish one, the duties of a deputy head are similar ... *he* deputises when necessary ... There are 5 assistant headmasters in the school and 3 of them act as heads of school ... It happens that the head of lower school is a woman *and so* she has been asked by the headmaster to look after the discipline of the girls in the school. She has also been asked by him to take part in Official Functions, acting as hostess when the school has visitors ...'

(Bennett 1972:50, my italics)[2]

Bennett's Scottish contrast is equally interesting. All five assistant headmasters are male. It appears to be accidental (and unusual?) for the head of lower school to be a woman, but as a result she is landed with girls' discipline and appears not to deal with boys – even in lower school? She too, predictably temporarily replaces the head's wife, by hostessing his school functions as his wife does the domestic events – instead of directing affairs.

Colleges of education

The training institutions which produce the teachers in the first place are of central importance not only in producing the basic teaching force but as potential agents of change, and as influences in inservice re-education of teachers. It is depressing, therefore, to see the same position mirrored yet again as in the schools sector – an overall predominance of women, their concentration in junior posts, but the steady, not to say rapid, decline in the proportion of women in leadership. During the rapid expansion of teacher training in the 1950s and 1960s, women outnumbered men by two to one overall, despite a higher growth rate for men (Ministry of Education 1964):

Students in training – colleges and departments of education

year	M	W	total
1953 – 54	6,825	19,858	26,683
1956 – 57	7,127	21,323	28,450
1959 – 60	10,571	24,013	34,584
1963 – 64	18,510	39,168	57,678
percentage growth 1953–63	171·21%	97·24%	116·16%

The position has been, however, reversed in the training colleges. In direct proportion to their reorganization from single sex to co-educational, from small rural to larger urban, and from single discipline teacher education to multi-disciplinary

223

higher education, women's representation in all levels, but notably the higher levels has steadily fallen:

Decline in proportion of women holding senior posts in Colleges of Education (teacher training)

| | Percentage of all posts | | | | | |
| | 1965 | | 1970 | | 1973 | |
	M %	F %	M %	F %	M %	F %
all lecturers	52.9	47·1	66·7	33·3	68·3	31·7
deputy principal	31·8	68·2	51·0	49·0	59·1	40·9
principal	36·9	63·1	45·9	54·1	57·0	43·0

Source: DES *Statistics of Education 1973*

Two-thirds of all principals and deputies were hitherto women; now nearly two-thirds are men. For the decade 1953–1963, the women's ratio was even higher: 71 per cent of all lectureships in 1953; 61·5 per cent in 1960; 55 per cent in 1962; 32 per cent in 1973. A reduction from two-thirds to one-third in twenty years can only mean a further decline in top women in teacher training. One alleged reason is that the women, carrying as many do, domestic responsibility, fight shy of the work commitment of reorganization, and of the staff-room conflicts and decision-making required. I question this. I suspect overt and indirect sex discrimination by both men and women on governing bodies who reproduce unfounded doubts and assumptions. ('But can she handle the difficult men in the staff-room? What would you do, Mrs Brown, if your children were ill at the peak of the summer term?') When did someone last ask *Mr* Brown? Moreover, a substantial number of women in teacher training are in fact single or have grown up children.

The time has surely come for some direct and decisive monitoring of the position of women in the policy making levels of education – or where will the leaders of the future be? Three sectors – and all in decline. But the situation in further and higher education is, if possible, worse. The position of women in further education for example is the least favourable of all

grade	men	women
principals	660	33
vice principals	501	39
heads of depts	2,371	225
readers	35	1
principal lecturers	2,513	126
senior lecturers	8,718	714
lecturer II	17,515	2,713
lecturer I	16,426	5,171
assistant lecturer	1,842	1,172

ource: DES *Statistics of Education* 1974: Vol. 4, Table 3a

ctors, as *Table 7(5)* illustrates. Only a handful of women hold
p posts at all and the latest statistics show a decline in women
rincipals from 8·3 per cent in 1961 to 4·0 per cent in 1975, a
ow familiar pattern.

In universities fewer than 10 per cent of professors are
omen; only 6 per cent of all readers and senior lecturers; and
omen account for only 10 per cent of all university staff
DES *Statistics of Education 1974*). Women academics like Tessa
lackstone and Margherita Rendel are more qualified than I to
rite of the masculine ethos of Academe, not to say its hidden
iscriminations. We ought perhaps in justice however to register
hat although higher education was the first barrier to be
reached by the Victorian and Edwardian pioneers (in terms of
tudy; Oxford and Cambridge refused women degrees until well
nto the twentieth century), our great-grandmothers would be
lisheartened to see that today women academics are the least
vell represented of any sector of education in relation to male
eers.

This is of greater significance educationally than the simple
ase of personal injustice to women academics. It means the
ack of an adequate feminine (or feminist) voice in the constant
estructuring of higher education, and the lack of enough in-
pired women to lift the horizons of women students to seek
dvanced positions in life and – one hopes – to care about lifting

the position of the less fortunate in life who did not get throug
the net.

My discreet spark on behalf of my university colleague
nevertheless remains a pale flash, compared with my mor
combustible blaze of frequent indignation at the complacer
chauvinism of schools and FE colleges who declare that all
right with their world – which houses not the 8 per cent o
so of girls who make the graduation lawns, but the 90 per cer
of girls who are steadily feeling their way towards greate
understanding of their mothers' frustrations, are determined no
to follow them, but lack insightful people in their environmer
to teach them how to think clearly, and to aim higher. If th
most highly educated 1 per cent of women in Academe canno
fight their battle on their own ground, it would augur ill fo
the rest of us. The compelling voice is still needed back at th
ranch.

There is no question but that there must be discriminator
practices in the staffing and promotion policies of the educatio
service, and it is difficult to see how far these will be expose
until both women staff in each sector and the Women's Right
groups of the teachers' unions (of which NATFHE is by far th
most thoroughly researched and most belligerent) rouse all thei
field forces to challenge practices that prevent women from
attaining leadership (like regarding leadership in polytechnic
as immutably linked with engineering or computer studies an
not with training in personnel and welfare studies?). The battl
for crèches in colleges and polytechnics has seen reversals ever
in its preliminary skirmishes – while more sports halls and dis
cotheques spring up like mushrooms. A policy of social priority

Hidden barriers

It will be clear from earlier illustrations that men and wome
teachers see their roles differently and that men in leadershi
tend to see women's role as subordinate, caring, and more peri
pheral to central and major planning. In the same way in whic
one can identify a 'hidden curriculum' of structural and at
titudinal constraints on girls, a collection of hidden barriers
less obvious but more pervasive than the alleged simplisti
causes of women's under-achievement (marriage, family, breal
in employment) can be detected by a keen and interested eye

They also see themselves differently according to their sex and domestic status. A. Walters' study of 104 mature women students in Surrey suggested that even the women on higher status jobs and on vocational courses described themselves first in terms of their domestic role (e.g. married, mother of three) rather than their past working life or present external role (former teacher, student). This is continuing evidence of women's ambivalence to the loyalty to an economic and productive role (Walters 1975).

Hidden constraints also include the difficulty of married women and of single women with dependents in taking part in training courses, whether evening classes at the Teachers' Centre or longer residential courses. It must be said that unconscious chauvinism on the part of the mainly male Assistant Education Officers and Principal Advisers who share out the diminishing in-service education budget in times of recession in selecting for courses, is not unknown ('She'll only be leaving soon to have a family' or 'she'll miss half of the course if the children are ill'). Since many women teachers are married to men teachers it is worth remarking indeed that the most effective key to unlock one door for married women is for LEAs and heads to make it clear to their male staff as part of in-service education that they are expected to divide the staying-home-to-look-after-Jeannie absences evenly with their wives. A head teacher can in fact often be spared more easily for a day than a class teacher – but his wife, pegged on Scale 2 because she followed his promotion, will be expected to cope with all domestic crises still. More attitude changing is needed here.

Women teachers are often less frequently groomed for seniority and for responsibility by their mainly male heads. Their apparently natural gravitation to pastoral work, tutor groups, and counselling places them on the tramlines for a senior mistress post, not a future headship, for which attendance at administrative meetings, local and regional policy discussions, timetabling experience, and curricular restructuring in reorganizing schools, is a better foundation. But a deeper question may be, why do not more apply for senior posts – as many do not who are qualified? Some suggest that women staff tend to create self barriers unconsciously. Evidence is quoted of the self-perception of women as lacking in confidence; less willing to apply fifty times for promotion, but cutting out after five because of rejection; less sure of capacity to tackle work several jumps ahead rather than one step up; less willing (perhaps rightly?) to relinquish the personal satisfaction of classroom teaching and pupil contact, for the chimaera of administration (c.f. Ollerenshaw and Flude 1974; Assoc. of Assistant Mistresses 1976; Hilsum and Start 1974).

For married women, the blind acceptance that they must follow husband's career promotion (and not he hers, if it occurred first) is a major hurdle, but one to which the remedy lies as much in their hands as in their husbands'. One small but extremely interesting survey of the problems of women teachers, described the cost to women held back by husbands' career as:

'nineteen years in one school on Scale 1' and
'five full-time and one part-time jobs in seventeen years.'[3]

It is curiously interesting how, also, the Cinderella hierarchy of subjects operates indirectly to the detriment of women teachers both in financial terms and in confidence-building and their personal development (or otherwise) for leadership. After twenty years of school reorganization, since the mid 1950s, it is daunting to see how, even though the shortage areas of teachers (the demand factor) has shifted constantly, the rank order of Burnham top allowances and of prestigious importance in school terms remains constantly in favour of male-dominated areas. It is rarely related to educational and curricular ideologies clearly defined in advance. Thus a typical school of from 1,000–1,500 pupils will possess four or five head of department posts for maths and sciences, often under an overall head of faculty and mostly at scale 4 or 3, to every one allocated for English, languages, the humanities (not only part of core studies but pursued by more pupils overall). Handicraft and technology rank for higher allowances than housecraft and needlework (does equal mean the same?). Economics will frequently outclass history. The logic may be individual; the effect when analysed is that because women dominate the arts subjects and remedial work, they draw lower allowances regardless of size of department or importance of work in the schools' scheme, and women teachers' average salaries tend therefore to be less than men's who have comparable years of service.

To the extent that the conditioning analysed earlier has trained the women of the past that decision-making and conflict are 'unfeminine', it would not be surprising that they eschew the trauma of several years of both, in the task of unceasingly reorganizing schools and colleges. The larger organizations, replacing as they do schools which twenty years ago averaged from 400–850 in size, mostly homogeneous in intake, and often single sex, have produced many new dimensions which require training and new attitudes. Decision and conflict acquire a new sharpness as opposing ideologies have to be discussed, stitched, welded, or moulded into a coherent whole. (Mixed ability or streaming? Integrated studies or history and civics?)

Supervision of 160 mixed staff represents a very different scale and cast of management problems from the oversight of three separate and again, identifiable, groups of fifty in three small schools. Requirements for senior posts in both larger schools and merging colleges and polytechnics include vastly increased reading of local reports, internal documents, the endless flow of government national discussion documents or Commission reports.

The gradual integration of teacher training into polytechnics is also steadily reducing opportunities for women staff. Of all trends, the removal of single sex institutions seems to me to be the major adverse factor affecting women staff. Believe in co-education as I do, I cannot but believe that if we continue our present headlong flight to totally unisex provision, we should consider two courses of action concurrently. First, some nationally validated research into the performance and skills of men and women in co-educational establishments with a view to counter remedies against under-achievement and polarization of roles; and second, a deliberate manpower/womanpower planning strategy for teacher redeployment which will ensure more balanced recruitment to the different sectors and levels of education. If we do *not* develop a national policy of deploying teachers in schools and colleges towards a policy of equality we will soon end up with an all-male leadership, thus turning full circle of Victorian times. Conversely, no true educationalist can accept unquestioningly any variation of 'the best person for the job'. There is meat for a substantial national debate.

The answers are no more simple than the problems. Staff

development programmes, aimed clearly at both sexes, should take special account of women's needs for management experience and retraining. Credit should be given for work not traditionally accepted as an equivalent gift (e.g. home-making) and compensation allowed for the illogicality of career pattern solely caused by sacrifice to husband's promotion. Women returning to teaching who held a scale post before, should be given some incremental benefit and not returned to basic scale, unless there is genuine well founded doubt about present capacity. The child-care problem is well rehearsed – but remains central. Married women who leave for a family should be encouraged to keep up contact, even in-service training while away – with support from the LEA or Training Services Agency for local schemes if need be.

Quota, sex roles, and the Burnham test case

In 1976 the newly introduced provisions of the *Sex Discrimination Act* resulted in our challenging the ruling of the Burnham report on teachers' salaries and conditions, that the third-tier post in co-educational schools had to be of opposite sex to the deputy head. We should be clear that rule was not, in fact, replicated in the Burnham FE report for colleges, the Pelham report on teacher training staff, nor in universities. It was limited to the schools sector for reasons which are not clear if the need for students to have access to both sexes at senior level were upheld.

The argument ran roughly thus. Girls in school need a senior woman at the top to 'look after them', a euphemistic phrase. Boys need a man. Therefore if one already had, for example, a male head and deputy, one needed a woman at third tier – and vice versa. Authorities were legally obliged (they thought) to advertise for the third tier of the opposite sex to the deputy head. Since most heads and deputies are men, the teachers' unions welcomed this as a protection for senior women teachers.

The rationale behind this rule was ambivalent. If the unions on the Burnham Committee really wanted equality, why was it not mandatory to appoint a deputy head of opposite sex to the head – a much more influential move. No way was this conceived. Nor, given an existing male deputy when the head resigned, was it mandatory then to advertise for a woman head-teacher to preserve the alternation. Equality and balance were apparently only designated as necessary at the support, not leadership, levels. Finally, and most specious of all, if the senior master/mistress were ones appointed of deliberately opposite sex to the deputy head, and the latter left, there was no obligation under the original Burnham rule then to restrict the *deputy head* advertisement to the opposite sex to the existing senior master/mistress, so carefully appointed to obtain sex balance. Thus, although in theory the rule preserved a mix at the top of the school, it was only at third tier level, and this automatic alternation vanished whenever the deputy head teacher moved.

In 1976 the Equal Opportunities Commission supported Mrs Castle against Surrey County Council in the industrial tribunal, in a challenge of this Burnham rule on the technical ground that the provisions of the Burnham report were only mandatory in so far as they were covered by the *Remuneration of Teachers Act, 1965*, i.e., were *financial* provisions. The real case being fought behind this technical argument, was, however, the fundamental principle laid down in the *Sex Discrimination Act* that all jobs must be open to both sexes (Section 6) unless a case can be established for a 'genuine occupational qualification' (Section 7). Neither the local authorities nor the teachers' unions could, however, make up their minds whether they were arguing for a preserved quota system (which is now unlawful) or for a 'genuine occupational qualification' for which no case has yet been proven.

Mrs Castle won her case, was appointed senior mistress at her primary school although the deputy head was also a woman, and that particular Burnham rule was removed from the report by the relevant authorities, rightly recognizing the ruling was applicable nationally and not merely to Surrey County Council. The value of the case was that it exposed the whole debate on why both sexes were needed at the top of the school and how this should be achieved. What became immediately clear was the fog of mythology surrounding staffing policies. The preservation of posts for both sexes at the top of the schools can only have originated in the minds of the Burnham Committee from one of two principles; that is a protected promotion avenue for the minority sex in each case (broadly women in secondary

231

schools and men in primary schools) or – in my view more soundly – that it was necessary for the welfare of both boys and girls to have both sexes at the top of the school.

What we did was to call the bluff of the authorities and unions and make them attempt to define which of the principles they thought they were applying. First, to look at the quota angle is to raise the whole principle of professionalism. It is clear from the statistics already given that qualified women and men are not available in equal numbers in all subjects. The fact moreover that substantial numbers of women leave teaching for a period and return after a gap of from 3–10 years, places in question whether as many women as men have the kind of experience (as distinct from the ability) defined by most LEAs and governors as necessary for an early headship or senior post. Imposition of a predetermined quota may and almost certainly would mean a breach of the right to appoint the best candidate for the job. Even the AAM's report on promotion of women teachers confirmed the widely known lack of women applicants for advertised senior posts. Eleven out of 110 applications for headships, eight out ninety-five for head of house; but while the lack of women applicants for head of maths was predictable, the absence of women prepared to take on head of history or head of English – in which the graduate teacher numbers are almost even in history and higher for women in English – must be a matter for especial concern (AAM 1976:3).

The opposite sex rule, if justified on quota grounds, would be impossible to justify logically. It could only be validly applied if made compulsory for all three top tier posts – head, deputy, and senior master/mistress. Supposing it to be applied arbitrarily in 1979. The accident of the then existing pattern of senior staff in each school as at January 1, 1979 (i.e. mostly men) would mean that nine out of ten secondary deputy headships would have to go to women. Since more deputy heads are male, the same thing would apply at third tier. Even if experienced candidates were not available? This would, moreover, predetermine an alternating sex balance in perpetuity on the accidental 1979 model.

The argument then shifts to teachers' roles. How, ask my male headteacher and Chief Education officer colleagues, do I then obtain advice on girls' problems? Who can I place in charge of girls' welfare? This strikes at the root of two fallacies criticized in earlier chapters, that only women can deal with the curricular and pastoral needs of girls and only men with boys; and second, that either sex will look to the same sex or the same person for every problem simply *because* the counsellor is a woman or a man. The curriculum should be common to both sexes and there should be no question of detailing women off to supervise 'girls' courses' or vice versa. Is it suggested that only a senior member of staff in a 1,500 place comprehensive school, can deal with pastoral problems? Demonstrably it is not so. It is, let me stress, crucial that there is the best mix of women and men at all levels, overall, that we can achieve, to avoid the teaching of small children in an excessively feminized environment, and of older children in what often can only be described as girls attending a boys' school and women teaching in a male environment. To designate this sex-balance at senior level on the basis that men and women will each deal only with their own sex is effectively to reject the whole ideology and principles of co-education. It would, even if not invalid psychologically, socially, and developmentally, be logical only if the terms of reference for both sexes were the same. Twenty years of staffing schools has taught me that senior masters, apart from occasionally caning boys, typically deal with school organization, curricular reconstruction, major administration, CSE examining, and resource allocation, while senior mistresses typically deal with social functions, pregnant schoolgirls, difficult parents, coffee for and entertaining of visitors (in my experience), and school attendance. Equal is not held to mean the same here. Any one of these functions can quite adequately be either dealt with by either sex or delegated to an appropriate woman or man on the school staff (PE teacher, head of house, year group leader, class tutor) who happens to have the characteristics needed for the problem. It is interesting that men are regarded as able to deal with girls when appointed as head of maths or science in girls' schools; and women with boys when teaching English and remedial work in boys' schools, as so many do. Matrons in boys' boarding schools are women.

Deeper than the reflex born perhaps of fear of personal misunderstandings in dealing with adolescents of the opposite sex who are past puberty, is the problem of how one reaches balance either without quota, or without definitions of 'genuine occupational qualification' on grounds that the job could not possibly be done by the opposite sex. One quite simple method, would be for appointing bodies to give priority to the minority sex *provided that the successful candidate is equally qualified and suitable.* It has never been wrong to select the person most fitting the idiosyncratic staffing position. It may be that a married woman will bring a maturity, understanding of adolescents, and acquired patience lacking in the younger man with drive. Credit for personal qualities and experience as well as professional background is a perfectly valid additional criterion for selection.

This question affects not only schools and colleges, but the youth service, careers education service, and all of the caring professions where adolescents need counselling as well as the professional service being offered. It is the practical demonstration of the polarity of perceived masculine and feminine qualities and characters that I criticized in the opening chapters. Those responsible for training and in-service education have a direct responsibility to question, to rethink, and to retrain their colleagues in diagnosis and not reflex, in matching personal qualities to pupils' and students' needs, regardless of sex stereotypes.

One important footnote should be recorded. It was a widely held view that the Burnham 'Senior Mistress' rule preserved avenues for promotion for women teachers. This may well be true in the case of comprehensive secondary schools, nine-tenths of whose heads and deputy heads are male. But from 1965 to 1973 (when the rule still operated) women actually *declined* as a proportion of senior mistresses in the primary sector, in secondary schools as a whole, in 'other secondary' schools, and in grammar schools, although they increased in comprehensive and secondary modern schools. It cannot therefore be argued that this intermittently applied quota worked universally in women's favour.

Women or people?

I suggested earlier that we should not generalize about women and men, but about functional status differences – that is, the difference between married and single women, women with and without dependents is more influential than between women and men. A single woman (including divorced, deserted, etc.)

with three children may be more hindered from promotion than a married woman with no children or whose family has grown up. A widower with three children may be equally constrained from promotion-prone activities like residential training courses, leadership of teachers' unions, or take-up of extra curricular duties. This diagnostic approach is supported by the preliminary findings of a study of the Higher Education Research Unit being conducted at LSE into supply and demand of teacher supply (Turnbull and Williams 1974) and which includes an examination of sex differentials in teachers' pay. Women earned generally less than men; but single women earned consistently more than married women. Differentials emerged that crossed the sexes – men graduates did better in the secondary sector while male non-graduates did better in primary schools. But while women graduates overtook male non-graduates in secondary schools, they do less well in financial terms in primary schools than men. But women non-graduates were more advantaged in *secondary* schools – a reverse of the male pattern. The two factors which predictably appeared to be most influential were the tendency for married women to have a break in service, and the restriction of geographical area in which they can apply because of the socially-induced assumption that they will follow their husbands' promotion pattern and not vice versa.

Turnbull and Williams, however, suggest that their analysis establishes that both men and women who come back to teaching after a break of two years or more, suffer no loss of earnings when they return in relation to others with a similar length of service, and question, therefore, whether lower pay is solely due to an interrupted career. More influential may be women's limited field of application and their lesser drive for either greater responsibility or more money because of their satisfaction in home life and their protection of a double income. There is no question but that my married women colleagues have a choice that I do not, of deliberately remaining in non-leadership roles for reasons of personal satisfaction at field level, because their double income is not in fact matched by double expenses, and is cushioned by income tax allowances for family. The central costs of mortgage, house maintenance, heating, and car are almost constant to single-income and to double-income families. A double-income married woman teacher has therefore

a lesser desire for increased financial security against inflati
(or incapacity). Hence the small differences between pay
single women teachers and male colleagues.

A second finding of this research is equally interesting. Th
position of married women *vis-à-vis* single women deteriorate
markedly from 1963 to 1971. The authors postulate that c
educational reorganization has resulted in the replacement
male/female discrimination by a form of married woman
single discrimination.

The part-timer and married returner

The whole structure of the profession has changed in tw
important respects in the last twenty years, the effect of whic
we underestimate both in terms of the structure of schools an
in the attitudinal effect on pupils. First, the proportion
teachers who are either married and have continued without
break, or who have returned to teaching after a break has in
creased steadily (the abolition of the marriage bar is post-war
Second, proportionately more of the total labour force has bee
made up by part-time staff, of whom nine-tenths are women
In 1954 there were only 5,000 part-timers in all schools. From
1964 to 1974, part-timers doubled from about 11,000 women i
each of the primary and secondary sectors (but only 429 an
2,782 men respectively) to 21,601 women part-timers in primar
schools and 15,881 in the secondary sector (but no equivalen
increase in male staff – 568 and 3,100). I do not propose t
debate the conditions of the teachers themselves but to questio
the cause and effect of this sex imbalance. My Northern fift
formers were incredulous at the idea that Ted also had the righ
to opt in and out of economic work and that they might take o
the breadwinner role. This attitude of assumed dependence b
girls and assumed responsibility to work fulltime of boys, is no
likely to change while they see throughout up to twelve year
of basic schooling only women combining marriage with par
time work. The sextyping of subject areas of teachers high
lighted in Chapter 5, is also replicated. Part-timers tend to b
found in 'feminine' activities like infant teaching, remedia
work, music and drama, and in minority subjects not regarded a
important enough to warrant inclusion in the core (e.g. foreig
languages in smaller schools, the craft areas which ar

lready sextyped). In the eyes of both girls and boys, part-
ime work becomes then pervasively if unobtrusively identi-
ied with a female role, and an 'additional', dispensable, external
ole.

The original rationale for encouraging recruitment expansion
f both part-time teachers and married women returners, was
n no way a conscious attempt to improve opportunities for
vomen. It was a response by government to the crisis of the
rastic shortfall of teachers needed to cope with the very high
irthrate of the 1940s as the pupils worked their way through
he system. Despite, however, the obvious skills, gifts, and
ariety that the part-timers and returners have brought, it is a
natter for serious concern, not to say strong disapproval, that
ll the educational, social, and organizational arguments brought
nto play in the 1960s to persuade LEAs to retrain and to recruit
his rich new labour source, have unaccountably vanished as the
ecession has caused authorities to look for convenient savings.
ven some teachers' unions have seriously debated (at least at
ranch level) policies of (a) part-timers out first, or (b) married
vomen to be declared redundant before men. We simply do not
dvance permanently on any front. When women were a con-
enient emergency resource, we heard of their own need for
ob satisfaction and creativity, and the 'earning for pin money'
yndrome began to fade. We were told by inspectors and ad-
isers of the special skills that bringing up a family and dealing
vith interpersonal relationships had given wives and mothers,
vith which our schools would be enriched (as in my view
hey are). Now that it is convenient to look for cuts by formulae
nd not by diagnosis, instead of weeding out the poorer quality
male as well as female) or the more dispensable curricular
reas (however we define these), government is supporting im-
licitly, a reversion to the previous pattern of a mainly full-
ime and constant teaching force, by allowing the nature and
haracteristics of financially recessive cuts and redeployment
o go unmonitored.

A policy of refusing to employ married returners was fore-
een and criticized in the DES/Lancaster study on returning to
eaching.

'Moreover, although women who have left teaching to bring
up a family have no prescriptive right to an opportunity to

237

return, to deny them effectively any reasonable chance be
cause of oversupply of those newly trained would be tanta
mount to the old marriage bar.'

(Ollerenshaw and Flude 1974:X)

There is no easy answer except that of learning to deploy our
staffing resources in an overall plan, nationally and locally, to
balance the profession with college leavers and with married
returners. The Lancaster Survey estimated that given the mas
sive expansion of students in the 1960s who will be ready to
return in the next decade, at intervals, there could be 6,500
trained teachers seeking a return by 1984 and 8,000 by 1989
Falling birthrate or no, our school standards are not so high that,
as an educationalist, I can accept that we cannot use the skills
locked up there – for which we have paid and in which we
have invested – for a further twenty years. Nor do I see how
any concept of personal or social justice can use women when
we are in crisis, and then dismiss them as without rights, without value, and without relevance when economic pressures and
therefore increased male competition makes it expedient to
do so.

Dare I suggest that if it were married and part-time men who
were so affected, they would have used the organized influences
at their disposal (unions; the subject associations to defend the
preservation of the threatened discipline – music, languages,
remedial work) more efficiently than the women have? Why is
it, still, that so many women shy away from organized, effective,
economic, political, or controversial battles even in their own
interests?

The problem is even more acute in further education, which
depends heavily on part-time staff. In the tertiary sector part-
timers tend to be equated with lower level, non-advanced work,
and are more often vital to the maintenance of courses in
smaller or rural colleges or those with little advanced work.
The policy of part-timers-out-first is therefore placing at risk
the courses on which girls in fact also predominate as students
and women as staff. The adult education service is almost entirely staffed by part-timers of whom two-thirds are women.
There is a growing cycle of deprivation developing, of cuts
simultaneously preventing women from retraining and of depriving those who have, of the one outlet for creative, non-

home based satisfaction which is compatible with home and family.

Geoffrey Partington's study documents a thorough but depressing historical survey of discrimination against married women teachers (Partington 1976:28–36). Depressing, because I have heard all of the quotations repeated in modern form in the last three years, and used to justify staffing cuts. The *Sex Discrimination Act, 1975* outlaws discrimination on grounds of marriage as well as of sex; and defines a new concept of indirect discrimination. Any woman teacher dismissed on grounds of marriage or because she is a part-timer (including, in my view, redundancy as part of any overall policy of priority for male 'breadwinners') should take expert advice from her union and/or a lawyer, to challenge the practice either under the SDA or, possibly, as a case of unfair dismissal under the other relevant Acts.

It is, in this context, revealing to note that no mixed teachers' union has a majority of women on its executive; some not even a significant minority. And with women still the majority in the profession as a whole, that the Burnham Schools' Committee has only five women out of thirty members of the Management Panel; and four out of twenty-seven on the Teachers' Panel, must be a matter for concern. Do women not stand for election? Or do men (and women) not elect them when they do? And if not, why not? The Equal Rights Panels of the unions ought to be examining in some depth the causes of women's absence from this key leadership role.

Traditions, of course, die hard. Despite the merger of the National Association of Schoolmasters and the new Union of Women Teachers in 1975, the General Secretary (Terry Casey) took no women representatives at all to the House of Commons Expenditure Committee when (using, however, the union figures expanded as a direct result of the merger) he went to argue stronger representation on the Burnham Committee. The women members 'had not won their spurs yet', said Mr Casey. Perhaps the fact that the reprinted NAS/UWT constitution still enshrines a clause, 'To ensure that schoolboys come under the influence of schoolmasters and girls under the influence of schoolmistresses' (*Education*, February 20, 1976) accounts for the union's Nelsonic eye to its prominent and vocal women. Their place is clearly, for the male leaders, still supervising girls' cookery and not arguing teacher politics in the House. If the deliberate reprinting of this clause embodies conscious union policy, the new approaches I have outlined in the early chapters are even longer overdue than I suggested.

During the discussion of the teachers' role in the primary and secondary school environment, the pupils' perceived image of her or his teachers on the child's future adult roles has emerged as of some importance. This is not to underestimate the effect of *parental attitudes*, which have not been reviewed principally because this is a book about the education system, and cannot embrace all aspects of the complex social educative process in one compass. Since, however, the attitudes of small girls are often very strongly conditioned before they enter school, parental re-education in more positive ways of bringing up their daughters must be an important task for schools – especially nursery and primary schools; and for the adult education service. Parent–Teacher Associations are an important voice in pressing for change and in the post-Taylor reforms, should be increasingly influential.

Re-training

The re-training problem is perhaps most acute in the area of numeracy and science. As long ago as 1959 the Crowther Committee recorded its concern about innumerate women teachers – they noted 'the considerable number of training college students, especially in the women's colleges, who have done virtually no mathematics *for three or four years before admission*, and had been unable to secure an O level pass' (Crowther Committee 1959 : para 150). Innumerate teachers qualifying then in 1959 still have twenty years teaching ahead of them. Many will even have achieved leadership positions in primary schools. In 1974, 75 per cent of maths teachers in secondary schools were male. A small research survey of thirty-nine schools in the West Midlands in 1976 revealed only five women heads of maths departments out of the thirty-nine (four in girls' schools, significantly). But of the men, four were in girls' schools, four in boys' schools, and twenty-four in mixed schools – a typical pattern which may well illustrate not only the shortage of women maths teachers but a likely bias against appointing women heads of departments in mixed schools (Hall and Thomas 1977).

In 1977, the Secretary of State for Education and Science has enlisted the aid of the Chancellor of the Exchequer, the Training Services Agency, and the Local Government Training Board to mount and fund a special programme of training and retraining, to produce more teachers of mathematics, physics, craft, design, and technology. Some useful characteristics of the pilot scheme create precedents on which we might build. Special one-year courses for graduates or trained teachers are funded either by secondment by LEAs (for which the TSA, through the LGTB will pay a premium to the LEA of £3,500 for each seconded teacher), or by paying training grants direct to applicants; and tuition fees direct to the training institution.[4] One weakness of the scheme is that *mandatory* grants for this scheme were not available to women (or men) wishing to return to teaching after a break in service. These – as usual – are at the mercy of the discretionary grant system. It is too early yet either to estimate the success of the scheme, or even to analyse the characteristics and distribution of applicants and trainees. Its value, however, is not only the obvious one of productivity of a shortage skill. It is the model that is set for future programmes. Retraining of teachers of cookery and needlework for example; of the alleged 'surplus' of college-trained teachers because of the declining birth-rate; and the retraining of secondary school teachers for further education and vice versa, are obvious next candidates for special programmes. Section 47 of the *Sex Discrimination Act, 1975* allows for programmes of positive discrimination' solely for women or for men where either sex was not previously represented in an employment sector. It would be interesting to explore this to establish follow-up programmes for re-training redundant men teachers for infant teaching and redundant women teachers specifically for handicraft (without the technology if need be) and for the apparent male preserves of 'dealing with the boys', discipline, and decision-making – in other words, for school management and government.

As today's five-year-olds reach the leaving age in 1991, the tertiary or FE colleges to which they may move, will still have a totally male leadership and women locked up in the typing room and the catering kitchen, unless the FE sector develops a counteractive positive staff development programme, particularly for its women staff. Natural trends make no impact; positive discrimination is needed. Nelson and Colne College under the leadership of David Moore has created a staff development system one of whose main purposes is to help to counteract the 'illogicality' of a woman's career because of the domestic burden, the precedence that the husbands career tends to take, and so on. This is well written up in a Coombe Lodge Report (1977) and points the way both for more research into women's position in FE and the need for interventionist programmes to 'level more women to the top' in the interests of the further education sector as a whole. We have thirteen years before today's school entrants reach FE; but next year's girl leavers will still be disadvantaged, in lacking women leaders. Regional Advisory Councils for FE/HE and the DES have a clear duty urgently to investigate the problem of women staff in FE as an act of national policy issue. Perhaps the new area Manpower Service Commission Boards can be used as leverage.

HM Inspectorate have recently, probably for the first time in the inchoate history of the educational pragmatism so characteristic of this country, produced a series of reports on the core curriculum. With equally anxious diffidence however they reassure us that there will be no national plan as such.

> 'the case for a common curriculum, as it is presented here deserves careful attention and that such a curriculum, worked out in the ways suggested, would help to ameliorate the inconsistencies and irrationalities which at present exist, without entailing any kind of centralised control.'
>
> (HM Inspectorate 1977:1)

I do not believe, in the light of the present accidental distribution of undergraduate entry and the equally incoherent relationship between the actual distribution of specialist teachers (see Chapter 4) and the attainment of a balanced curriculum, that we will have the tools for the job, without more central sponsorship. Alison, Jane, Fiona, and Liz, sitting in today's reception class, will reach eleven plus in 1986, by which time teacher training will be cut by nearly half. If they are to have a *full* opportunity to learn the handicrafts, two foreign language (*pace* the channel, we really are in Europe now), the physical sciences, enjoy real careers education, and profit from new programmes of transition from school to work, we need double

242

the number of specialists *pro rata* in some subject areas, that we now have.

This means positive, conscious, and long-term re-training of many existing teachers and some mature returners to newer subject areas with a transfer value. If an undergraduate can become a specialist in three years from the sixth form, a graduate or college-trained teacher with experience can re-specialize in two years. This would both ease the current level of teacher unemployment and call the bluff of those who allege we cannot offer a common curriculum to all because we do not have the resources. Teachers are better re-trained and re-deployed than on the dole or wasting their skills.

Such programmes would give many women teachers an especially valid second chance to top up their deficient earlier imbalance. It would also, ideally, include a national planning dimension for a proper, permanent, and protected staffing establishment of part-time specialist staff – of both sexes – to give greater flexibility in sparsity areas.

Since this is not a book about teaching as such, but a synoptic glance across the whole spectrum of women in education, much has been left out, many problems under-discussed. The complexity of women's under-achievement and stereotyping of roles in the teaching profession will not be solved in one short chapter highlighting some strands only of a complexly woven mix of historical tradition, politics, prejudice, vested interest, and – on the part of many women still – passivity to accept the status quo. It will be solved by sophisticated enquiry across the related fields of training institutions and their recruitment, post-experience education, good school practice, and investigation of discriminatory practices.

It is arguable whether yet another national commission would be competent to handle such an enquiry but any attempt at a national policy must spring from a nationally validated work respected by the education sector itself and therefore handled by qualified innovators. Perhaps the first task of a recalled Central Advisory Council for Education should be to examine the re-deployment of the teaching profession (and hence the re-structuring of the whole historical tangle of Burnham structures) towards a balanced profession geared to educating and encouraging girls and boys (in that order) to equal, higher attainment.

A formidable list of action programmes begins to emerge. To conclude at sunset is romantic but valedictory. If we are looking for a way ahead, we need to look for innovation, fresh approaches, and beginnings, even if only dawning. The concluding chapter touches lightly on some of these.

EIGHT

The way ahead – a development plan

'Certum est quia impossibile est.'
(*It is certain because it is impossible*)

TERTULLIAN, 225 AD

Late in the evening, late in November 1975, the telephone rang in the study. The voice of a colleague from Westminster came over the line, succinct, tired, but satisfied. 'It's through.' 'With education and training still in?' 'Yes.' The *Sex Discrimination Act, 1975* had finally received the Royal Assent, with, as Huxley would have said, 'all its parts of equal strength and in smooth working order' – or nearly. We had won the first hurdle in legislative terms, in the race to convince government that it is useless to attempt to tackle inequality in employment, in pay and salary, or social discrimination, without simultaneously attacking their causes and counter-remedies – the formative

245

years of education and training. This chapter is not, however, about discrimination legislation as such. It is too soon to judge, even accurately to assess in the context of education, the merits and demerits of the Act, or of the Equal Opportunities Commission set up under its powers to monitor progress and to act as an agent for constructive change. That is for another, perhaps a later book. We are here concerned with translating the messages, problems, and diagnosis of this albeit incomplete account of the education of girls and women into a positive action programme for change. And to do this is only possible if we use the same kind of unstructured, widespreading, but loosely coordinated network of caring people across the country, as that which had helped to haul the many draft Bills and their amendments safely up Sisyphus' hill. The word is partnership; of government, professional staffs, community groups, voluntary organizations, collectives, caring individuals. Each has a different but related part to play in bringing about radical but constructive change. I began by translating Kurt Waldheim's declaration, back to the classroom, the High Street, the home. I end by a similar call – for every reader who is in touch with children, young people, women in need, to accept their own individual responsibility (not only that of the governmental and detached 'They') to help to alter the structure, attitudes, and policies of society, that we shall not be debating womens' under-achievement when, in retirement, my generation sees the twenty-first century safely in.

Inequality and discrimination

'... discrimination against women violates the principle of equality of rights and respect for human dignity, it is an obstacle to the participation of women, on equal terms with men, in the political, social, economic and cultural life of their countries and hampers the growth of the prosperity of society and the family, and makes more difficult the full development of the potentialities of women in the service of their countries and humanity.'[1]

It is important to distinguish inequality from discrimination, because the measures needed to deal with each are radically different in some tactical respects. To combat inequality we need an overall strategy and policy of positive discrimination in investing our resources, based on diagnosis of the greatest need and the most immediately effective of a choice of intervention and affirmative action programmes. These will be carried out through the tools of the policy makers, committees, leaders of the service, as well as through the community. Discrimination is an individual act by an identified person or body (the authority, the Principal or head teacher, the admissions officer, the interviewing panel) and can be attacked at precise decision-making stages along the way. Since the new Act, we now have two kinds of discrimination: *unlawful* – that is, which fits the way the drafter of the Bill drafted it, and apparently '*lawful*' – that is discrimination which is blatantly conscious, overtly indefensible if equality means the same, but which does not happen to fit the wording and terms of a legal document. In educational terms, neither is acceptable. While the law is a useful, indeed a vital tool of human rights, effective overall change (test cases apart) will come by convincing the leadership of education that discrimination is wrong, unrespectable, non-u, bad education, uneconomic, and harmful to social stability.

Thus the Principal who wrote to a married woman applicant for a further education course that

> 'We regret that we are unable to offer you a place at the present time. The reason for this is that it is not our policy to offer places to mothers with children under school age. However, we should be very willing to reconsider your application as soon as your youngest child is at school'

was practising blatant discrimination, not just even accepting inequality, if only because young fathers are not so denied. This breathtaking arrogance of a college principal is based on several complacent assumptions: that he is a better judge than Mrs X of her family's needs and capacity to cope with her part-time absence; that on the magic day of five-years-old, all children, regardless of circumstances, can suddenly be adequately cared for, but at four and a half cannot; that Mrs X is a better mother at home in any circumstances, regardless of her own financial, mental, psychological, or intellectual needs which will also affect her relationship with her children; that he has the right unilaterally to decide on a desirable policy for society, and so on. Some mothers are better at home, and some children need a homeparent until their teens. Other children and parent are better adjusted and stretched with shared lives from th outset. This is for individual families to decide for themselves not for the men who control the education service to determin as acts of policy.

Similarly, the under-achievement of girls in the sciences ma or may not spring from innately inferior capacity; or fron psychological or even sociometric difficulties influencing thei competitive learning environment. But the former practice, nov unlawful, of rationing scarce physics laboratories in favour o boys and teaching girls biology in a converted classroom, on th grounds that the boys needed physics for later vocational train ing and work and girls did not (a widespread practice in my 196 survey), was clearly discriminatory.

Women's failure to raise their expectation to advanced F courses rather than shorter skills-based training may sprin from conditioned environmental inequalities. But a consciou policy of denying (rationed) discretionary awards to girls and women to enable more grants to be given to boys and men, be cause the latter are expected to be breadwinners, would be discrimination; as is the continued denial of equal day releas to girls under eighteen and to young women seeking caree training, at nineteen or twenty.

The aggregation of inequality – jam tomorrow

The education expenditure cuts which have been cumulatively intensified since 1973 have now produced the basis of a decade of recession and compound deprivation which will make i doubly difficult to persuade government – central or local – tha the time to redress the balance in favour of girls is now. It always seems a problem to be dealt with when resources (later) permit Jam tomorrow, as usual. One reason is the triviality with which the feminist debate is still treated by many who control re- sources. This, like most aspects, has roots in the past which cling tenaciously to their hidden subsoil, in the present. The OECD survey on educational opportunity in the mid 1960s – when the golden expansionist days meant increased available resources for new developments – merely confirmed male neglect and imperviousness to the emergence of girls as a social risk group.

For Westergaard and Little do us scant justice. They sweep aside girls' inequality as of little importance – yet going on to illustrate themselves how stark it actually was ten years ago.

'There are other inequalities of educational opportunity besides those of social class – *inequalities between the sexes for example. But these – so far as the present data go – are of little importance until sixth form level* ... But fewer sixth form girls than boys leave with the minimum qualifications for university entry; and fewer even among the qualified, in fact gain admittance to a university. Moreover, the disparity between the sexes widens as one goes down the social scale. The resources – cultural, economic, psychological – necessary for a working class child to overcome the obstacles on the way are very rarely expended on behalf of a girl. At the extreme of the scale, an unskilled manual worker's daughter has a chance on only one in five or six hundred of entering a university – a chance a hundred times lower than if she had been born into a professional family.'

(Westergaard and Little 1965 : 222, my italics)

This major contribution to the OECD study group predictably concentrates on academic opportunity, selective secondary and higher education. There is no mention of further education, day release, or extended (non-academic) secondary education. They concluded that the overall expansion of educational facilities has been of greater significance than any redistribution of opportunities. But as the published statistics now show, this expansion has benefited men at a consistently higher rate than women.

I believe it is now essential for us to find methods of identifying particular risk groups among our girls and women by the kind of aggregation of factors of deprivation which lay behind the EPA programme, and the National Children's Bureau's risk groups who were 'Born to Fail' (Wedge and Prosser 1973). For example, rural girls in schools in a mainly working-class or lower middle-class catchment area (i.e. excluding the developed rural commuter villages in which we all tend to live in a well-cushioned ring around the towns), who are in the East Midlands or the North East, and who are in the bottom two quartiles of ability, who are thirty miles from a college and have little public transport, will have five or six indices of potential deprivation.

They are five times more at risk than urban girls in a large mixed school in the residential outskirts of a large, well serviced South Eastern town. The choice of sample schools, of pilot areas for investment in new approaches to careers education; for development and grant aid for 'bridging courses' for school leavers and adult returners; for the first range of new in-service training courses, should be guided by *aggregated* factors of deprivation, and not by the accidental willingness of Chief Education officers and heads to experiment – for those areas still in most need are unlikely necessarily (with distinguished, but few, exceptions) to have the liveliest of leaders.

A national policy

'We do not believe that there is any hope of carrying out the measures we have outlined ... unless they are worked out and adopted as a coherent, properly phased development programme'. (Crowther Committee 1959:para 396)

Teachers' in-service training courses regularly hum with the immediate impact of the major strands of new (or reinforced old) philosophies in the wake of each prestigious report. But rarely are they seen as a diagnostic whole.

Unfortunately no post-war committee has been prepared yet to look diagnostically at either the special situation of girls as others have discriminatorily planned for them on the one hand; or, ironically, to look at them in precisely the same light as boys, on the other. We now need not a simple national declaration that it is no longer British to discriminate, but a positive, planned policy for which national and local resources will be allocated to achieve certain defined objectives by, say, 1985 and 1990 and which will improve the educational opportunities and achievements *of those girls and women most in need*. If, as many hope, the Central Advisory Councils for England and Wales are recalled, moreover, to look at the educational needs of girls and women as the *present* system educates them and to make recommendations for improving their opportunities, there should be no deferment of immediate measures, pending publication of their report. The task is sufficiently great for no interim measures to be regarded as abortive.

There are encouraging signs internationally. It is interesting hat it is the Nordic countries that principally are seen to share he UK's concern to include education and training in measures o enforce equality. The Nordic Council of Ministers of Education issued a statement on Sex Roles in Education in 1974, declaring that

> 'the educational policy is an important tool for endeavours to achieve equality ... for all levels of the educational system the Nordic countries should take measures to increase the individual's opportunity to *choose* an education, a trade, and an adult role without being bound by expectations originating in sex roles.'

taly, one the other hand, has passed its Anti-Discrimination Act in response to the EEC's Equal Opportunities Directive, in December 1977, but excluding education and training from its provisions.

> 'Attempts to widen the Act's scope to bring general education and training within its ambit, and to include more detailed and potentially stronger enforcement provisions on the model of the UK Sex Discrimination Act, were firmly rejected.'[2]

Similarly, Ireland now has an Employment Equality Agency, set up under the *Employment Equality Act, 1977*; but has no legal monitoring of education and training. The Dutch Emancipatie Kommissie, however, set up in 1974, keeps an interested eye on education. It was asked, for example, to review the 12–16 comprehensive scheme prepared in 1975–6 by the former government in order to monitor its suitability in the context of equal opportunity. On the European level there are encouraging signs. In addition to the increased attention being paid to equal opportunity in education and training in individual countries, the Commission of the European Communities has now started a phased project to attempt to diagnose the prevalence and cause of inequality of education and training in the secondary years n its nine member states, the first stage of which is the production of a diagnostic report to be considered by government experts and, later, by the Minister of Education in 1978 with a view to action programmes to speed the achievement of real equality. Simultaneously, the Ministers of Education of the twenty countries that make up the Council of Europe have designated equal opportunity in education and training for women as the theme for their 1979 biennial conference. One of the many benefits that will come from these international enquiries into the causes and scale of and remedies for inequality between the sexes, is the increased exchange of information and ideas between experts of the different countries – as well as the implicit endorsement of the growing respectability of the sex inequality debate.

In terms of this country, there would be benefit in replacing our pragmatic and decentralized fatalism which accepts, decade in, decade out, the unevenness of our provision and our achievements as between LEA areas, regions, town, and country, by a national policy that has certain common national strands which are binding on all LEAs. The next section suggests some of the contents and principles that might be included.

The curriculum and common core

The oversensitive reaction of the English teaching profession to suggestions of defining a common core of subject areas which every child should study will, if there is not a relaxation and some concession to the accountability of the educational system to pupils, parents, and to the world of work, soon lead to a counter-reaction seeking some national control over the structure and standards (not the detailed content) of the curriculum. We are the only European country to reject so constantly even the concept that there is a proper minimum which children ought to learn and which teachers ought to teach not primarily so that both are 'happy', but so that both are socially useful and competent and that children are equipped both for survival and to meet the demands of the world of work competently. We should stop being ashamed of our mill chimneys and power stations, of business and commerce (as if we were still Voltaire's nation of shopkeepers), and of our factories and industrial technology.

This means common core of some kind, and an end to any options system for those under statutory school age which enables them to discontinue subjects vitally necessary for recruitment to skilled employment, further training, and later stages of re-education. This final message could not have been more starkly endorsed than by the 1974 report of the (then) National Youth Employment Council, whose title of *Unqualified*

ntrained and Unemployed summarizes its main theme in three
words, for the 300,000 school leavers who leave every year
with no marketable qualifications or skills, and end on the unskilled labour market or unemployed. The Council recommend
especially that employers should open boys' jobs to girls and
vice versa (now legally mandatory under the employment provisions of the *Sex Discrimination Act, 1975*), and asked the
new Manpower Services Commission to research into interchangeability of boys and girls in employment. The Council
pressed for investment in training for the less able 'in the
interests of the nation as well as of the young people concerned'
to match the 'great deal of money in educating those who have
academic ability'.

It is a nonsense to say that examinable qualifications do not
matter, and that external examinations distort the system to
the disadvantage of children. We do not adequately stretch
either sex today. Twenty years ago academically able children
attempted up to ten subjects out of the twenty-five or so generally taught, in School Certificate; and four or five at eighteen
plus. That system had some major faults of inflexibility, and
over-specialization, and the examination syllabuses left much to
be desired educationally. Nevertheless the pendulum has swung
too far, and today far too few able girls now study for more
than five subjects at 'O' level or CSE, or for more than one or
two Advanced levels. There is no better investment than
measurable attainment, not because it is educationally 'better'
but because society in the shape of employers, training bodies,
colleges, and universities, demand it. Until they cease to do
so, educationalists should cease to argue that they are right and
the rest of the world is wrong.

For those, nevertheless, for whom the examination system
is held to be inappropriate (although with a 7-grade CSE which
can be moderated on school based assignments, these should
always be a minority) there should always be a constant second
and third chance. Many colleges of further education do now
exercise considerable discretion in waiving recruitment requirements for mature (i.e. not school leaver) entrants who lack
formal qualifications, and this has been adopted as a policy
principle by the new Business Education Council, preserving a
route for the motivated student with an educationally disadvantaged past.

Equal means the same

Perhaps the most fundamental curricular question facing t*
education service is that underlined by the United Natio*
Resolution of 1967 (see page 19) which declared that equ*
rights in education at all levels, meant the *same* curricul*
examinations, staff, and grants. Does equal mean the same, *
'of equivalent value'? One major weakness of the wording *
Section 22 of the *Sex Discrimination Act, 1975* is that it speal*
of 'not less favourable treatment'; not of the same treatmer*
Circular 2/76 of the Department of Education and Scien*
which heralded the new Act to the LEAs, regrettably interpret*
this as not necessarily meaning identical classroom provisi*
for girls and for boys. I challenge, refute, and reject this. It*
impossible for me as an educationalist to reconcile the historic*
thousands of pages of educational philosophy demanding educ*
tion for personal fulfilment we have printed over the years, *
the millions of words we have poured out on the need to tre*
every individual child in their own right on the one hand, wi*
any deliberate construction of different and separate education*
objectives, curriculum, routes, and practical resources for*
classified and defined group of pupils whose only comm*
element is a collection of hormones which has determined the*
sex – sex; not gender. The physiological distinction betwe*
girls and boys is a matter of sex. Gender is the collection of att*
tudes which society stitches together (dress, behaviour, att*
buted personality traits, expected social roles, etc.) to clotl*
girls and boys in order to help image identification.

The Green Paper on what has come to be known as t*
'Great Debate' – curricular reform in our schools and the vex*
question of national standards – was, moreover, considerabl*
more ambiguous on this issue of 'equal' or 'equivalent' than*
desirable, given an apparent national policy of full equality *
education and training. Regrettably, the Consultative Doc*
ment, *Education in Schools*, stated that

'Equal opportunity does not necessarily mean identical clas*
room provision for boys and girls but it is essential that, *
translating their aims into day-to-day practice, schools shoul*
not by their assumptions, decisions or choice of teachir*

254

materials, limit the educational opportunities offered to girls.'   (DES 1977 : para 10.9)

reject this utterly. With respect to both policy maker and drafter, it is a nonsense. If girls are deliberately not offered the same subjects, practical resources, and teachers as boys (e.g. biology and not physics, cookery and not metalwork, mixed tennis but not mixed cricket, typing but not economics), then schools are in fact quite deliberately limiting educational opportunities not only to girls, but also conversely to boys. The Green Paper goes on to recommend that schools must prepare pupils for the transition to adult and working life, and that since 'the traditional division of labour between men and women is rapidly breaking down, the curriculum should reflect this by educating boys and girls according to their needs and not according to sexual stereotypes' (para 10.10). This is surely irreconcilable with different courses for girls and for boys. Breaking down the tradition of men's work and women's work starts way back in the schools which educate for adult roles; not at sixteen plus. The latest output from HM Inspectorate (*Curriculum 11–16*, HMI Working Papers, December 1977) make reassuring progress. The introductory paper says among other things that

'There is the responsibility for educating the autonomous citizen, a person able to think for *herself or himself*, to resist exploitation, to innovate and to be vigilant in the defence of liberty ... The role of women and men continues to change and with it inevitably the role of men. Both contribute to the care and upbringing of children ... Society tends to expect a finished product from schools whereas it appears to need young people who have acquired certain essential skills ... whose earlier education will enable them to benefit from further education and training. *This is as true of the education of girls as of boys* ... This country is committed to equal opportunity in education, which must lead to some redistribution of responsibilities within the home as well as in the world of work.'

The wider relevance of mathematics to other curricular areas, and the reciprocal relationship with language is well explained in the Working Papers and is a further justification for insisting that *every pupil* studies mathematics to the highest examinable level up to the compulsory school age. The case for an education in technology which is not work- and employer-centred ('school leavers should be equipped to look at technology critically and to be part of a society that seeks to master technology, not to be enslaved by it. It is essential to be well-informed in those matters ... to strengthen the foundations of democracy') also makes its own case for its wider relevances to our future young women.

Meanwhile, whatever continuing debate about the legal effect of Section 22 of the *Sex Discrimination Act,* educationally there can be no question but that the continued denial of the technical crafts for girls is proportionately 'less favourable treatment' than the denial of cookery and needlework to boys, for all the reasons that are spelled out earlier. Girls lose the transfer value of underpinning their spatial development which the handicrafts offer (and which some psychologists rightly or wrongly suggest they need because of alleged innate deficiency). They are less qualified to enter technical vocational training or skilled trades in industry. And, more insidiously, they miss the whole impact on pupils' attitudes to transition from school to work which the outward-looking design and technology programmes (based on earlier exposure to the crafts) offers to boys. In its place, they receive a conditioned drive to the inward-looking domestic and child-rearing role, which further restricts their horizons. Ironically, the denial of cookery and needlework to boys is a positive *advantage* to them, and not a parallel detriment; but further disadvantages girls. It frees boys for career-based school studies, and it removes from them the expectation of the later need for them to share in domestic responsibility, enabling them to concentrate in training and career advancement, often at the expense of their wives' outward lives.

Nor can biology be regarded as of equivalent value to physics and chemistry, its transfer and foundation value for later study and training being considerably more limited. Separate physical education programmes are not always necessary. The denial of the higher social status and standing of male sports and PE activities, to girls, removes from them the resultant spin-off benefits of the wider clubability and competitiveness beyond their immediate environment, which is one indirect foundation for men's later tendency to organize themselves in business, indusry, and society in exclusively male supportive groups.

For the less able, my second curriculum reform would therefore be the replacement of the present domestically oriented skills by different practical work which looks to the external field of *work*, of community involvement in their locality; and of personal relationships and their tools for survival in a complex world; and consumer education, not cooking. I personally would remove the latter from the first to third year altogether, and reinstate it as a compulsory minority element in an overall 'transition from school to career' course for the fourth and fifth year (for both sexes), equipping them with a wider range of survival skills. Failing this, the alleged though not in fact universal reslanting towards 'home economics' should reflect the economics, more than the home.

It will be evident that much of the principal argument in this work, rejects current social mythologies. Elizabeth Janeway exposes with delicate but perceptive common sense, much of the social mythology surrounding the 'woman's place is in the home' syndrome, and by a different route, arrives at a common remedy to that which is implicit throughout my own argument: what can prevail against these myths? Not logic alone, and not compulsion, but instead an answer in *reality* to those needs which the myths answer in fantasy' (Janeway 1977:333).

One answer in reality, which she seeks, lies with the restructuring of our curriculum on the lines suggested.

Priority of development programmes for the less able

T. H. Huxley wanted a ladder from the gutter to the university. We do not appear, a hundred years later, to be able to build adequate rungs, even to the intermediate tertiary range, even from the safety of the school's secure pavement, for our less able girls. I have also, in all of the argument so far, completely omitted the very substantial programmes now currently being promoted by the Manpower Services Commission and Training Services Agencies, in offering second-chance retraining to mature entrants. They are described in detail in MSC and TSA publications[3] and are well worth the study, for two reasons. First, the government has, for reasons which are politically understandable but educationally less obvious, swung all of its resources into a massive MSC/TSA programme of short courses, mostly of a maximum of twenty-six weeks and which are clearly job related. With escalating unemployment and rapidly changing employment patterns, this is short-sighted. In ten years time, a short term TSA course will be of less value than a BEC or TEC vocational qualification with a substantial transferable core of generic studies and it is questionable how far the swing of mature women's recruitment to TSA's 'TOPS' (Training Opportunities Courses) is in their long term interest. Many, however will be attracted not only by the hope of early employment in the relevant skills-area but by the substantial training allowances which contrast advantageously with the bleaker outlet for LEA grants and awards. Mature entrants are almost all by definition limited to 'discretionary awards' (see Chapter 2) of which women suffer the greatest vulnerability. The public expenditure cuts have hit the discretionary sector very hard, by the admission of the DES itself. In a recent survey, they concluded that authorities made 2,000 *fewer* full value discretionary awards instead of the 5,000 extra needed to keep pace with the 18–19 age group (that is 7,000 fewer than needed). They also found that 45 per cent of LEAs made grants to 16–19s less generous than the LEA national standard, and 80 per cent grants to over nineteens less generous than those recommended as necessary. The aggregation of inequality bites again – where women live determines their level of grant.

Opportunity and a ladder are merely paper power if the resources needed to climb are denied. The overall national policy for which I am pressing should include a major review of the whole mandatory and discretionary antithesis, and its replacement by a system of resource allocation based on real educational diagnosis and need, and a conscious priority for a decade, for the less able – for the first time this century.

Research and review

Recommendations have already emerged implicitly in each chapter, for further research and enquiry. Research into the factors of conditioning which affect girls and boys in different kinds of schools; experimental work in non-sexist teaching materials; in-service training and re-education programmes – these are for both national bodies and local education authorities. Their co-ordinating policy makers (the Association of

258

County Councils, the Association of Municipal Authorities, and he Society of Education Officers) will need to devote time in heir national debates on policy priorities for their declining resources, to this new, imperative need, if we are not only to achieve this equality, but keep up with our European neighbours economically and developmentally.

There seems to me, however, to be a deeper and wider need, which the recommendations of the Taylor Committee (1977) on the increased involvement of parents and governors in the running of our schools, enhances. We are long overdue for a new Education Act.

The current principle Act of 1944 (for England and Wales) was at that time, one of the finest, most visionary, and far-sighted to reach the statute book. It has been amended by a score of smaller Acts and Statutory Instruments but its principles remain little altered. There is need to sit down and redefine that which should be legislatively binding on all areas as a minimum standard of provision, investment, entitlement, and that which is more appropriately delegated to local education authorities to vary according to the needs of their area. Written into a new Act, should be citizens' rights – regardless of sex, race, creed, or region of origin – to a certain level of *recurrent* education throughout life, including adult education after retirement; and as a right, not a privilege to be argued for with 120 different LEA Committees or officers whose differing philosophies, prejudices, and resources create differing inequalities of access. This would be a major life-chance for the 'lost generations' of women whose first chance education has not equipped them for economic adult life outside their homes.

A quintessential characteristic of the education service at its best, is that the word impossible does not figure in our vocabulary. With the future lives of children and the country's economic and social future in our hands, there can be no room for failure; only if necessary, prolongation of the fight. Somehow, ways have to be found; an act of faith. Ray Strachey tells an anecdote which, if apocryphal, is nevertheless characteristic, of Emily Davies and Elizabeth Garrett in their early years, discussing at Aldeburgh all the great causes to be fought in order to combat the many social injustices suffered by Victorian women. Emily summed the matter up.

' "Well, Elizabeth", she said, "it's quite clear what has to be done. I must devote myself to securing higher education while you open up the medical profession to women. After these things are done", she added, "we must see about getting the vote." And then she turned to the little girl who was still sitting quietly on her stool and said "you are younger than we, Millie, so you must attend to that".' (And Millicent Garret Fawcett, of course, did.) (Strachey 1978:101)

I cannot promise my predecessors that we have succeeded as well as they; nor that we will do so in the next two decades. The progress of the last five years, however, gives us a more secure foundation that ever before – if the men as well as women in leadership in the classroom, in government, and in the home care to combine in coherent planning for an equal future for all. I cannot do better than to end with Octavia Hill's parting words:

'When I am gone, I hope my friends will not try to carry out any special system, or to follow blindly in the track I have trodden. When the time comes that we slip from our places and they are called to the front as leaders, what should they inherit from us? Not a system, not an association, not dead formulas ... what we care most to leave them is not any tangible thing however great, not any memory, however good but the quick eye to see, the true soul to measure, the large hope to grasp the mighty issues of the new and better day to come – greater ideals, greater hope, and patience to realise both.' (Edmund 1913:583)

What she did, we can do. That, readers, means you.

Sextyping of textbooks

Check list of the Swedish Board of Education's Sex-role Project Group

Educational publishers and teachers should ask the following questions about textbooks and readers:

1. Does the content or form of the publication distinguish clearly between values (whether the writer's or other people's) and facts concerning
2. differences between the sexes – physical, physcho-physical and mental,
3. sex roles – individual and social, sexual discrimination – materially, psychologically, and socially speaking?
4. Is the reader made to realize that facts also constitute/ can constitute a subjective selection? The point is that this selection can be influenced by masculine and feminine

values in accordance with our existing masculine an
feminine cultures.

5. Is any information provided, everywhere and in practic
ally all subjects and contexts, as to who does what, i
which function they do it and why they do it? Are th
students given tasks inducing them to find out somethin
about the person (man/woman) behind the scenes? Ar
there different roles? If so, why? Are there different work
ing conditions? If so, why?

6. Do text and illustrations depict both traditional and ur
traditional sex roles? Captions and student tasks shoul
be capable of encouraging debate and criticism.

7. Does the text avoid polarizing 'masculine' and 'feminine
characteristics, as in 'she was technically gifted bu
feminine' or 'he was a good sportsman but gentle'?

8. Are the proportions between masculine and feminin
examples, nouns, pronouns, etc. fairly balanced?

9. In other words, is the author aware that his product ma
bear the marks of his personal values or attitudes – o
the sex role which he himself occupies?

Source: Report of the Swedish National Board of Education
Sex Role Questions and Programs for Equality, 1976.

Notes

Chapter One

1. The Board of Education's 1923 report on the *Differentiation of Curricula between the Sexes in Secondary Schools* is now followed by *Curricular Differences for Boys and Girls*, Education Survey 21, HMSO, 1975, for England and Wales, and by *Differences of Provision for Boys and Girls in Scottish Secondary Schools*, Scottish Education Dept., 1975.
2. Resolution No. 2263 adopted by the General Assembly of the United Nations, November 7, 1967, under Article 9, the 'Declaration on the Elimination of Discrimination against Women'.
3. HNC/HND are advanced courses requiring one or two relevant subjects at GCE advanced level before recruitment.
4. See the report of HM Inspectorate *Curricular Differences Between Boys and Girls* (1975).

Chapter Two

1 The case is spelled out in Byrne (1976).
2 'As regards the *individual* nature, woman is defective and mis
   begotten for the *active* force' (Aquinas).
3 Unquestionably one of the early major influences was Havelock
   Ellis, whose *Man and Woman* first published in 1894 was up
   dated, reprinted in 1934, and used extensively in training courses
   at that time.
4 'The Queen (Victoria) is most anxious to enlist everyone who
   can speak or write to join in checking this mad, wicked folly
   of "Woman's Rights" with all its attendant horrors, on which
   her poor feeble sex is bent, forgetting every sense of womanly
   feeling or propriety' (quoted in Cole 1946).
5 The 'noble mission' is 'what God intended she should be –
   a helpmeet to her husband'.
6 Unpublished report on 'Improvement of the Situation of the
   Education and Professional Training of Women' by the Federal
   Minister for Education and Science in the Republic of West
   Germany – December 8, 1977 (II A3/2861-2)
7 *The Position of Women in Society*, report of the Commission
   appointed by the Prime Minster (Copenhagen 1974:81).
8 *L'ecole maternelle francaise*, La documentation francaise illus-
   trée, April 1975, page 15.

Chapter Three

1 'The Council's practice is to appoint a headmistress to take
   charge of an infant, junior mixed or girls' department, and a
   headmaster to take charge of a boys' department' *The London
   Education Service* (1972: 36).
2 Given in full in Appendix I for the guidance of English teachers.
3 Ormerod and Duckworth (1975) is more directly relevant to the
   UK than the equally interesting evidence from Frazier and
   Sadker (1973).
4 Jill Watson's drawings are in fact of at least 8-*year-olds*, and the
   activities well beyond the average nursery school child.

Chapter Four

1 We were still writing on the back of requisition forms in 1949,
   because of paper rationing.
2 'The girls were busy with their sewing and the boys were
   making raffia mats or cane baskets or bowls ...' (Miss Read 1955).
3 As Honorary Research Associate of Hull University Institute of
   Education. The Research report is as yet unpublished.

Ruth Miller's excellent *Careers for Girls* (1973) spells out the complexity of subject combinations and levels needed for different careers.

'True, some boys who have little interest in physical activities can compensate for this by performance in other directions but unless this is done successfully the adolescent may find himself in difficulties our personal relationships with his contemporaries' (Lovell 1963 : 228)

Natural sciences into human biology, mircobiology, botany, zoology; history into social, political, economic, mediaeval, European; maths into pure and applied.

It was, after all, a woman – Octavia Hill – who pioneered the whole discipline of housing and estate management.

Chapter Five

'That's the worst of factory work for girls. They can earn so much when the work is plenty that they can maintain themselves anyhow' (Mrs Gaskell, *Mary Barton*, page 7).

Set up by the Secretary of State in 1974 to restructure education for industry and commerce.

Single, divorced, widowed, separated, deserted, wives of long-term prisoners, long-stay patients, etc.

'Dost thou not know, my son, with how little wisdom the world is governed?' Count Oxenstierna to his son, 1648.

Interestingly, the Gittins Committee, the parallel for Wales, could only produce 28 per cent women members.

Chapter Six

Public Expenditure to 1978–79, Cmnd. 5879, which replaced the 1972 White Paper 'Education : a framework for expansion', moreover, reasserted (para. 11, page 97) the Robbins' principle of the right to a place for all qualified and seeking one; but then cut HE places from 750,000 to 640,000 on economy grounds.

See, for example, *The Employment, Education and Training of Girls and Women* (ATTI 1973; the Association of Teachers of Technical Institutions has now become NATFHE), as well as the annual DES statistics.

Part-time study for professional qualifications in insurance, banking, accountancy, business administration, membership of technical and professional institutes, etc.

Adult education provision is well documented. Interested readers should contact the National Institute of Adult Education at Leicester, and read the Russell Report (1973) for further background.

Chapter Seven

1 The school-leaving age went up to 15 in 1947; but my rur
   district did not acquire a fully equipped secondary school un
   1955.
2 Because the legislation, organization of schools, and gener
   system of education in Scotland differs radically from that i
   England and Wales, it is not possible to extend the scope
   this book to include it generally.
3 Suffolk deputy heads and senior mistresses' unpublished 197
   report.
4 DES Admin. Memo 9/77 (26 May, 1977) and accompanyir
   brochure.

Chapter Eight

1 Preamble to Draft Convention on the Elimination of Discrimin
   tion against Women. Status of Women Commission, Genev
   December 1977.
2 *European Industrial Relations Review* No. 49 : January 8, 197
3 See especially *Training Opportunities for Women* (MSC an
   TSA 1975) and the Annual Report of MSC 1976–77 for the lates
   statistics and programmes.
4 Discretionary Awards 1975–76 – 1977–78 (DES 1977).

Selected bibliography and references

A. History of education of women

BURSTAL, SARAH (1937) *English High Schools for Girls*. Manchester: Manchester University Press.

KAMM, JOSEPHINE (1958) *How Different from Us* (Dorothea Beal and Frances Buss). London: Methuen.

—— (1965) *Hope Deferred*. London: Methuen.

OLLERENSHAW, KATHLEEN (1961) *Education for Girls*. London: Faber & Faber.

STEPHEN, BARBARA (1927) *Emily Davies and Girton College*. London: Constable.

TURNER, BARRY (1974) *Equality for Some*. London: Ward Lock Educational.

B. Historical – general

ALLEN, MARY S. (1925) *The Pioneer Policewoman*. London: Chatto & Windus.

ACWORTH, EVELYN (1965) *The New Matriarchy*. London Gollancz.

BIBBY, CYRIL (1972) *Scientist Extraordinary: T. H. Huxley* Oxford: Pergamon.

BISCOE, VRYNWY (1932) *300 Careers for Women*. London Lovat Dickson.

BOARD OF EDUCATION (1904) *Regulations for Secondary Schools*. Code 2128. London: HMSO.

—— (1923) *Differentiation of Curricula between the Sexes in Secondary Schools*.

BROWNLOW, J. M. E. (1911) *Women's Work in Local Government* London: David Nutt.

CENTRAL BUREAU FOR THE EMPLOYMENT OF WOMEN (1919) *Careers Guide to the Professions and Occupations of Educated Women and Girls*. London.

ELLIS, MRS (1842) *The Daughters of England*. London: Fisher & Son & Co.

H M GOVERNMENT (1919) War Cabinet *Report on Women in Industry*. Cmnd. 135. London: HMSO.

MACARTHUR, MARY (1908) *Woman in Industry*. London: Duckworth.

MARWICK, ARTHUR (1977) *Women at War 1914–18*. London: Croom Helm.

MAURICE, EDMUND C. (1913) *Life of Octavia Hill*. London: Macmillan.

NEFF, WANDA (1966) *Victorian Working Women*. London: Frank Cass.

REANEY, MRS G. S. (1884) *Our Daughters: their lives and there after*. London: Hodder and Stoughton.

STRACHEY, RAY (1978) *The Cause*. London: Virago.

C. Sex differences and sex roles

ADAMS, CAROL and LAURIKIETIS, RAY (1976) *The Gender Trap*. London: Virago.

BARKER, DIANA L. and ALLEN, SHEILA (eds) (1976) *Sexual Divisions and Society: Process and Change*. London: Tavistock.

BEAUVOIR, SIMONE DE (1949, reprinted 1974) *The Second Sex* Harmondsworth: Penguin.

BELOTTI, ELENA GIANINI (1974) *Du coté des petites filles* Paris: Des Femmes. (*Dalla parte delle bambine*, Fetrinelli, Milan 1973).

BRIERLEY, JOHN (1975) Sex Differences in Education. *Trends in Education*, February.

CENTERWALL, A. and STRÖMDAHL, B. (1974) *Boy, Girl does it matter?* Stockholm: Swedish National Board of Education.

CHETWYND, J. and HARTNETT, O. (eds) (1978) *Sex Role System*. London: Routledge & Kegan Paul.

CHILDREN'S RIGHTS WORKSHOP (1976) *Sexism in Children's Books*. London: Writers' and Readers' Cooperative.

DISSY (1974) *Sexism in Children's Books*. London.

COLTHEART, MAX (1975) Sex and Learning Differences. *New Behaviour*, May.

DAVIE, R., BUTLER, N., and GOLDSTEIN, H. (1972) *From Birth to Seven* (Report of the National Child Development Study). London: Longman.

DOUGLAS, J. W. B. and PIDGEON, A. (1960) A National Survey of the Ability and Attainment of Children at Three Age Levels. *British Journal of Educational Psychology* 30: 124-31.

DOUGLAS, J. W. B., ROSS, J. M., and SIMPSON, H. R. (1968) *All our Future*. London: Peter Davies.

DEPARTMENT OF EDUCATION AND SCIENCE (1975) *Curricular Differences between the Sexes*. Education Survey 21. London: HMSO.

ELLIS, HAVELOCK (1934) *Man and Women*. London: Heinemann.

FRAZIER, N. and SADKER, M. (1973) *Sexism in School and Society*. New York: Harper & Row.

GELB, LESTER A. (1974) Masculinity and Feminity. In J. Baker Miller (ed), *Psychoanalysis and Women*. Harmondsworth: Penguin.

HUTT, CORINNE (1973) *Males and Females*. Harmondsworth: Penguin.

JONES, A., MARSH, J., and WATTS, A. G. (1976) *Male and Female*. Cambridge: Careers Research and Advisory Centre.

KLEIN, VIOLA (1946) *The Feminine Character*. London: Routledge & Kegan Paul.

LAINÉ, PASCAL (1974) *La Femme et Ses Images*. Paris: Stock.

LOBBAN, GLENYS (1974) Presentation of Sex Roles in British Reading Schemes. *Forum* 16(2).

— (1975) Sex Roles in Reading Schemes. *Education and Sex Roles. Educational Review* (27)3 June.

LOVELL, K. (1963) *Educational Psychology and Children*. London: University of London Press.

MACCOBY, E. E. (1966) *The Development of Sex Differences*. Stanford: Stanford University Press.

MARKS, P. (1972) Feminity in the classroom. In J. Mitchell and A. Oakley (eds), *The Rights and Wrongs of Women*. Harmondsworth: Penguin.

MILLER, JEAN B. (ed) (1974) *Psychoanalysis and Women*. Harmondsworth: Penguin.

OAKLEY, ANN (1972) *Gender and Society*. London: Maurice Temple Smith.

ORMEROD, M. B. and DUCKWORTH, D. (1975) *Pupils' attitudes to Science*. Slough: NFER.

PIAGET, J. (1952) *The Child's Conception of Number*. London: Routledge & Kegan Paul

PIAGET, J. (1953) The Origins of Intelligence in the Child. London Routledge & Kegan Paul.

—— (1956) *The Child's Conception of Space*. London: Routledge & Kegan Paul.

REYERSBACH, A. (1974) Ladies don't play football. *The Making of the Second Sex. New Era* 55(6) July.

ROSSI, ALICE (1964) *Equality between the Sexes. Daedalus* Spring.

SCOTTISH EDUCATION DEPARTMENT (1975) *Differences o. Provision for Boys and Girls in Scottish Secondary Schools* Edinburgh.

SHARPE, SUE (1976) *Just like a Girl*. Harmondsworth: Pelican.

SWEDISH NATIONAL BOARD OF EDUCATION (1976) *Sex Role Questions and Programmes for Equality*. Stockholm.

SWEDISH USSU STATE COMMISSION (1975) *Handbook in teaching on Sexual and Personal Relationships*. Stockholm.

TERMAN, L. H. (1919) *The Measurement of Intelligence.*

THOMAS, A. and STEWARD, B. (1975) Counsellor Response to Female Clients with Deviant and Conforming Career Roles *Journal of Counselling Psychology* 18(4):352-57.

TOLSON, ANDREW (1977) *The Limits of Masculinity*. London: Tavistock.

VALENTINE, C. W. (1963) *The Normal Child*. Harmondsworth: Pelican.

WISENTHAL, M. (1965) Sex differences in Attitudes and Attainment in Junior Schools. *British Journal Educational Psychology* 35: 79-85.

ZILLBOORG, G. (1974) Masculine and Feminine. In Jean B. Miller (ed), *Psychoanalysis and Women*. Harmondsworth: Pelican.

D. Teachers and teaching

ASSOCIATION OF ASSISTANT MISTRESSES (1976) *The Promotion of Women Teachers*. London.

COHEN, A. and GARNER, N. (1965) *A Student's Guide to Teaching Practice*. London: London University Press.

DEPARTMENT OF EDUCATION AND SCIENCE (1963) *Staffing of Schools*. Reports on Education 6. London.

—— (1964) *Training the Teachers*. Reports on Education 7. London

HALL, A. and THOMAS, B. (1977) Mathematics Department Head ships in Secondary Schools. *Educational Administration*, Spring

HILSUM, S. and START, K. B. (1974) *Promotion and Careers in Teaching*. Slough: NFER.

HORNSBY-SMITH, M. and NEWBERG, C. J. (1972) Subject Specialisation in School. *Education Research* 15(1), November.

ISAACS, SUSAN (1932, reprinted 1963) *The Children we Teach* London: London University Press.

MCNAMARA, D. R. (1972) Women's Commitment to Teaching. In *Research Forum in Teacher Education*. Slough: NFER.

OLLERENSHAW, K. and FLUDE, C. (1974) *Returning to Teaching*. University of Lancaster.

ONE PARENT FAMILIES (1974) *Please Ms!* At 255 Kentish Town Rd., London NW5 2LX.

PARTINGTON, GEOFFREY (1976) *Women Teachers in the 20th Century*. Slough: NFER.

TROPP, ASHER (1957) *The School Teacher*. London: Heinemann.

TURNBULL, P. and WILLIAMS, G. (1974) Sex Differentiation in Teachers' Pay. Unpublished report.

E. General

ALLPORT, GORDON W. (1954) *The Nature of Prejudice*. Reading, Mass.: Addison-Wesley.

ATTI (1973) *The Employment, Education and Training of Girls and Women*. London.

AUSTRALIAN SCHOOLS' COMMISSION (1975) *Girls, School and Society*.

BANTON, MICHAEL (1965) *Roles*. London: Tavistock.

BARKER-LUNN, J. C. (1970) *Streaming in the Primary Schools*. Slough: NFER.

BENNETT, S. J. (1974) *The School: An Organizational Analysis*. Glasgow: Blackie.

BOYD, DAVID (1973) *Elites and Their Education*. Slough: NFER.

BRITTON, MALCOLM (1975) Women at Work. *Population Trends* 2 (Winter). London: Office of Population Censuses and Surveys.

BROWN, GAVIN (1964) *The Careers Handbook for Girls*. London: Arthur Barker.

BULLOCK COMMITTEE (1975) *A Language for Life*. London: HMSO for DES.

BYRNE, EILEEN M. (1974) *Planning and Educational Inequality*. Slough: NFER.

—— (1976) *The Rationale of Resource-Allocation*. Unit 16, Course E321. Milton Keynes: The Open University.

COLE, MARGARET (1938) *Woman of Today*. London: T. Nelson and Sons.

COOMBE LODGE (1977) Study Conference 77/8. *Women in Further Education* 10(4).

CROWTHER COMMITTEE (1959) *15 to 18*. London: HMSO for DES.

DALE, R. R. (1969) *Mixed or Single Sex Schools*. London: Routledge & Kegan Paul.

DAHRENDORF, R. (1974) The Natures and Types of Social Inequality. In J. Beteille (ed), *Social Inequality*. Harmondsworth: Penguin.

DANISH COMMISSION ON THE STATUS OF WOMEN (1974) *The Position of Women in Society*. Copenhagen.

DEPARTMENT OF EDUCATION AND SCIENCE (1970) *Student Numbers in Higher Education*. London: HMSO.

—— (1973) *Careers Education in Secondary Schools*. Education Survey 18. London: HMSO.

—— (1977) *Educating Our Children*. DES for 1977 Regional Conference on Education.

—— (1978) *Higher Education in the 1990s*. London: HMSO.

FOGARTY, M., RAPOPORT, R., and RAPOPORT, R. (1972) Women and Top Jobs – the Next Move. Planning XXXVIII. PEP.

FOGELMAN, K. (1972) *Leaving the Sixth Form*. Slough: NFER.

FRIEDAN, B. (1963) *The Feminine Mystique*. London: Gollancz.

GIROUD, FRANCOISE (1972) *Si je mens* ... Paris: Stock.

HADOW COMMITTEE (1931) *The Primary Schools*. Consultative Committee of the Board of Education. London: HMSO.

HENNIKER-HEATON COMMITTEE (1964) *Day Release*. London: HMSO for DES.

H M GOVERNMENT (1973) *The Employment of Women*. 6th report of the Expenditure Committee. Session 1972–3. London: HMSO.

II M INSPECTORATE (1977) *Curriculum (11–16)*. December. London.

HUNT, AUDREY and RAUTA, IRENE (1975) *Fifth Form Girls: their Hopes for the Future*. London: HMSO for DES.

IRISH DEPARTMENT OF EDUCATION (1977) *An Roinn Oideachais an Taonad Curaclain* (Research Report on Mathematics). Dublin.

JANEWAY, ELIZABETH (1977) *Man's World, Woman's Place*. Harmondsworth: Penguin.

LONDON AND HOME COUNTIES RAC FOR TECHNOLOGICAL EDUCATION (1976) *The Vocational Education of Women*. London.

MACINTOSH, N. (1973) Women and the Open University. *Women in Higher Education*. Staff Development Unit, London University, Institute of Education.

MACKAY, D., THOMPSON, B. and SCHNAUB, P. (1970) *Breakthrough to Literacy*. Harlow: Longman for Schools Council.

MACKIE, L. and PATTULLO, P. (1977) *Women at Work*. London: Tavistock.

MCMEEKING COMMITTEE (1959) *Report of the Advisory Committee on Further Education for Commerce*. London: HMSO.

MILL, JOHN STUART (1869) *The Subjection of Women*. (1974) London: Everyman.

MILLER, RUTH (1973) *Careers for Girls*. Harmondsworth: Penguin.

—— (1978) *Equal Opportunities*. Harmondsworth: Penguin.

NATIONAL UNION OF TEACHERS (1976) *Equal Opportunities for Women*. London.

NEWSOM COMMITTEE (1963) *Half our Future*. London: HMSO for DES.

NEWSOM, JOHN (1948) *The Education of Girls*. London: Faber & Faber.

NOVARRA, VIRGINIA (1976) *Right on, Sister!*

NUNN, SIR PERCY (1945) *Education, its Data and First Principles*. London: Edward Arnold.

OAKLEY, ANN (1976) *Housewife*. Harmondsworth: Penguin.

OECD (1965) *Social Objectives in Educational Planning*. Paris.

PLOWDEN COMMITTEE (1967) *Children and their Primary Schools*. London: HMSO for DES.

RAPOPORT, ROBERT (1974) *Mid-Career Development*. London: Tavistock.

'READ, MISS' (1955) *Village School*. London: Michael Joseph.

ROBBINS COMMITTEE (1963) *Report of the Committee on Higher Education*. London: HMSO.

ROWBOTHAM, SHEILA (1973) *Woman's Consciousness, Man's World*. Harmondsworth: Pelican.

RUSSELL COMMITTEE (1973) *Adult Education: A Plan for Development*. London: HMSO for DES.

RUSSELL, BERTRAND (1961) *A History of Western Philosophy*. London: Unwin University Books.

SANDBERG, ELIZABETH (1975) *Equality is the Goal*. Report of the Advisory Council to the Prime Minister of Sweden. Stockholm: Swedish Institute.

SCHOOLS COUNCIL (1968) *Enquiry 1 – Young School Leavers*. London: HMSO.

SPRINGRICE, MARGERY (1939) *Working class Wives*. London: Pelican.

ST. GEORGES, G. (1971) *La Femme Soviétique*. Paris: Stock.

SULLEROT, E. (1973) *Les Françaises au Travail*. Paris: Hachette.

SYMONDS, A. (1974) Phobias after Marriage. In Jean B. Miller (ed), *Psychoanalysis and Women*. Harmondsworth: Pelican.

TAYLOR COMMITTEE (1977) *A New Partnership for Our Schools*. London: HMSO.

TAYLOR, L. C. (1971) *Resources for Learning*. Harmondsworth: Penguin Education.

UNESCO (1975) *Women, Education, Equality – a Decade of Experiment*. Paris: UNESCO Press.

—— (UK Commission) (1976) *The Status of Women in Britain*. Paris: UNESCO Press.

VAN DER EYKEN, W. (ed) (1973) *Education, The Child and Society 1900–1973*. Harmondsworth: Penguin Education.

WALTERS, A. (1975a) *Women Students in Further Education*. Paper presented to Standing Conference on Sociology of Further Education. Blagdon, Somerset: Coombe Lodge; Information Bank No. 1052.

—— (1975b) Unpublished M.Sc. dissertation, University of Surrey.

WEDGE, P. and PROSSER, H. (1973) *Born to Fail*. London: Arrow Books.

WESTERGAARD, J. and LITTLE, A. (1965) *Education Opportunity and Social Selection in England and Wales*. Paris: OECD.

WORKERS' EDUCATIONAL ASSOCIATION (1934) *The School Leaving Age and Juvenile Unemployment*. London.

Name index

Subject index